Language

W9-BOE-743

Grammar and syntax   137
Dialects and speech   137
Grammaticality and
   correctness   139
Subjects and predicates   141
Finite verbs   143
Reference   147
Transformations   153–162
Restrictive/
   nonrestrictive   161

Words

Grammaticality and
   correctness   139
Jargon   170
Euphemisms   171
Pompous words   172
Words and grammatical
   context   173
Prepositions   177
Word confusion   180
Mistakes with metaphor   186
Clichés   187
Written slang   189
Colloquial English   189
Wordiness   190

CLEAR SENTENCES

Problems

Fragments   143, 238, 246
Ambiguity:
   Dangling modifiers   145
   Pronouns and reference   147, 201
Monster sentences   164

Techniques

Writing complex sentences   144
Preposing   148
Subordinating   150
Highlighting   151
Using active / passive   153, 265
Using BY phrases   156
Sentence embedding   157
Making relative clauses   160
Clause reduction   162

Mechanics

Punctuation

End punctuation:
   Period   228
   Question mark   228
   Exclamation point   226
Comma 222
Semicolon   234
Colon   221
Dash   226
Quotation marks   229, 107
Parentheses / brackets   227

Word Forms

Abbreviations   193
Capitals   196
Hyphens   204
Italics   207
Numbers   210
Plurals   216
Possessives   219
Pronoun forms   204
Word division   243
Spelling   239

Sentence Faults

Agreement:
   Subject-verb   196
   Pronoun-antecedent   200
Parallel structure   214
Run-on sentences   236
Sentence fragments   143, 238, 246
Split infinitives   242
Shifts in tense and person   199

Passages for Editing

for practice in applying rules   245–260

The College Writer's Handbook

University of Hawaii | **Suzanne E. Jacobs**

JOHN WILEY & SONS, INC. | *New York London Sydney Toronto*

The College Writer's Handbook, Second Edition

and Roderick A. Jacobs

Copyright © 1973,1976 by Suzanne and Roderick Jacobs

Library of Congress Cataloging in Publication Data

Jacobs, Suzanne E
  The college writer's handbook.

  Includes index.
  1. English language—Rhetoric. 2. English
language—Handbooks, manuals, etc. I. Jacobs,
Roderick A., joint author. II. Title.
PE1408.J25 1976   808'.042   75-28036
ISBN 0-471-43591-0

Printed in the United States of America

10 9 8 7 6 5 4 3 2

Preface

Like its predecessor, this edition serves two main purposes.

1. It is a compact reference book for students faced with various kinds of writing tasks, including course assignments, essay examinations, papers for freshman writing courses, and bread-and-butter writing that many students will have to do after college.
2. It is a standard writing textbook with exercises on which the students and the instructor work together, and it may be used with a book of readings, reading material from other courses, library resources, newspapers, films, interviews and, of course, the students' own experience.

   As a reference book the emphasis is still on the immediate writing task: how to write, control, revise, and perhaps revise again. In continuing to work with students in standard courses and in a college writing clinic, we have found that their most troublesome writing problems involve structure, clarity, introductions, wordiness, and word choice. Here, we provide conveniently organized, easily applied advice about these matters.

To find what is needed the student should consult the index, the table of contents, the list of margin symbols inside of the back cover, or the branching outline inside of the front cover. The number of margin symbols has been increased, and the index has been considerably enlarged. A new chapter (Chapter 1) has been included to orient students to college and postcollege writing. It contains a variety of sample papers with comments on their approach and technique. The samples are from freshman English, the humanities, and the social and physical sciences. There are a short list of books on technical writing and notes on proposals and on-the-job writing. Although the samples do not provide an instant formula for success, they show the beginning student, unsure what to say or how to approach a topic, the kind of writing that other students have done.

Even though Chapter 1 will be helpful to classes that use this book as a standard text, we think that Chapter 2 is a logical starting point for course work, since it provides the basic ordering of the course assignments. The subsequent chapters give advice and suggestions for dealing with problems that arise while these assignments are being written.

Here is a plan for a single-semester freshman course, using this book with outside source material. The first few assignments involve the students in description, illustration, and narration (see the first part of Chapter 2). A film, some extracts of professional and student autobiographies read aloud in class, and the students' own experience serve as raw material or subject matter to be integrated with that already provided by the book. For these assignments the stress should be on detail—the quantity of it as well as its freshness and appropriateness. Consequently we would stress the fact that students must be good observers. The next assignments, according to this plan, direct the student toward comparison and contrast, definition, cause and effect (or *reason* writing), and dealing with counterarguments. These are techniques in the ordering and developing of ideas—techniques taught in the latter part of Chapter 2. In this portion of the course the subject matter is oriented toward argument, issues, and ideas. Although the emphasis still is on the use of detail, there is now additional stress on the problems of organization and structure. Subject matter of this kind almost inevitably generates organizational problems, and at this point in the course the student is ready to tackle them. Techniques such as comparison and contrast can then be used by students on various kinds of papers:

> A data-gathering paper requiring summary, conclusions, and recommendations (the data to be collected in interviews, perhaps).
>
> A problem paper on a local issue, requiring the collection of news articles or other written material (perhaps interviews) and again a summary, conclusions, and recommendations.
>
> A literature paper on a short literary work, or a history paper done by students enrolled in a history class.

Chapters 3 to 7 (which discuss mapping; criticisms to anticipate; grammar; word choice; research papers; and mechanics) provide the instructor with material on various kinds of writing problems or skills. From this material he can select the skills that seem most important for a particular class or most relevant for a particular writing project. Thus students writing about a local issue will need to use appropriate documentation such as is discussed in the footnoting section of Chapter 5.

At the back of the book there are rules for punctuation, agreement, spelling, and other "mechanical" matters. They are included at the back because the need for this kind of checking comes late in the writing process, after all other revisions have been made and the paper is almost ready for final typing. Closer to the front of the book is instruction in the skills needed earlier in the writing process—first the organization of the paper, then sentence structure (as dealt with in Chapter 6, "A Writer's Grammar"), then word choice and a short section on wordiness. Chapter 4, "Criticisms to Anticipate in Writing a Paper," which follows the organization chapters, defines and illustrates faults such as "incoherence" and "overgeneralization."

We know that there are many students (and instructors) who can make good use of a grammatical apparatus. For them we have included "A Writer's Grammar" (Chapter 6), based both on recent transformational analysis and on the most useful traditional concepts. We were pleased by the quantity of favorable comment we received on the first version of the "Grammar" and we invite further comment and suggestions. This component has now been extensively revised so as to focus in more depth on the needs of the writer. Sentence fragments, dangling modifiers, run-on sentences, and other mistakes are discussed within a unifying grammatical framework that will allow for exploration as much as for correction. Through analytical discussion, illustration, and practice, we try to make the would-be writer more sensitive to the rich range of choices offered by the English language and to the consequences of particular choices.

We express our gratitude to many people who sent us suggestions for this new edition. We particularly thank William Mahaney, Harry Crosby, and Fran Osborne for their detailed recommendations. We also thank editors Chris Jennison and Tom Gay and three University of Hawaii faculty members, physicist Peter Crooker, botanist Eleanor Saboski, and anthropologist Linda Alexander. Our special thanks go to student writers Jon Okada, Harry Hill, Dianne Elliott, Sylvia Yuen, Joel Matsunaga, Eilyne Matsumoto, and Robin Stroll.

Suzanne E. Jacobs
Roderick A. Jacobs

Honolulu, 1975

Contents

Some Preliminary Suggestions   1

1

Kinds of Writing You Can Expect To Do   7

General Purpose Writing   8
Essay Exams   16
Course Papers   22
Science Writing   35
Proposal Writing   40

2

Organizing and Developing A Topic   43

The Unifying Idea   43
The Relation of the Paragraph to the Paper: the Plan
    or Outline   48
Beginning and Ending Paragraphs   50

Idea Development Through Description   55
Idea Development Through Illustration   58
Idea Development Using a Time Sequence   59
Idea Development Through Definition and
  Classification   61
Idea Development Using Cause and Effect   64
Idea Development Using Comparison and Contrast   67
Paragraphs That Take Note of Counterarguments   73
Idea Linking and Linking Words   76

3

Mapping: a Way to Check Your Organization and Coherence   79

4

Criticisms to Anticipate in Writing a Paper   87

Vagueness   88
Repetitiousness   89
Irrelevance   90
Incoherence   95
Overgeneralization   97
Oversimplification   100
Confused Reasoning   101
Undefined Terms   103

5

Research Papers   105

Some Basic Rules about Research Papers   105
Guide to Punctuating Quotations   107
The Sample Research Paper   108
Footnotes   127
The Bibliography   131
Standard References in the Library   132
Suggested Topics   133

6
A Writer's Grammar   137

Grammar and Syntax   137
Dialects and Speech   138
Written Dialects   139
Grammaticality and Correctness   139
Subjects and Predicates   141
Predicates, Finite Verbs, and Fragments   143
Dangling Modifiers   145
Pronouns and Reference   147
Preposing   148
Subordination and Finite Verbs   150
Highlighting with IT   151
Highlighting with WHAT   152
Active and Passive   153
BY Phrases   156
Sentence Embedding   157
Relative Clauses   160
Restrictive and Nonrestrictive Relative Clauses   161
Relative Clauses and Clause Reduction   162
A Final Note of Caution: Monster Sentences   164

7
Word Choice   167

Words and Implication   168
Jargon   170
Euphemisms   171
Pompous Words   172
Words and Grammatical Context   173
Prepositions   177
Pairs of Words Commonly Confused   180
Metaphorical Words   185
Clichés   187
Written Slang   189
Colloquial English   189
Wordiness   190

8

Mechanics   193

Abbreviations   193
Agreement   196
Capitals   204
Hyphens   207
Italics   210
Numbers   211
Parallel Structure   214
Plurals   216
Possessives   219
Punctuation   220
Run-On Sentences   236
Sentence Fragments   238
Spelling   239
Split Infinitives   242
Word Division   243

9

Passages for Editing   245

Editing for Fragments and Run-On Sentences
  (Passages 1, 2)   246
Editing for Tense Shifts (Passages 2, 3, 4)   246
Editing for Punctuation (Passages 5, 6, 7, 8)   249
Editing for Vague "This" (Passage 9)   252
Editing for Subject-Verb Agreement (Passages
  10, 11, 12)   253
Editing for Parallel Structure (Passages 13, 14)   254
Editing for Active/Passive (Passages 15, 16)   255
Editing for Wordiness (Passages 17, 18, 19)   256
General Editing (Passage 20)   258
Passage Not Ready for Editing (Passage 21)   259

Index   **261**

The College Writer's Handbook

Some Preliminary Suggestions

1 AT THE BEGINNING, THINK OF WRITING AS SPEAKING

The first thing to conquer is fear of the blank page. If you can write down the thoughts in your head, no matter how garbled, useless, or wrong these thoughts may be, then you have at least accomplished Step 1 and should stop reading this item and go to the next one.

If a blank sheet of paper fills you with dread, however, or if it makes you feel tight in the area of the heart or suddenly hungry, then you might use one or more of the following gimmicks:

a. Imagine you are talking to someone about your topic. Concentrate on this conversation until you can actually hear the words. Write down what you hear.

1

b. If you're mathematically inclined or like to think in terms of maps or diagrams, then draw a picture or write a formula. Explain this to an imaginary listener and write down your explanation.

c. If it's difficult to start at the beginning, then start in the *middle* of what you want to say. (Also see p. 4: *Separate the Writing Task into Stages.*)

2 MINIMIZE THE AGONY

If you are past the stage of fear but still go through considerable agony in the process of writing, then you might do well to forget temporarily about writing well. Don't think about good sentences, exact words, spelling, or punctuation. Think about getting all the material onto the page as quickly as possible. If you find there are often long pauses between writing one sentence and the next, and your mind wanders off the topic, then give yourself a time limit, say half an hour for a page of writing. Set the alarm clock and promise yourself a reward for accomplishing your goal, even if you are not satisfied with what you have written.

3 FORGET ABOUT FANCY LANGUAGE

Many students honestly believe that they must imitate someone else's style when they write papers for college courses. All too often the result is that their writing sounds inflated and phony and the ideas themselves unoriginal. Feel free to be yourself when you write, to say what you mean in clear, straightforward terms of your own.

Unless you are already a fairly skilled writer, a thesaurus may do you more harm than good. It may tell what a word means but not what context to use it in. If you are a reasonably competent writer, use it if it helps you recall a word you already know but have momentarily forgotten.

4 CONSIDER YOUR AUDIENCE

A general rule in writing is to find out who you are writing *for,* and then to imagine at every step that some member of this audience is sitting by your side listening, arguing, and questioning. Assume that this person is willing to listen but rather slow to catch on. Many examples may be needed before this person can grasp a general idea. He has to be led, step by step, through a reasoning process because he cannot or will not make the logical leaps that might help him grasp your meaning. Such a reader—or listener—may lose interest if a general idea is repeated. He is likely to become bored and stop reading altogether if he cannot make connections between what you have said on paper and his own experience. Different audiences require different words, different kinds of concrete examples, different syntax or ways of ordering the words, and sometimes even quite different content. But any audience is slower to comprehend your message than you may, at first, believe.

5 FIND OUT ABOUT THE MEDIUM

It helps a writer to know the medium he is writing for. Of course he will know whether he is writing an article for a magazine (say, *Consumer Reports* or *Playboy*), a letter to the editor of the *Los Angeles Times,* or a short manual of instructions for building a canoe. In each case, the writer knows what kind of writing he should do, how formal it should be, and generally what sort of style his readers are used to.

A writer of course papers in the first year of college, however, is often totally in the dark about the medium of course papers. You may never have read any, may never have seen any published, and you may assume that the sole reader of a course paper is a graduate student grader or the course instructor. You may not be at all sure what style of writing your reader expects, or for what purpose anyone would read what you've written. You may assume that the grader is not reading your paper for information but rather for purposes of evaluating the work you have done, and this fact means that he's not really an audience at all but rather someone between you and your audience.

What can you do? First, you can become familiar with the medium of course papers. Look ahead in this book to the sample course papers for literature, anthropology, and science. Ask your professors to show you samples of course papers. Second, assume that your instructor or teaching assistant is not only an evaluator but also part of an audience made up of all the students who took part in your course as well as all the people who have done the reading you have done. Third, assume that what you write could conceivably be published in a student journal to be read by anyone, student or nonstudent, interested in the subject matter.

6   SEPARATE THE WRITING TASK INTO STAGES

For many amateur writers of course papers the following plan will be helpful:

a. Write whatever random notes on your topic you can think of.

b. Decide, after looking at your notes, what general statement the paper, as a whole, will make. This is often a personal response to the material—your considered view of it. It does not have to be profound, startling, or even very original. But it must be what you really think.

c. Make an outline, putting your notes in order. (See the discussion of planning and outlining, pages 48–50.) Your outline represents the structure your final writing will have.

d. Consider now whether your topic is too broad to be covered in detail in the amount of space you have; or whether it is so narrow that you will have to pad out your material to fill up the space. If it is too narrow, then decide what bigger or wider question your topic is part of, and take this as a new topic. (If you are in a real quandary, this is a good time to go see the instructor or teaching assistant.)

e. Write a first complete draft with all possible speed. (Don't do another version of your notes. Write complete sentences.)

f. Put the draft away in a drawer for at least two days. (Some people, when they take it out again, find it completely disorganized. If this is the case with you, consider what you have written as notes only. Start again at Step *b*).

g. Revise. Much of this book consists of suggestions for revision.

h. Type.

i. Proofread. If possible, put the paper away again for a day or so before proofreading. If this is not possible, try to wait at least an hour. As proofreader, try to imagine you are reading some-one else's paper for the first time.

Because you know the content of your paper thoroughly, you will probably have a tendency to skim it when you proof-read. You can force yourself to be more careful by reading the paper backwards, from right to left and from the last page to the first. You will be surprised at the number of typographical and spelling errors you discover.

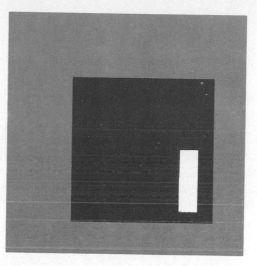

Kinds of Writing You Can Expect To Do

This chapter is like a display of writing. The various samples exhibited here were written for tasks both easy and difficult by freshmen, more advanced students, and professional writers. What these show is that the principles of writing apply to subject matter that varies from physics to poetry and from elementary observations to quite sophisticated matters of theory.

What assignments were these writers given? What was written? What form did their writing take, and how long was it? Five kinds of writing are covered here:

GENERAL-PURPOSE WRITING. Writers record their observations, argue a point, react, reflect, or recommend a course of action. The freshman in a writing course, the professional writer, and the ordinary person on the job all must write responses based on their personal experience or point of view. See p. 8.

7

ESSAY EXAMS. These require not only knowledge of the assigned reading and lecture notes but also skills in thinking, organizing, and writing. Speedwriting is rarely necessary if the writer organizes first. See p. 16.

COURSE PAPERS. The kind most frequently assigned asks you to explain, describe, evaluate, and/or comment on some fairly narrow part of the subject matter that makes up the course. See p. 22.

SCIENCE WRITING. Informal write-ups and notes have to be written in clear, straightforward English. Formal articles customarily follow a rather set pattern to allow colleagues to read them easily. Technical language is a necessity, but writers should work for simplicity in style. See p. 35.

PROPOSAL WRITING. College students, some of them undergraduates, have initiated projects and have been granted money by state and federal agencies. This is an outline of what most fund-granting agencies want to know about a project. See p. 40.

General-Purpose Writing

A DESCRIPTION

Writing instructors frequently assign a short exercise in description. The object is to look closely and memorize as much as possible of a visual scene, then to write out the details so that someone reading the description will come close to seeing exactly the same scene. In this case the assignment was to watch a short documentary film, without narration, and then to describe one very short part of it (15 seconds to 1 minute) so that the reader could nearly see the film himself. One student remembered a scene in a dance hall. She remembered balloons, streamers, women in long tight dresses, lacy ruffles, flabby stomachs bulging, and hips swaying. She remembered a teased hairdo and hair hanging loosely, a face with an intent expression and one with deep grooves in the skin. Her technique was to write out a list of things remembered, then to rewrite the list in full sentences.

Anna's Lounge

Fat balloons and colorful crepe streamers hung from the ceiling of Anna's. Olive-skinned women wore long, tight dresses that ended in a large lacy ruffle just below their knees. Creases in the taffeta and satin fabrics not only showed their feminine curves but also every flabby stomach bulge. Their black hair was either carefully teased high or left hanging loose below their shoulders. Every woman seemed intent on appearing beautiful as each one swayed well-padded hips to the music.

—excerpt from paper by Sylvia Yuen

A NARRATIVE

Writing courses, even those in expository writing, sometimes require a narrative paper. The object is to tell what happened. The purpose is much the same as the purpose of writing a description—to teach techniques in the use of details, since it is these which make writing come across to the reader. In this case the student was told to narrate a rather ordinary event in his life (perhaps something that happened a number of times). Before writing he was to run this "happening" through his head as though it were a film. The writer was to concentrate, trying to see scenes and also to hear words or bits of conversations. Then he was to write it out exactly as it happened.

Parts of two student narratives are printed here. The first one gives a few moments from an ordinary day's surfing; the second gives the preliminaries to the writer's sewing lesson. While the passages contain "just the facts," something more is communicated.

Surfing Moments

Clifford picked up his surfboard and jumped off the rocks into the water. It was very cold and it made me shiver when it closed around my knees. Slowly, I walked farther out until the water reached my waist. Grabbing the sides of my board firmly, I slid onto it and felt the water wet my stomach. As I paddled and picked up speed, I could feel the water streaming around my stomach all the way down to my legs. The water around me was a deep blue-green color that made it impossible to see the bottom. It made me uneasy not to be able to see what was in the water around me. I paddled faster, half from fear and half from excitement. As I got closer to the surf, the roar of the waves made me stop. Sitting up on my surfboard, I watched the waves as they formed and broke. As I was sitting, I saw a swell begin to form and get bigger. It hissed as it got bigger and gave a roar when it broke into whitewater. My attention suddenly focused on Clifford trying to catch a long swell. Just as the wave reached its biggest size, Clifford stood up and raced across the face of the wave. It excited me to see Clifford surfing and I hurried out to get some waves for myself.

As I paddled into the area where the waves were, he saw a perfect swell coming behind him. At first it was just a long green hump of water, but it quickly turned into a high wall. I turned around and paddled furiously as the wave approached. I felt myself

Sewing Lesson

I walked along the lane carrying my red carpet bag making sure there wasn't a car coming in or going out since it was only a one-car lane and there were no sidewalks. I stopped at the third house, which, like all the others in the lane, was old and made out of wood. This one had a picket fence about three feet high. The gate was old and termite-eaten and made a creaking noise when I pushed it open. It took only four steps along the narrow cement walkway to get to the steps of the porch. I left my slippers on the porch and without knocking, opened the white door which had a screen on the top half.

"Good morning," I said, raising my voice a little so that she could hear me.

"Hai, gudu mawning," she replied from the kitchen.

It was about 8:15 and I was the first student there. I took out the contents of my bag and put them on the side of one of the two drafting tables in the living room and stowed the bag under the table. Then I hurried over to the sewing machine in the middle of the room. There were four other machines: three Sears Kenmores and an old-fashioned black Singer machine with an old, brown, wooden cabinet. But this particular machine was a new model Singer and whoever was the first to arrive in the morning would always set their thread and bobbin in the machine before anyone else could get to it.

I pulled the stool out and sat

rising and knew that I was on the wave. My speed suddenly increased and I stopped paddling. I reached down and grabbed the sides of my board; I could feel my hands being pushed back by the water streaming by. Quickly I pushed my body up and brought my legs up under me. I stood up in a crouching position and began to work on the wave that was mine. I streamed down the face of the wave and made a wide left turn back up the wave. I felt the board rising under me and my knees bent as they absorbed the force of the wave. Shooting to the top of the wave, I hit the lip of it and watched it break into a million glittering drops. Dropping down to the bottom of the wave, I cranked a hard left turn, forcing part of the board and my feet into the water. I streaked back to the top of the wave at an angle going upwards. Seeing that a section of the wave was about to break, I streaked toward it with streams of water flying from my board. As the wave broke right on top of me, I could feel the water splashing on my head and shoulders. Maintaining my balance, I wiped the water from my eyes and cruised to the end of the wave. Bending down, I grabbed the sides of the board and lay down on it. I could feel my heart beating rapidly and my mind was spinning.

—student writer, Joel Matsunaga

down trying to adjust it to make sure I could sew comfortably in that position. It was a small stool with four black metal legs and a little, round, flattened-out cushion on the top. I could never sit on it for more than 30 minutes and since every machine had a similar stool, there was no chance of me exchanging stools for a more comfortable one.

—student writer, Eilyne Matsumoto

A PAPER ABOUT AN ISSUE

This kind of assignment asks the student to argue a point. The emphasis is on convincing or persuading the reader, and the techniques are similar to those used by a debater. In this case the assignment was to argue the question: "Is capital punishment uncivilized?" One student writer, whose approach is given below, argues that it is *not* uncivilized. Here is how the writer proceeds.

In her first paragraph she claims that capital punishment is a necessary right of a society even if it is not the right of an individual member of the society. She distinguishes between the functions of a society and those of its individual members. Society can force private land to be sold and can draft men for defense, but an individual cannot. These transactions may be necessary to a society. These two examples point up the distinction between these functions and show that a society cannot be judged by the same standards as an individual.

In her second paragraph she tries to show that taking human life may be justifiable. First, she says, taking life is not a crime even for an individual if it is done in self-defense. The same rule applies on a larger scale. An army is permitted, even compelled, to kill in order to ensure the survival of a society. In both these cases killing is permitted when it means self-defense. The writer is using them as analogies and claiming that capital punishment is essentially the same kind of necessary behavior. Capital punishment is a way society has of defending itself.

In her third paragraph she deals with possible counterarguments. She argues that innocent lives will rarely if ever be taken through capital punishment—and that far more lives will be saved since criminals will be deterred by fear of capital punishment. She provides descriptive detail and a few examples to justify these arguments. So, she concludes, capital punishment is really a civilizing influence since it enables society to take ultimate sanctions against those who violate an essential prohibition.

The writer using this approach has really given a three-part answer to the question, or three reasons why she believes that capital punishment is more civilized than uncivilized.

THE PROFESSIONALLY-WRITTEN ARTICLE

Here we include part of a professional article. What it shows is that this writer had an assignment not too different from one given in many college classes. As a reporter for the *New York Review of Books* he was asked to read books on the subject of Walt Disney and Disneyworld in Florida. Then he was to visit Disneyworld, observe, participate, and write up his observations and comments in an article. In the paragraphs quoted below the writer uses a combination of the techniques just demonstrated: description, narration, and a form of argumentation, although he may not have been conscious of using them.

In the first paragraph there are descriptive details from the scene around him: moving cars, hanging mosses, dead trees, billboards, and neon signs. In the second paragraph there are narrative details: he went to the hotel, he talked to the clerk, he waited in a restaurant, he talked to the waitress. The last paragraph tells not what he saw nor what he did but what he thought about the fantasyland. For him Disneyworld is a world of contradictions. At Disneyworld humans do what robots ought to do, and robots do the human jobs. The reader is perhaps half aware of this meaning by the time he reaches these sentences because he has been prepared by the description and narration already provided.

> With every automobile moving at the same speed, as if remotely controlled, driving to WDW during the energy crisis was more dreamlike than any experience in Fantasyland itself. But the landscape anticipates WDW—the Haunted Mansions, at least—in the thick drapes of Spanish moss, and in the weird gray forests of dead cypresses and live oak. "Mickey & Minnie are Waiting for You," a billboard proclaimed. . . .
>
> At WDW's Polynesian Village Hotel, a sidewalk hostess cheerfully informed this reporter of a long delay before his room would be ready, and suggested waiting in one of two restaurants. In spite of People Movers, the Monorail, and a highly-touted mass transport system, every visit to WDW entails a great deal of queuing, waiting, and being told that this or that "attraction" is temporarily closed, or not yet opened, or still on the drawing board. In what seemed to be the less disastrous of the two restaurants, the aforementioned reporter managed to question some of the waitresses: "Are you well treated here? Do you like the job? Are you paid well? What induced you to come?" Answers: "It is a thrilling

place to be. I feel connected with a great thing. The money is pretty good. Everybody here is just great."

But the restaurant work seemed robot-like. And this proved to be one of the contradictions of WDW, that of people performing jobs that robots might be expected to handle very competently, and of robots accomplishing tasks that until very recently were widely regarded as human.—Robert Craft, "In the Mouse Trap," *The New York Review of Books,* May 16, 1974

See also the passage from *Summerhill* (p. 84) written by A. S. Neill. Again the author's task was to write up what he had seen, heard, or felt, and to make some sense of it.

Another writer with a similar task was Martin Mayer when he wrote *The Schools.* In this case the book was written after 30 months of traveling in the United States and Europe, talking to people in schools and watching classes. He also read a good many books. One of his techniques is to slip a snippet of pure narration, like a piece of film, in between the pages of general discussion. Here is a piece that shows what happened in a French classroom on the day that he was there.

The school is built into a hillside, two stories high facing the road and one story facing the dirt playground at the rear. It was put up about fifty years ago, and has received no special care. The floors creak and the furniture is scarred. The class is the equivalent of an American sixth grade, taught by the principal of the school (elementary-school principals teach full time in France; indeed, principals everywhere except in the United States carry some teaching load as well as administrative duties). There are about thirty-five boys in the room, ranged in seven rows facing front. One of them, a handsome boy with well-brushed black hair, is called upon to recite, and to the accompaniment of some ragging from those in his row strides to the front, where he does not slouch. The teacher, a faintly shabby but highly dignified man in his early forties, ignores the ragging.

On request, the boy draws the femur of a rabbit on the blackboard. It is assumed in France that all children can draw accurately—and, oddly enough, the assumption seems to be correct. The teacher says to the visitor, in a stage whisper, "The son of the mayor. He will go to the *lycée.*"

Oh.

The teacher turns to the child, pleasantly. "What kind of animal is the rabbit?"

"Herbivorous."

"A complete sentence, please."

"The rabbit is an herbivorous animal."
"Why is he an herbivorous animal?"
"Because he eats plants."
"Only plants?"
"Only plants."
"Good."

—Martin Mayer, *The Schools,* (Harper: 1961), p. 11

An account of this episode sheds light on the topics Mayer wants to discuss: the student's expectations of what he is to do in the classroom, the teacher's conception of his own role, and ways of segregating or "streaming" students at the high school age. (The *lycée* is a college preparatory school.)

SAMPLE JOB ASSIGNMENTS

Much of the writing you might be expected to do on the job will be "technical writing," or assignments like these:

Do a population study for a school board.
Write up a progress report on a psychiatric patient.
Summarize the results of a soil analysis for a corporate farmer.
Write up detailed specifications for a patent application.
Do a report on the potential building safety of a factory still on the drawing board.

For nontechnical jobs the writer is more likely to depend on his own experience and observations. His assignment is apt to be: describe or narrate what happened, draw conclusions and make recommendations, suggestions or comments, possibly for future action. Here are two examples:

1. The personnel manager of a company returns from a recruiting trip to college campuses. He writes out a five-page report for his company's president, saying how many management people he hired, with a sketch of each, and for what positions they were hired. He names the colleges producing potentially good employees. He describes the kinds of changing attitudes he noted among those interviewed and how his company's hiring

policies might profitably be changed in the future to take the changing attitudes into account.

2. A hospital administrator attends a Washington conference. New federal money, he learns, will be granted to those hospitals willing to install certain equipment, give certain kinds of training programs, or cooperate with the people in the neighborhood of their hospital by giving classes. He writes up an account of this meeting for his staff, followed by a list of particular ways his hospital might be able to use the federal money. He calls for the support of his staff and asks them to respond to his suggestions.

Essay Exams

AN ESSAY EXAM FOR A BOTANY COURSE

The following essay question from a botany exam has two parts:

> When the first Polynesians arrived on the Hawaiian Islands, they had to sustain themselves on the materials they found there (native plants). *a.* Using what you know about the native plants, describe a hypothetical life style developed by these first settlers. Consider the essentials in this life style: food, clothing, shelter and medicine. *b.* How did this life style change when their *introduced* plants grew to harvest?

The professor warned the students that they would be judged not only on the extent of their knowledge about plants but also on their ability to organize and to keep their answer down to three bluebook pages.

What is meant here by the ''ability to organize''? As our sample answer on the next page should make clear, it means first, not to write down everything one knows—a rule surprisingly hard to follow because the pen, once it begins to race across the bluebook page, has a will of its own. The student, in spite of himself, finds himself writing details that are interesting perhaps but not relevant to the question. Second, ''organizing'' means dividing the answer into parts or categories and gathering up the evidence for each part so that it can be written down in an orderly fashion, without unnecessary repetition and without rambling.

For this exam a hastily drawn up chart was useful, with ''native plants'' and ''introduced plants'' across the top and ''food, clothing, shelter, and medicine'' down the side. The student jotted down the names of all the native and introduced plants he could think of, for quantity of detail was important here. The more evidence or detail he could produce to support his answer the better.

For this essay exam, as for most, an introduction and conclusion were not really necessary. The conclusion is taken for granted in the question: the life-style of the new settlers was largely determined by the plants they found when they first arrived, and later their life-style was changed by the use of their introduced plants. As for an introduction, the first statement of the essay is usually enough, and a whole paragraph of introduction is almost always a waste of space.

The general rules are these: make a statement and back it up with detail. Once you have given all the detail you know, stop. Make sure you have answered the question.

Hawaiian Plants and Life-styles

Restating the question may help a beginning exam-taker.

When the migrating Polynesians arrived in Hawaii from the Marquesas and/or Tahiti, they probably came equipped with the seeds and cuttings of some of their most useful plants from the homeland. After several years, they would have incorporated into their lives the products of these plants brought with them. What would the native flora contribute to their lives, and how would the introduced plants have changed their life-style?

But the writer could have begun his answer here.

This is essentially a listing technique.

Initially the migrants would have relied heavily on the limu for a food source (e.g., limu kala, limu kohu, lima manauea). These were very similar to or even identical to seaweeds of the southern hemisphere. We can speculate that niu (*Cocos*) was native and that this provided its nutritious solid and liquid endosperm to the newcomers' diet. Native berries ('ohelo berries) and the hapu'u, a source of greens (fiddleheads) must have been a relief in a plant diet otherwise dominated by starch from the tree fern trunks (hapu'u and ama'u). Not only was their diet bland and somewhat harsh, but their clothing would have been also. Mamaki, found growing wild, would have made a rough grade of kapa cloth. The strong native fiber, 'olona, which made some of the best cordage in the Pacific and helped these people to net fish, might have been used in some way for clothing also. Medicines would have come from the flowers of the plant 'olona, and also from the lehua and limu kala. As for housing, the native pili grass provided a good thatching material, but it was used in conjunction with less-than-ideal frame materials of 'ohia and mamane, plus the native 'ohe.

Now let's consider the relative golden age of later years. For starters, the dinner table has improved tremendously. We've enriched our starch selection with various pois of the taro, 'wala, and 'ulu origin, and have these same plants either in puddings with niu, or just cooked but unpounded. Cooking is probably easier now with ti leaves as food packaging and banana "trunks" as water sources. The men can eat bananas (these are kapu for women), and to make everyone feel good we might find a mild narcotic drink made from the pounded root of the 'awa. The kitchen is complete with a set of proper ipu's and wooden calabashes made from breadfruit or milo woods. Now people wear the much finer wauke kapa cloth. And now the hau plant, in addition to the niu and 'olona, can be made into cordage. For medicine there is the 'awa as well as the ginger and banana plants. And finally housing has improved too since hala and ko leaves can provide a heavier, more permanent thatching material for walls, floors and mats. Many, however, might still prefer the softer native pili grass for roofs since it is much quieter when the wind blows through it.—student writer, Bernie Hill

There is no harm in this rather abrupt ending, and it is better than ending with a restatement of the general idea. Graceful endings are not a hallmark of essay exams.

And here is a sample showing what one should *not* do. Read the examination question once again, then read this answer. At what point does it stop restating the question and begin to veer away from the question entirely?

Hawaiian Plants and Life-styles

When the first Polynesians arrived, they brought with them plants that could help them sustain their lives. There was an ecosystem that had already been established, and with the introduction of their plants and life, a new one was to be established. They would have to try out new native plants that grew there. The Hawaiian life-style was to live in harmony with nature. They would cultivate the plants that they brought with them and learn to use gradually what was native to the land. But they would always live in harmony with nature. With the cultivation of their new plants, some plants would have to be removed and their new plants might take over, killing the existing ones. (Example: The rat was brought here to Hawaii by the first Polynesians and this in itself upset the balance for the honey-creeper that made its nest on the ground.) When the plants were ready to be harvested the seeds would be able to scatter and grow elsewhere, with the possibility of killing the plants that inhabit that region. (Example: depletion of sandalwood by man; but there was another plant that could also grow there to take its place.) Hawaiians would inevitably experiment with the native plants to incorporate them into their culture.

With the coming of Cook again the ecosystem was to be re-arranged. The introduction of new diseases that were new to the Hawaiians took a toll on their lives. Even with new plants the same thing could be seen, but not to such a great extent. The native plants then had been wiped out by newer, stronger introductions; the growth range became smaller and smaller. And in some cases some plants became extinct.

A HISTORY ESSAY EXAM

The question was this:

The Trade and Navigation Acts were a major factor in provoking the American Revolution. Discuss.

The word ''discuss'' means that the writer has some choice in the direction he takes. He could discuss the statement by showing these acts were *not* the major factor because there were other factors more important. Or he could say that there were good reasons to believe that these acts *were* the major factor. Or he could dispute the implication that *all* of the acts were provocative. Here is the approach chosen by one student.

This student writer chooses the last alternative above. He shows that the acts as a whole were not a cause of the revolution; only a particular group of them were.

How did he proceed? His first paragraph claims that these acts were two very different kinds of legislation—one kind was intended to encourage trade, the other to tax it. The first kind, covering all major acts up to 1763, created strong ties of loyalty. The writer describes benefits such as guaranteed markets, plentiful credit, and efficient transportation. He details the wide support for this legislation in the colonies.

The writer then describes the later laws in some detail, showing that they were passed in Parliament over the opposition of both American and British commercial interests and were intended to benefit only a small Tory clique around the king.

In his last paragraph the writer concludes that these particular laws and their corrupt and ruthless enforcement led to the rapid weakening of American loyalities to Britain and to the justifiable conviction that the British government sought to establish a centralized control over the colonies that would destroy the self-governing powers they had already gained.

The writer using this approach has produced a three-part essay. The first two parts are a contrast between two different kinds of laws, from which the conclusion, the third part, logically follows. In this essay the conclusion is not a restatement of anything but is essential to the development of the main idea. (For ways of developing ideas in these ways, see particularly *Description,* and *Comparison and Contrast,* pp. 55 and 67.)

Course Papers

AN ANTHROPOLOGY PAPER FOR A FRESHMAN OR SOPHOMORE COURSE

The assignment was to write a detailed paper (5 to 8 pages) describing the norms and unwritten laws of a particular culture. The student was to write about a group that he had known or been part of himself (an ethnic group, an interest group like musicians or surfers, a religious community, a social class, or a group formed by members of an occupation). This was not an assignment that stressed the collection of data. Instead the emphasis was on the interpretation of personal experience.

One student writer chose to describe the culture of the military, especially that of military families, since she had been part of one. Her general statement was that the military society she had known had developed its own special norms and social rules.

This is how she develops her topic. *First,* she notes that, while the military service has several different branches and inter-service rivalries, military society as a whole is characterized by a major social division between officers and enlisted men. Here she lists many details regarding this split. *Next,* she describes the double role played by the military wife, double because both civilian and military demands are made on her. *Then,* she describes the pattern of frequent moves, the role of military neighbors in this process, the consequences of these moves for making and keeping friends, and ways of adapting quickly to new surroundings. What traits of character, then, does the military family reveal? The writer *concludes* by naming some of them. (To develop her ideas, she uses several kinds of paragraph development: description, cause and effect, and comparison and contrast. For more on these, see pp. 55, 64, and 67.)

For this assignment, as for many given in freshman writing courses, the writer had to recall particular people, happenings, and conversations. She had to produce the material for analysis out of her own experience. Some students, unable to remember enough from their own experience, did observations ''in the field''—in an old people's home, for instance, and in a high school.

Here is the student's paper.

Military Family Life

''The military family'' is usually viewed as a rather curious group of outsiders who are here today and gone tomorrow. Civilians often feel that the military is just one big blob of people—all of them the same—who generally take more from a community than they contribute. It would probably be very surprising to many to get an inside glimpse of the experiences, ideas, and unwritten codes which govern the social conduct of the military family life in general, and also the complex differences among military people. I have been a member of a military family for many years now. What follows is a description of cultural patterns and codes as I perceive them.

First of all, the military is divided into organizations: Army, Navy, Air Force, Marines, and Coast Guard. Within and between each service is a very definite pecking order with very strict rules of discipline and conduct. These are accompanied by the unwritten rules which govern the social actions between individuals and families.

The two main divisions in the military itself are enlisted personnel and officers. Enlisted people go through nine grades, E-1 (E for enlisted) being the lowest, through E-9. Officers' ranks are O-1 to O-10. Probably the main unifying factor in the military is the combination of rank and discipline, an absolute necessity for any large organization that must work as a single unit.

Approximately 85% of the total service personnel is enlisted, and are considered the labor class of the military. There are general basic differences between those of enlisted and officer rank regarding background, education, and personalities. The lower enlisted ranks most often are not educated beyond high school or maybe a year or two of college. As a matter of fact, many young men finish high school in the service. Many enlisted people come from lower income families, or had broken and troubled childhoods, or just didn't know what to do with themselves. The military offers great opportunity for people willing to put forth the effort. People are constantly being trained and educated in all types of fields—in the technical aspects of machines and electronics, in medicine, in both military and civilian kinds of occupations. By the time an enlisted person is in a higher rank he is well trained, has gained confidence and maturity, better pay, and probably a wife. If the strict conduct of the military is too much for a person, he has probably gotten out (his choice or the service's) long before he reaches say E-5 or E-6.

The officers (15%) are generally college graduates who have gone either to the Academy or an OCS (Officer Candidate School) and are the management level of the military. Besides being a little older than recruit enlistees, they have already experienced the discipline necessitated by college life and officer's training. Or, if they are not college graduates, they are exceptional, higher enlisteds who are selected to go to "knife and fork" school, or to any of several various other routes where the government pays for the schooling. These officers, men who were once enlisted, are known as mustangs.

There is also a warrant officer program. Their niche is between E's and O's; W-1, W-2, W-3. They are definitely officers, but generally are more specialized and fill specific billets. Their qualifications are similar to the mustangs in that they too generally come up from the ranks.

There is a specific no-fraternization rule between enlisteds and officers, especially if the parties involved are in the direct chain of command. The thinking is if an officer must give a life or death order under combat conditions, then friendship with one or two of his subordinates might bias him against the others. Also, since officers are human too, there may be diminished respect if the two groups have been out drinking and carousing together. Seeing an officer under such human conditions could tarnish the luster a bit. This rule is generally followed, but probably just as much because of the differences in interests, education, and financial levels as because of the rule. However, there are common grounds especially in the fields of sports, child rearing, organizations such as PTA, Scouts, other community services and church, where the rule does not appear applicable. But even then the attitudes and manners reveal that people feel they are ''enlisted'' or ''officer'' rank.

How does this life-style affect the family's social conduct? Approximately 35% of military men are married. The wives are definitely a part of the military way of life, but they are still civilians. They usually have a foot in each door. It is expected of the wife of a higher ranking officer or enlisted man to make the younger wives feel more relaxed and that they have a home away from home. But there is a thin line between playing the mother hen role, earning respect for oneself, and ''wearing her husband's stripes,'' attempting to take advantage of one's husband's rank. In many cases the unwritten rules of hierarchy among the women are as strictly followed as with the men, but in recent years, especially in the time of civil rights and women's liberation, this is taking on less importance. It used to be felt that a wife's conduct had a great bearing on how far a man could advance, but over and over it is being shown that this is no longer true. However, the group of wives still forms the core of ''military family'' that gives continuity to this life style. Mothers play a very decisive role in decision making in child rearing. About half the time she is the only parent.

That is another major point. Military men go away. Each service has some type of unaccompanied (that is, without families) tour of duty. For instance, the Navy has sea duty or outposts way out in nowhere, where the man will be gone from three to fifteen months. Of course, during war time it could be longer. Nevertheless, during his absence the wife is making all of the decisions. Generally, the children who are brought up with this way of life adapt even more readily than their parents — as children generally do.

Usually, during husbands' absences the wives become a more cohesive group. They get together more frequently for coffees, luncheons, theater, picnics, or community volunteer work. Even the working wives— and there are quite a few—try to get together more often. They generally share information from the husbands, problems, etc. In some instances a rivalry develops about who's getting the best information, or a problem discussion turns into a bitch session, but generally the more experienced wives tend to help keep things in proper perspective. They are not too tolerant of chronic criers, or those wives who feel they need super extra-curricular masculine attention.

Some wives use the time during their husbands' absence to pursue time-consuming activities that wouldn't really interest him—higher education, cake decorating, or sewing, for example. The long absences (six months or more) aren't easy every moment for even the best adapted. Every military wife can vouch for the fact that if something major is going to happen, it happens during a deployment—the engine falls out of the car, Suzie breaks her leg, a bill comes for the roof caving in on the Florida house. But the military has services for many of these types of problems: dispensary, legal advice, and various other specialists in various other fields. And there are usually some husbands around from other ships or squadrons who are willing to lend a hand because they know that when they're deployed some other at-home husband will return the favor.

If a baby is born during the father's absence (not too uncommon an occurrence) the wives generally play "Dad" taking turns at the hospital, getting the mother to and from, and if a grandmother doesn't come to help out, they also take turns staying with her till things are adjusted.

There is a plus side to the separations, though it may seem to be hidden. Once a military husband/wife bond has established itself, the separations tend to keep the relationship vital. This is provided the separation isn't a matter of years as in the cases of the POW's. Each homecoming, say greeting a ship after a six or seven-month deployment, is a very emotional experience, and serves to renew the cohesiveness and mutual respect. Of course, there is always the problem of having put one another too high on the pedestal, but one keeps this in mind when the husband sleeps for the first three days (he hasn't been on a picnic either).

Probably the one single aspect that has the greatest bearing on life style is the nomadic way of life. The unmarried military person is taken care of as far as travel goes, or his quarters. It is not much trouble. But a family has a different set of problems, especially where children are concerned. There are schools and organizations to transfer, pets to be considered, and an overall view of maintaining a consistency in their way of life. Very often families live in military housing where they are surrounded by others who experience the same ways. It is all really taken for granted. Neighbors often provide a meal or child care for families moving in and out, or some movers just prefer a cup of coffee and a fifteen-minute break to say that she has just discovered that half of Johnny's clothes that were to go with them on the trip have been crated in a big box and loaded on the bottom of the truck.

For the career family variety is the spice of life, but it still isn't easy to leave good friends. Because of their outgoing nature, and the hard fact of short-term residency, military families usually make friends quickly because they know they will lose them quickly. Very often, however, they will meet their military friends again halfway around the world. After a period of time, say ten years, one has a very long list of true friends (it is amazing how much talking one can do at 2:00 A.M. when the husbands are gone), and will probably correspond only once or twice a year, probably at Christmas via the family gram—a xeroxed annual diary with a short hand-written note.

For some families the variety they seek is almost completely within the military community, venturing out into the local scene with each other. For others, it is being in a new civilian community and partaking as much as possible of that new way of life. There's a fantastic and interesting difference between the locals of East Greenwich, Rhode Island and Kalihi, Hawaii, and Mobile, Alabama.

Some military families buy houses each time they move, and live on the local economy (while still partaking of exchange and commissary privileges). The children often go to local schools whether they live on base or not, and military wives take an active role in PTA, Scouts, and church. This is one way of providing continuity and stability to the life-style of the children.

The people who have successfully adapted to this way of life are usually very energetic people who I'm certain in the eyes of a psychoanalyst have all kinds of hang-ups and problems. I've heard the military man's job described as an outlet for aggression, men playing at war like little boys with toys. I've heard the wives described as dominant and overbearing with overtones of martyr need. Or that the high rate of mixed marriages is because the men are a bunch of misfits who can't make it with American women, or who are too stupid not to get hooked by a foreigner looking for an easy way out, or who need a person totally subservient to themselves. (That last one is pretty funny—how quickly foreign brides Americanize!) I am sure there is some validity in some of these opinions, but what I was trying to express here was a generally accepted view of how the successful military families see themselves. They are citizens of the world rather than a given community. They see themselves as individuals with a great diversity of interests, but they also recognize the common factors that they share, probably the most predominant of which is the desire for adventure.—student writer, Diane Elliott

A HUMANITIES COURSE PAPER (4 to 6 pages)

We include this assignment to illustrate what a student might write for a junior-level paper. This student, in a course stressing ideas and issues in literature, history, and philosophy, was asked to write a paper on any of Bertolt Brecht's plays. For her topic she chose what she believed to be an important idea of Brecht's—the value of knowledge itself and of the search for knowledge in human life. The play is *Galileo.*

In her paper she notes that the idea has always been an interesting one. Does knowledge do anybody any good? If so, whom? Galileo, the major character in this play, is sure at first that knowledge is good not only for him but for everyday people as well, but soon he comes to regard this belief as foolish and naive. Common people, he asserts, are unable to appreciate science and his scientific discoveries; furthermore it is none of his concern whether or not his discoveries are useful to anyone else. Knowledge has value in itself, quite apart from its application. Indeed the scientist need not concern himself with ways his knowledge might be used.

Later the reader is surprised, then, to find Galileo announcing that it is wrong for knowledge to be applied in ways that will oppress people. Here is a contradiction, for now Galileo seems to believe that knowledge and the applications of this knowledge *cannot* be separated from each other. The writer focuses on this contrast between the rather selfish Galileo and the Galileo suddenly concerned about the welfare of the people. The change in character, she says, is not adequately explained, and this makes the characterization inconsistent.

What might be the reason for such inconsistency? Between the first time Brecht wrote *Galileo* and a later time when he revised it, this student claims, he himself changed his mind about the role of knowledge. The revised version reveals Brecht's realization, after the explosion of atomic bombs, that knowledge could be used in horrifying ways. But parts of the revised version still indicate Brecht's earlier feeling that knowledge is in itself a thing of value, regardless of how it may be used. For Brecht, knowledge and the ability to think clearly were the weapons people must use against tyrants and their rise to power—an idea uppermost in his mind at the time when Nazism was first on the rise.

In the end, says the student, Brecht works around to cover both aspects of the problem: knowledge is good, but in order to be of real value it has to be used in a good way. There is no way one can separate knowledge from its use. (To develop these ideas, the writer used several techniques: description, comparison and contrast, and cause/effect. For more on these, see pp. 55, 67, and 64.)

Here is the paper that the student wrote.

Brecht's Concept of the Value of Knowledge in his Play *Galileo*

In *Galileo* Brecht asks whether knowledge pursued for its own sake can be of value to society. The issue is interesting. If knowledge is never applied, is it still good? Does knowledge make the knower a happier person? or a better one? Is the search for knowledge a worthy occupation? Should everyone seek it, or only a few? Brecht centers his play around two main considerations: the question as to whether knowledge helps the people for whom it is intended, and the newer question in this atomic age, whether knowledge in the hands of the government might not lead to the destruction of man.

At the beginning of the play Galileo is excited by the social context of his research. He sees his discoveries, which challenge antiquated beliefs, as part of a social movement from which both workers and intellectuals will benefit. "At last," he says, "everybody is getting nosy. I predict that in our time astronomy will become the gossip of the market place and the sons of fishwives will pack the schools."[1] He relates himself to the workers; like him they have discovered that there are contradictions between their observations of the universe and the ecclesiastical concept of the order of the universe. He tells the monks that even unread sailors and carpenters, not afraid to use their eyes, are discovering new ways of doing things.

But Galileo fails to consider that behind their similar discoveries there are quite different motivations. Curiosity motivated Galileo to study the sky, whereas the dockyard workers have jobs in which they are forced to take note of the sky. Whereas Galileo seeks to find the knowledge he acquires, the workers receive it without seeking. Galileo, excited by the fact that they have arrived at similar observations, falsely concludes that the workers are motivated by the same driving curiosity which motivates him—"that same high curiosity which was the true glory of ancient Greece" (p. 354).

It is the little monk who destroys Galileo's illusion that he and the workers are working for the same goal. He convinces Galileo that his new water pumps will never work wonders for the people because technological advance without parallel growth in spiritual maturity not only fails but is even harmful to people.

But the loss of the illusion that he is aligned with the workers does not disturb Galileo. It thereby becomes clear that the social context of his work is not really important to him and that he is motivated solely by personal curiosity. Later we see that his interest in research is so selfish that to see his work hurting others does not bother him. After his break with Ludovico, he is so excited about continuing his studies that he is not disturbed by the fact that he has just ruined his daughter's marriage. When he learns that the results of his continued study are causing great disturbance among the people, he says, "I have written a book about the mechanics of the firmament, that is all. What they do or don't do with it is not my concern" (p. 385). He accepts no responsibility for the way in which the people understand and act upon his discoveries.

It therefore comes as something of a surprise that this same Galileo

---

[1] Bertolt Brecht, *Galileo,* original copyright 1952, English version by Charles Laughton, included in collection edited by Eric Bentley, *Seven Plays by Bertolt Brecht* (New York: Grove Press, 1961), p. 335. All quotations from the play come from this edition.

becomes suddenly fearful that the government will use his research and knowledge to oppress the people. The same man who had asserted, "What they do or don't do with it is not my concern" now confesses with regret that he "surrendered [his] knowledge to the powers that be, to use it, no, not to *use* it, *abuse* it" (p. 400). Apparently he has simply changed his mind, for now he seems to feel the scientist's responsibility does not end with the acquisition of new knowledge. Now he asserts that valor must be a requisite for a scientist because through his discoveries he unleashes a powerful force into society and he must have the courage to guide its usage toward good ends. But the reader, or the audience, finds this change of character hard to believe. Brecht has failed to create a situation for Galileo which adequately accounts for his change from a selfish character to one so deeply concerned for others.

The reason for the inconsistency in Galileo's attitude is probably a change in Brecht's attitude toward the central question of the play between the first and second writings of it. Brecht first wrote *Galileo* when he believed that a man who pursued knowledge, in this particular case a scientist, would help society even if he had no concern for the welfare of the people. Living under Nazism, a regime which maintained its control over the people by keeping them ignorant, Brecht believed that the way to end oppression was to teach the people to think. This could be achieved within the restrictions of fascist states by familiarizing them with an academic field, such as science, which employed a method of critical analysis. As he states in one of his essays, "Propaganda that stimulates thinking, in no matter what field, is useful to the cause of the oppressed." [2]

Brecht assumed that people, having learned to doubt in a non-political field, would eventually doubt the right of the government to exploit them. As he explains, "the researches of physicists in recent years have led to consequences in the field of logic which might well endanger a number of dogmas that keep oppression going," ("Writing the Truth," p. 15). However, Brecht's later experiences in America changed his attitude toward this central question. He was in America when the atomic bomb was dropped on Hiroshima. He realized then that while the scien-

---

[2] Bertolt Brecht, "Writing the Truth, Five Difficulties," English version published in *Twice a Year, Tenth Anniversary Issue* (New York: 1948) and also in pamphlet form (publisher unknown).

tific method of inquiry might teach people to think critically, the effects of scientific research could be so destructive as to override any potential benefits. Consequently he reversed the message of *Galileo*. As he says, ''The atomic age made its debut at Hiroshima in the middle of our work. Overnight the biography of the founder of the new system of physics read differently.'' [3] In the second version of *Galileo* Brecht demonstrates that the pursuit of knowledge without the intent of helping society is necessarily detrimental to society.

Brecht's final conviction, that only knowledge pursued for a good purpose is beneficial to society, encompasses both aspects of the problem; knowledge must be directed toward the people for their use and guarded from use by the government. The playwright stresses the importance of considering the people's emotional and spiritual immaturity by demonstrating their inability to accept the truth even when they see it; the young boy sees that the girl is not a witch and admits this to Andrea, but he continues to lead his friends in shouting that she is. However, Brecht does not endorse the little monk's unrealistic solution of stopping research. He tells mankind to continue to ''kindle'' knowledge, but urges him to ''use it right'' (Esslin, p. 89). This admonition is an admission of the destructive power of science. Without proper guidance not only will science fail to instruct people to think critically and to govern themselves intelligently, but, in the hands of despotic government, it can become ''a flame to fall downward to consume us all'' (Esslin, p. 90). Brecht urges the intelligent and compassionate use of knowledge, warning that only knowledge which is pursued with the intent of easing human suffering can be of value to society.—student writer, Robin Stroll

A PAPER ABOUT A POEM

Here the student was to write a paper about any poem written by John Donne not already discussed in class. The assignment was to explain in detail what the poem said and also to show how the technique and form used by the poet made the message more powerful. The purpose of an assignment like this was to provide practice in close reading. The object for the student was to write a

---

[3] From Martin Esslin, *Brecht: The Man and His Work* (New York: Doubleday, 1960), p. 87.

paper that revealed his understanding of single words, of things being compared, of sentences, of the situation, of the feeling or tone of the one who is speaking, and also of how the poem builds as it goes along.

"Holy Sonnet X" is the poem discussed in the sample paper. The technique of the student writer is to talk about meaning by discussing first the attitudes of the speaker, then the use of personification and logical argument, then the variations on the sonnet form used by this poet.

Sonnet X

Death be not proud, though some have called thee
Mighty and dreadfull, for, thou art not soe,
For those, whom thou think'st, thou dost overthrow,
Die not, poor death, not yet canst thou kill mee.
From rest and sleepe, which but thy pictures bee,
Much pleasure, then from thee, much more must flow,
And soonest our best men with thee doe goe,
Rest of their bones, and soules deliverie.
Thou art slave to Fate, Chance, kings, and desperate men,
And dost with poyson, warre, and sicknesse dwell,
And poppie, or charmes can make us sleepe as well,
And better than thy stroake; why swell'st thou then?
One short sleepe past, wee wake eternally,
And death shall be no more; death, thou shalt die.

John Donne

The Concept of Death in Donne's "Holy Sonnet X"

Donne's Holy Sonnet X ("Death be not proud") reveals a speaker secure in his religious faith considering the power of Death. The sonnet starts with what sounds like a challenge to Death and builds to the final triumphant declaration "death, thou shalt die."

Death is personified as a "might and dreadfull [i.e., fear-inspiring] warrior," but one who turns out to be subject to the same conditions of mortality and dependency as ordinary men. Death has been deluded by pride, for those whom he thinks he has overthrown are not really dead. The speaker even expresses contemptuous pity for "poore death." Death, like all of us, is subject to dying, to "Fate, Chance, kings, and desperate men.'' All that death can do is cause a ''short sleepe'' prior to eternity. Donne's poem thus reduces a traditionally feared phenomenon to a pitiable and ineffectual foe, doomed to failure.

To achieve this Donne uses logical argumentation. The dead aren't really dead, for after death ''wee wake eternally.'' Sleep and rest, which look like pictures of death, bring pleasure; therefore, he argues, the real death must bring more pleasure. The speaker continues by showing that death, which allows rest for men's bones and freedom for their souls, must give way to the greatest ''pleasure,'' eternal life. Death, through the mechanism of eternal awakening, is reduced to a brief interlude between life and immortality. The final paradox then is that death must itself die. To those who have lost someone to death, death seems permanent, but only when viewed from the limited perspective of bodily life. Donne presents a broader perspective based on a secure faith. Eternal salvation is achieved by man through the vehicle of death, so death is not fearful at all.

''Holy Sonnet X'' conforms generally to the two-part division of the Italian sonnet. The first eight lines develop the more tentative argumentation, the last six lines reveal a firmer and eventually triumphant tone as if the speaker is himself realizing ever more strongly just how powerless death is. The last six lines, the sestet, depart from the usual Italian sonnet rhyme scheme cdecde—two triplets. Instead the rhyming is cddcef. This seems to break the sestet into a four (cddc)-two (ef) structure. The four line grouping is used to present the humiliating (to Death) list of phenomena which enslave death, on which death must depend. These contain the major reasons why death should not be proud. This use of a grouping of four lines is close to the way such quatrains are used in the English or Shakespearean sonnet form. But the final couplet, which in the usual English sonnet form is rhymed, is here unrhymed. Two distinct though related ideas are expressed. Line 13 summarizes: ''One short sleepe past, wee wake eternally.'' But line 14 has a different function, as we might expect from its failure to rhyme with (and thus unify itself more closely with) the previous line. Line 14 marks the speaker's culminating realization, a realization not achieved until this final line, that death is itself doomed to die. The Italian sonnet form indicates through its rhyme scheme an 8-6 grouping, a two-part division of the total experience. The English 4-4-4-2 allows a different division with a neat final couplet to tie up the ends. Donne manipulates and draws on both of the forms and creates a new variant at the end, to communicate the experience of a man of faith confronting death.—student writer, Duane Reinhart

Science Writing

A LAB REPORT

A student taking a physics course is required to hand in his lab data book at the end of each section of study. His assignment happened to be a long-term study of the properties of transistors. He was required to show the following in his lab book:

1. An understanding of the theory and a working knowledge of the equipment in the lab.
2. Records of the lab work: a list and description of equipment, drawings of diagrams, notes about what he did and when, tables showing the numerical results, graphs on which these results were plotted, and notes to himself (possible mistakes he made in method, peculiar results, and interesting general patterns).
3. General discussion of results or summary: How did his results vary from the theory, or from his calculated results? How can he explain the discrepancy?

The student follows the steps above.

STEP 1. His lab book contains first the student's "self-test," two or three pages of short answers showing that he understands the theory. Many of these are "thought" questions, for example:

In a *pnp* transistor, what determines the conductivity of the material in each section? Can you think of any advantages of having different conductivities in the two *p* sections? How might this difference be achieved?

The student's answer:

In any transistor, the conductivity of each region is determined by the number of charge carriers in that region. The number of charge carriers is in turn determined by the impurity concentration. Variations of the emitter and collection conductivities will produce a variety of input and output characteristics, which may be especially useful for some particular circuit application.

STEP 2. Next come the records of lab work: many pages of charts and graphs and diagrams showing exactly what the lab set-up was and then what readings were taken. (In this case, 15 pieces of equipment with the names and serial numbers, 13 diagrams of electrical circuits, 13 pages of tables, nine pages of graphs showing the curves resulting from the plotting of the data, and 12 pages of equations.) Also in this part the student writes notes to himself:

> I have made a change in the circuit. The Burgess battery is unable to supply sufficient voltage, so I am making the following change. . . .

> Data from pp. 12 and 13 is no good. I failed to keep *Vce* constant while varying *Vbe.*

STEP 3. Finally there is the discussion of his results. Why was his first set of results so different from the theoretical ones obtained through mathematical calculations? More experimentation revealed the answer to this problem:

> When I heated the transistor too much, I changed the characteristics of the transistor. When I repeated the process and checked my results, I found that my method was not to blame. The transistor had changed and drastically altered the gain versus frequency curves.

An article written by a scientist on the results of his experiments may contain much of the information from his lab book, but the format, of course, is different from that of a lab report. The reader will want to know the results *before* he comes to the details of procedure. The following is a traditional kind of ordering in scientific articles:

1. First, there is an abstract of half a page or so stating the problem under investigation and the results of the research or experiment. This is typed on a page separate from the paper.
2. Then, the introduction gives what background the reader may need in the history or theory of the problem.
3. Then come the details of procedure. What was done? In what way? In what quantities? With what equipment?

4. Next come the results, followed by a discussion of them. The discussion will be longer than the notes in a student lab book, since presumably the experimenter had a reason for doing the work that he wants to discuss. Did the results confirm someone else's work? Reveal something new? Disagree with the results of others?
5. The bibliography will be at the end.

Especially if the article or paper is long or complex there may be a need for acknowledgments, a summary section, table of contents, appendixes, graphs, drawings, and index, as well as sub-headings throughout the paper. To find more samples as well as the standard style and format of scientific papers, one should look under ''Technical Writing'' in the library's card catalogue. The following books may be especially helpful.

John H. Mitchell, *Writing for Professional and Technical Journals,* (Wiley, 1968). A useful reference. More than half of the 400 pages contain excerpts from the standard style manuals for journals in the following fields: engineering, biology, chemistry, and physics, as well as the humanities, arts, mathematics, medicine, and social science.

IEEE Transactions of Professional Communication, published by the Institute of Electrical and Electronics Engineers, is a journal about technical writing. Interesting articles. One such (December 1964, ''Project Literacy'' by W. D. Reel) prints two versions of engineering articles, where the second one is much improved.

The American Chemical Society's *Handbook for Authors* is a very useful style manual. 118 pages. Attractive, no nonsense, and easy to use. (The other academic journals have their own style guides, as listed in John H. Mitchell above.)

Jack T. Huber, *Report Writing in Psychology and Psychiatry,* (Harper, 1961). 100 pages. Pleasant to read. Addressed to those who act as consultants, therapists, and clinicians. Contains examples of whole reports together with commentary.

A THEORETICAL SCIENCE PAPER

Students in advanced science courses may be asked to write papers on the theoretical bases of science. One student doing a physics seminar course chose to write on the conflicting theories of gravitation, mainly on the work of the physicists Brans and Dicke. In his abstract he tells why it is important to do so and outlines the areas to be discussed in his paper.

His paper begins historically. How have scientists and philosophers in the past few hundred years explained the concept of space? (Newton, Berkeley, Mach, Einstein, and Brans-Dicke) He then focuses on Mach's Principle. If it is valid, what is its more general relevance?

Then at length and in technical detail he explains particular aspects of the work of Brans-Dicke, work that developed from Mach's.

Then, he discusses the implications of the Brans-Dicke work for astrophysicists and cosmologists. If valid, what predictions could be made on the basis of the theory?

Finally, he asks what experimental evidence could be used to shed light on the validity of the theory. He concludes by suggesting that present tests or procedures are not adequate but that ones yet to be developed might give better data for testing the theory.

This writer has proceeded in a manner not too different from that of a historian. The questions are the logical ones. Why is it important to argue for one theory rather than another? How did the theory in question develop? What is it? What is especially interesting about it? What are the implications of this theory for a particular group or a particular field of study? How can we evaluate it or judge its validity?

The introductory portion of the paper is printed here. The footnotes have been omitted.

The Brans-Dicke Theory of Gravitation

Abstract. A study of the Brans-Dicke theory of gravitation is important for two reasons. First of all, the theory is a well-developed one which has not

been conclusively invalidated by experimental evidence up to the present day. Secondly, the theory is based on a rigorous adherence to Mach's Principle, which in itself is an intriguing scientific and philosophical concept.

This paper surveys the Brans-Dicke theory, in particular the gravitational field equations, the weak field approximation, and reviews certain predictions of astronomical and cosmological interest. It discusses the validity of the theory, using comparisons of its predictions with experimental results.

Introduction. The detection of pulsars and other possibly relativistic phenomena has made it important to establish a correct theory of gravitation. Before they can postulate models of such phenomena, theoretical astrophysicists must know which, if any, of the several theories advanced so far holds true in the limit of highly relativistic celestial bodies.

Besides general relativity, one of the best developed theories to have survived the rather imprecise and inconclusive tests of relativity carried out thus far is that developed by C. Brans and R. H. Dicke.[1] Perhaps the greatest fascination of this approach is its philosophical differences with general relativity.

The principle of Mach. Dicke[2] traces the origins of the principle of Mach and of relativity itself back to the writings of Bishop G. Berkeley, an eighteenth century British philosopher. In Berkeley's time the dominant concept of space was that of Newton, wherein space is regarded as an absolute structure imbued with innate geometrical and physical properties. Bishop Berkeley questioned this belief,[3] arguing rather practically that for an empty physical space all the Newtonian physical and geometrical properties cease to have any meaning. Instead, Berkeley reasoned, the only meaningful motions and physical and geometrical relationships are those of material bodies relative to other matter.

Nearly a century ago the Austrian philosopher Ernst Mach[4] expanded upon the philosophy of Bishop Berkeley, developing his now famous principle, which serves as the basis of the Brans-Dicke theory of gravitation. Assuming the validity of Berkeley's principle of relativity, Mach argued that all inertial forces observed locally in an accelerated laboratory are due to the distant matter in the universe, since such inertial forces may equivalently be regarded as gravitational effects originating in the distant matter being accelerated relative to the laboratory. Mach's principle, then,

is the statement that the inertial effects at a point are determined by the mass distribution of the universe about the point of interest.

If he assumes the validity of Mach's principle, the physicist must note its cosmological implications. If, in fact, the inertial effects in the laboratory do depend on the distribution of matter even in the farthest reaches of the universe, then physics cannot be investigated without considerations of cosmology. The laboratory is intimately connected with and influenced by the rest of the universe.

The strong motivational influence of Mach's principle on the Brans-Dicke theory necessitates philosophical and quantitative departures from Einsteinian general relativity. In general relativity mass distribution about a point of interest only influences the orientation of locally inertial coordinate frames. Moreover, such frames are not uniquely determined by the distribution of distant matter. Other than in the determination of the locally inertial frames, distant matter exerts no locally observable effects upon an experiment in general relativity. On the other hand, in the Brans-Dicke theory the "strong" equivalence principle, upon which the field equations of general relativity are based, is incompatible with Mach's principle. Instead, locally observed inertial effects are closely tied to the distribution of mass about the laboratory. A further conclusion is that locally observed physical laws are quantitatively position-dependent. This will be reflected in the position dependence of the values of physical constants, which can no longer be regarded as constants unless by assumption.

The last few points are rather startling at first glance and deserve further attention. . . . (At this point the writer begins his technical discussion of those areas outlined in the abstract.)—student, Jon P. Okada

Proposal Writing

A PROPOSAL

A student majoring in chemistry decides, on the advice of a professor, to apply for a small research grant. His plan is to study the effects of trace amounts of arsenic in streams and rivers on certain plant and animal life in the water. He knows how to collect his samples, conduct the laboratory work, and write up his laboratory results. But what should he say in the proposal? The plan

followed by this student was to answer a list of questions the granting agency might ask.

What is the problem that prompts the study? What does the student know about the history or background of the problem? Is the student aware of other research in the area? Do the teachers of this student believe he is competent and dependable? (He arranges for recommendations to be sent.)

Exactly what are the objectives of the study? In very specific terms, what does the student plan to find out? What will be his procedure? How will he have access to laboratory equipment? The agency wants to know, in other words, not only that he knows the subject area well but also that he is practical and well-organized.

What is his budget? How does he plan to allocate the time? Will other people be involved, and, if so, what will their specific roles be?

What will happen to his results? How does the student plan to make them available to the community of scientists?

Complete guides to proposal writing are available in most libraries. Look in the card catalogue under Proposal Writing, Research Grants—U.S. Grants Register, or Endowments.

Organizing and Developing a Topic

The Unifying Idea

Every piece of writing, if it is to be understood, has a central idea. Even a set of instructions for filling out an income tax return will communicate some main thought, such as *Don't make mistakes on this form,* or *It's important to do this form carefully.* Here are the central ideas from four other pieces of writing:

> The graylag goose has elaborate courtship rituals.
>
> Eustacia was selfish.
>
> Justice can mean different things to different people.
>
> Caesar was, in all, a fair man.

None of these ideas in themselves are very exciting. They all

sound vague, general, dull, and perhaps obvious. But then it is usually the detail, and not the general idea, which carries interest or excitement.

The unifying idea may be stated in the first sentence, the second sentence, any sentence of the first paragraph, or it may not be stated at all. A novelist or poet, even a writer of essays may write about characters, events, places, and feelings. Yet even for such writers there has to be an overall viewpoint or focus around which to organize his ideas. If not, there is nothing to explain why the writer chooses to include some kinds of detail and to omit others.

The scientist, unlike the novelist, will almost always state his unifying idea in some single sentence, probably in the opening paragraph, and perhaps more than once. An article might begin as boldly as this:

> Recent research has shown (x . . y . . z). I will argue here that the cause of these symptoms lies particularly in the diet of Western rural Americans.

(See *Beginnings,* p. 50, for more ways to state the main idea in the first paragraph.)

Whether stated or not, some sort of unifying idea is *there.* The reader senses it, and the writer, of course, uses it to give shape and coherence to the bulk of his words and sentences.

The problem for the writer is how to turn a topic into a unifying idea. If you start with a topic like

> *A college course in writing*

then you are obligated to say something about it. For example:

1. Here is a plan for *a college course in writing.*
2. *A college course in writing* should not be required here because almost everyone writes quite well.
3. The *writing course I had in college* was very practical.

4. Writing cannot be taught in *a college course in writing.*
5. *A college writing course* is a quick and frightening way of finding out exactly what one has—or doesn't have—to say.
6. *A college writing course* should teach students how to ask questions.

So the topic is what you write about, and the unifying idea is what you say about the topic. *War* is a topic. *War is tragic* is a unifying idea.

Suppose for a paper on the novel, *Pride and Prejudice,* which you have just read, you were given the topic:

     Mr. Darcy's pride

The problem is to decide what your own feeling about this topic is and then to state your feeling as a unifying idea. For example:

1. Mr. Darcy's reputation for "pride" was mainly a creation of jealous, nosy townsfolk.
2. Mr. Darcy was proud in the sense of being reserved—appropriately reserved.
3. Mr. Darcy's pride changed to humanness, concern, and love.

If for a sociology assignment you choose to investigate *Occupations in California Chinatowns from 1900 to 1970,* then this area is your topic. But once the research is finished and you must write the paper, then you have to formulate a main idea, to say something about occupations in California Chinatowns from 1900 to 1970. Here are several possibilities:

1. People from California Chinatowns were excluded by law from certain jobs in the years between 1900 and 1970.
2. The skills many people learned from the Oriental cultures were not used for earning a living as much as they might have been.
3. The kinds of jobs held by people from Chinatowns in these years show a gradual but steady change.

This topic for a biology paper:

> *Our recent experiments on dentalium eggs*

might be transformed into this unifying statement:

> *The experiments on dentalium eggs* showed the exact location of the genetic material responsible for the growth of the apical tuft.

A unifying idea, unlike a topic, is a statement of some sort. It is often a personal response that someone could argue with if he cared to. But responses can range all the way from very personal opinions to impersonal statements practically devoid of feeling. For instance, it is hard to disagree with anyone who says, "The gray-lag goose has elaborate courtship rituals," but at least it is conceivable to do so.

In writing essay examinations it is especially important to think in terms of the unifying idea. One student who failed to do so was asked this question:

> Some historians argue that the causes of the Great Depression were more psychological than material. Do you agree or disagree?

The student said he agreed. Then he gave the dates of the stock market crash, some facts about poor distribution of foodstuffs, and the failure of banks—none of which really argued for or against a psychological explanation of the Depression. What he said related to the general topic, the Depression, but it did not answer the specific question.

The writer might have argued that the Depression was not caused by lack of food or productivity (i.e., material things) but rather by too much optimism on the part of American businessmen, too little candor in criticizing business abuses, an unrealistic belief on the part of most Americans in a "permanent plateau of prosperity"—and, by contrast, a sudden loss of confidence in generally sound banks and people's fear of spending what money they had left. All of these factors, it could be argued, are psychological.

Examination questions often begin with the word "Discuss." For example:

> Discuss the concept of equality in Rousseau's *Social Contract*.

The word "discuss" is usually a signal which means:

> Here is a topic.
>
> Make a statement about the topic.
>
> Provide supporting evidence for your statement.

The student writer given the question above decided to approach it by making her first statement a general definition of equality as Rousseau saw it:

> What Rousseau meant by equality was that all men, regardless of appearance, culture, or the state of their civilization, were equal in that they possessed the same general rights and privileges.—student

After first naming some of these rights and privileges, the student spelled them out. She showed that in Rousseau's view "uncivilized" peoples and Western European "civilized" man, different as they might seem, possessed some of the same rights and privileges.

The same procedure can be used in discussing a long quotation. For example, suppose you were asked to write about some aspect of this quotation:

> There is an ideal that has long been basic to the learning process as we have known it, one that stands at the very center of our modern institutions of higher education and that had its origin, I suppose, in the clerical and monastic character of the medieval university. It is the ideal of the association of the process of learning with a certain remoteness from the contemporary scene—a certain detachment and seclusion, a certain voluntary withdrawal and renunciation of participation in contemporary life in the interests of the achievement of a better perspective on that life when the period of withdrawal is over. It is an ideal that does not predicate any total conflict between thought and action but recognizes that there is a time for each.
>
> —George F. Kennan, *Democracy and the Student Left*

In your essay you would have to deal with the central argument—
that intellectual "thought" should not be undertaken at the same
time as "action," possibly political or social action. But there are a
good many possible approaches, or, in other words, many different
unifying statements you might choose to make. Here are a few of
them suggested by student writers:

1. A modern university could model itself after the medieval university in ways that would allow for such seclusion. (Then a
   listing and description of these ways, followed by thoughts on
   how this seclusion would change qualitatively the kind of learning received.)
2. Thought and action must not be thought of as separate activities; without action, or experience, the thoughts a student has
   are of very little value or substance. (Then a listing of the kinds
   of worthless knowledge gained by those isolated from action or
   experience.)
3. The writer agrees: One is likely to have a better perspective on
   contemporary events after a period of secluded study and con-
   templation. (He then gives examples of contemporary events
   and the ways people who have acquired perspective from a period of academic seclusion would view those events.)

The Relation of the Paragraph to the Paper:
The Plan or Outline

The first major task of the writer facing a topic is to select a unifying idea, a viewpoint on the topic. (See pp. 42–48 for discussion
of this.) Then he must decide how to deal with the idea, or what
approach to take. Perhaps the idea will be stated first, or perhaps
a necessary definition will be given. The remainder of the paper
may be devoted to explaining, illustrating, or developing his idea.

    You should—in your own way—write out your plan for the
topic. An outline of this kind can take many forms. Some writers
like to work out a neatly set-out outline like this:

Topic: Local Control of Schools

Unifying idea: Present methods of organizing and financing our schools do not provide for real local control.

Approach:

I. How the present system developed
   A. Need for community integration
      1. Schools organized to serve local community needs
      2. Needs and policies defined by regular meetings of citizenry
   B. Growth of community
      1. Immigrant desire for upward social mobility

Other writers prefer a less formal way of sketching out their approach:

I want to show that local control of schools is neither possible nor desirable.

I'll start with a statement of present problems in the schools—dictation of requirements by state bodies, rejection of school bonds for financing schools, low status of teachers, irrelevance of curricula. Then I'll show how well the system worked in the eighteenth and early nineteenth centuries.

Whatever your approach, you need to break down the unifying idea of the whole paper into parts, perhaps into a number of narrower ideas or into a logical sequence of steps, or some combination of narrowing and sequencing.

Note, for example, the sample paper on page 23 about military society. The unifying idea, that military society has its own norms and social rules, breaks down into subideas.

There are different norms for enlisted men and officers.
The wife of a military man plays a double role—both military and civilian.

Frequent moves have been one reason for the growth of certain kinds of behavior.

Members of the military family possess certain character traits.

Each subidea above becomes the unifying idea of a paragraph (or more than one paragraph). Sometimes the paragraph idea is stated by the writer in a single sentence, called the "topic sentence." The ideas expressed by each paragraph make up the whole unifying idea.

Paragraphs are thus the major units of a piece of writing. The purpose of this section is to suggest ways to develop ideas within the narrower framework of a paragraph. We start with two kinds of paragraphs that present somewhat different problems: paragraphs which begin and paragraphs which end papers.

Beginning and Ending Paragraphs

Novelists have often complained that the hardest task of writing any novel is figuring out how to begin. Other writers have the same problem. And endings seem almost as hard, since writers of articles and short papers are often tempted to end with some impressive-sounding phrases or else a boring repetition of what has already been said elsewhere in the paper.

BEGINNINGS. One favorite maxim for speechmaking was: "Tell them what you're going to tell them, tell them, then tell them what you've told them." Speechmaking, however, is quite different from expository writing. A reader can always look back; a listener can rarely "hear back" unless he has a tape recording.

The length of the introduction—whether a single sentence or several paragraphs—is determined by the complexity of the material, the kind of audience one is writing for, and how familiar they are with the general topic. In the case of course papers, the audience is usually fully familiar with the general nature of the topic, and so little is needed by way of introduction.

The word "beginning" is perhaps better than "introduction." The latter word suggests long and unnecessary openings like:

> People of all ages and climes have been concerned with the problem of . . . (whatever it is you are discussing). In this paper I can only deal superficially with a problem whose impact has been as stunning as . . . (some other impressive problem).

or the coyness of

> Have you ever seen magnolia trees in bloom?

or perhaps the unattractiveness of

> In this essay I will give some causes of the 1812 War and then I will give some examples of why it was unnecessary. Then I will give some effects of the War and summarize.

The third of these beginnings is better as a plan of action for the writer than as an actual opening. It does, however, embody one essential ingredient of any beginning: it sets a direction. It is not an extra little decorative touch stuck onto the paper but the first essential step in the development of the paper.

Compare the following beginnings of a paper on the structure of the Chinese family:

First Beginning

The Chinese family consists of some sets of relationships with regard to tradition which have remained fairly constant. Many traditions, however, have been weakened and new ones have been formed to take their place. Two family types will be represented in this paper and their differences and the reasons for these differences will be the topic of this paper.—student

Revised Beginning

The complicated structure of the Chinese family has changed considerably in the past sixty years. The Lim family described by Harrison in 1918 lives in Shanghai but still functions like the rural peasantry of the previous six centuries. The T'sou family, reported on by Weinstein in 1970, functions more like members of an industrialized nineteenth century European society.

—student revision

The revised beginning reveals the writer plunging more directly into the subject matter of his paper. Parts of the first are a little

too much like his private outline. It is wordy and boring to read. However, both beginnings show that the writer has thought a great deal about his topic. The following strongly suggests that the writer has thought little and does not yet know what he wants to say:

> War is the topic. These two writers have expressed opinions and ideas. Each writer is convinced of his own opinion. They appeal to the reader's pity and sympathy. Some of what they say may be true; some may be untrue.—student

This version should be scrapped. The writer must first decide what he wants to say.

The kinds of beginnings are almost as varied as the writers or the topics chosen. If a writer has thought long enough about his topic and decided how he is going to develop it, then beginning should not be difficult.

BEGINNING WITH AN EFFECT. If he is using a cause-effect structure, he would do well to begin with the effect:

> Hikers in the southern end of the Appalachians have been noticing that treetops are turning brown and that once-solid rock surfaces are beginning to crumble.—student

> By the end of the 1960s, Indonesian children who had once spoken any one of fourteen different languages and dialects now spoke Bahasa Indonesia, a language that did not exist fifty years earlier.—student

BEGINNING WITH A "CONCESSION STATEMENT." The "concession statement" is a particularly useful opening when the author is going to explain something that might not easily have been predicted. The writer first concedes that something is commonly known or superficially true, then he proceeds to the more important statement. Notice how this procedure works:

> Although the universities were the scenes of intense political activism in the sixties, they did not alienate long-term public opinion as much as one would expect.—student

Helping poorer nations was once the keystone of a liberal foreign policy. But today liberals seem to say, "Leave other nations alone. Don't interfere!"

—student

Despite the lack of population growth in this country in the last few years, consumption of non-durable goods almost doubled.—student

The two works are concerned with notions of power, but the authors start with very different presumptions.—student

EXERCISE

Think about what must have followed these beginnings.

1. Perhaps the major problem this country has to face is the decay of the American city. If this decay is not halted, some horrifying possibilities await us. What is happening, what might happen, and what could be done?
2. Los Angeles has been called the America of the future. What Los Angeles is today, America will be tomorrow. Los Angeles, a huge tangle of concrete freeways, contains within it some ten million people, embracing Orange County in the south and extending to Riverside in the east.
3. In the last three presidential elections every major candidate has promised to help our cities. Yet almost no improvement can be detected. To understand why this is so is to understand something important about our system of government.

ENDINGS. Rarely is an elaborate "conclusion" needed, one constituting a major and important part of a paper. Sometimes it is as well to stop when you have finished what you have to say. If the focus of the paper is clear and the reader has understood the relationship of the ideas, then the ending should not have to tell him the point of the paper. On the other hand, summarizing can be useful, even necessary, where very complex matters have been discussed in some detail.

In general, think carefully before ending with

1. a paragraph that summarizes or repeats what you have already said

2. a rhetorical question:

    Is the youth of today going to allow such a takeover?

3. a row of dots:

    And so the wheel has turned full circle once more and . . .

4. an impressive quotation:

    The answer to the problems facing the present generation is not obscure. The prophet has written:

    "Look within: thou art Buddha."

5. a suggested new direction or sudden change of attitude.

(Examples 1–4 are taken from student papers.)

EXERCISE

To help you as you go over your own papers, think about what must have preceded the following endings:

1. We will need a much clearer realization all around that culture *does* cost money and that it usually cannot pay its own way.
2. Mohican civilization had its own integrity and vitality. It was this that enabled the Mohicans not only to learn from the white man but also to add richly to the white man's civilization.
3. Sir Herbert Read said that education is the creation of happiness. The really creative work must be done to enable happiness to grow and flower in a child. The young delinquent, the maladjusted child, is just an unhappy person.
4. The more basic characteristics of U.S. television are thus quite

distinct from those of the British network. By and large, these characteristics arise from one solid fact. Fundamentally, American television is controlled by three groups of people: the broadcasters who are concerned with making profits from advertising; the sponsors, who are concerned with making profits from the sale of cars, breakfast food and female toilet requisites; and the advertising agencies, who live off both. The yardstick for a program is still "Will it sell a product?" No one influential in either political party seriously questions such a yardstick.

Idea Development Through Description

You can develop an idea by means of *description*. Notice the way this writer piles one detail on another. Notice also the kind of detail he has selected. Together they add up to a central idea or a unified impression:

> The Park Hill project is a particularly interesting development in large-scale housing. Built in a slum area it stands on a sloping site so that the height of the building varies. It has elevators for vertical communication and decks for horizontal communication. These decks are wide enough for the movement of goods and furniture, for children to play in, and for adults to meet and gossip. All the front doors open onto the decks. They are, in fact, streets without fast-moving traffic. The recessed balconies and solid masses of pre-stressed concrete are integrated into a varied and exciting pattern.—student

The details provided in the passage above indicate that the writer favors certain human values—the need and desirability of neighborly intercommunication and the visual pleasures afforded by skillful design—above, say, purely financial considerations. Description is more than just a pretty word picture of a landscape. It may be a particularly powerful vehicle for important ideas.

You can use description more profitably in college writing than you may realize. When an assignment calls for analysis, or when you are asked a particular question in an examination, the bulk of your writing can be descriptive, or a kind of descriptive definition

of a problem or situation. Suppose the question is

> What seems to you to be the most serious problem faced by urban schools?

You could select, say, the problem of student disabilities arising from malnutrition and begin your essay by describing malnutrition. Or suppose in a literature class you were asked

> What was Huckleberry Finn's attitude toward the society in which he lived?

Your unifying idea, or the statement you choose to make, might be

> The violence, false charity, and religiosity of the society around him are quite foreign to Huck, and almost certainly repellent to him. Yet whenever he encounters such behavior, he seems toler-ant, even indifferent.

The writer could then *describe* in more detail Huck's tolerance, re-ferring to particular incidents.

> Or suppose the question was this:

> In what way do automobiles shape our culture?

Then one answer might be

> Automobiles determine the way we design and lay out our cities.

The writer could then *describe* typical city roads, parking lots and garages, service stations, advertising space and the size of it (big because of fast-moving cars), the layout of shopping centers. He might then contrast these with the amount of space given over to other functions of society such as recreation, farming, and hous-ing.

Description is a powerful technique. Describing hunger in Ire-land or the effect of napalm on a Vietnamese child may in itself be more powerful than marshalling arguments and reasons. Descrip-tion, of course, serves other valuable functions. The workings of

the automobile transmission system or the difficulty of learning
Chinese can be described without necessarily implying moral
values or arguing for a certain point of view.

   Whatever the goals of particular descriptions, it is the depth
of the description, the truth of it, sometimes the sheer amount of
it that makes it powerful. To say, ''Adolescence may be confusing
and painful,'' is a bland, even trite, pronouncement. But a novel
like Carson McCullers' *A Member of the Wedding* is neither bland
nor trite because it describes, it brings to life, situations that moti-
vate such a statement. Here this author speaks of Frankie, an ado-
lescent girl, also called F. Jasmine. Frankie's brother had just been
married. The bride's name is Janice.

> She wanted to speak to her brother and the bride, to talk to them and tell them
> of her plans, the three of them alone together. But they were never once alone;
> Jarvis was out checking the car someone was lending for the honeymoon, while
> Janice dressed in the front bedroom among a crowd of beautiful grown girls.
> She wandered from one to the other of them, unable to explain. And once
> Janice put her arms around her, and said she was so glad to have a little
> sister—and when Janice kissed her, F. Jasmine felt an aching in her throat and
> could not speak. Jarvis, when she went to find him in the yard, lifted her up in
> a roughhouse way and said: Frankie the lankie the alaga fankie, the tee-legged,
> toe-legged, bowlegged Frankie. And he gave her a dollar.
>
> —Carson McCullers, *A Member of the Wedding*

EXERCISE

Think of descriptive details from your own experience which would
develop the following ideas:

1. Parents are (are not) particularly perceptive about their own
   children.
2. The kind of housing available affects the quality of the life of
   the dwellers.
3. Some character in a novel, poem, or play seems very real.
4. Some particular location arouses particular emotions in you.

Idea Development Through Illustration

You can develop an idea by giving examples, or illustrations. Here the writer first states his general idea, then gives several illustrations:

> The previous elections were also a mockery of democratic processes. The administration, to ensure that the results were predictable, ruled off the ballot the most likely threat, the popular General Minh, and also the only avowed "peace" candidate, An Truong Thanh. The Tri Quang Buddhists were excluded as "pro-neutralist" and the entire trade-union tickot was eliminated because of faulty certification of one candidate. When, after receiving the election returns, a committee of the Vietnamese Assembly recommended invalidating them, the decision was reversed under the eyes of a gallery containing armed members of the secret police. After the elections, the runner-up, like many others active in the campaign, was arrested and thrown into prison. He will probably die there.
>
> —student

Note that the example, if it is well stated, can itself communicate a general idea. In each of the items below, for instance, it is easy to tell what general point the writer has in mind.

(1) You can't put your purse down any longer without someone snatching it. Even my neighbors steal my potted plants.

(2) No one in Congress has less than a hundred thousand dollars in assets. I know of several senators who have spent a million and more of their own money to get themselves elected.

An alternative method of illustration is to begin with one very long example and then turn to the general points illustrated by the example. A discussion of inflation might begin with John H. Leeburger of Terre Haute, Indiana, who worked hard all his life and looked forward to the then-ample pension of $3,500 per year. Today he is spending his old age in the most degrading kind of poverty. Then, after some more detail, would follow a more general discussion of the nature of inflation. Here again the honest writer will take pains to ensure that his particular case is both representative and relevant. Notice how Lawrence Wylie in his sociological study, *Village in the Vaucluse,* uses a specific incident to il-

lustrate community awareness of the family unit and the roles assigned within it.

> . . . One day Madame Favre was sitting in front of her house sewing. Three-year-old Dédou, who was playing in the street, went too near the gutter and was about to get muddy. His mother looked up and called sharply to him:
>
> "Dédou, you'll get yourself dirty. Get away from there!" Dédou was usually a docile child, but this time a naughty urge got the better of him. He looked up impudently and shouted:
>
> "Why?"
>
> His mother gave him a glance that he would remember and said through her teeth:
>
> "Because I tell you to be good. Because you're the child and I'm the mother. Because we're not animals. That's the way it is! So!"

} This is the illustration.

> Madame Favre was not merely exerting her authority. She was unwittingly explaining that there was a principle involved in this situation over which Dédou had no control. He could only recognize it and accept it. She was explaining that both she and he were part of a family and that each had a role that must be maintained. She was emphasizing the importance of human dignity. She was saying that those were the facts, pleasant or unpleasant, and that his only reasonable course of action was to conform.

} Here is the author's interpretation.

> —Lawrence Wylie, *Village in the Vaucluse*

EXERCISE

In each case below think of one example which will develop the topic in an interesting and accurate way.

1. The effects of prolonged unemployment
2. The portrayal of marriage in family television programs
3. The social role of churches today
4. Speech patterns and employment

Idea Development Using a Time Sequence

Perhaps the most common way to develop an idea like the following:

> Christopher Columbus was in some ways an irrational man.

is to tell the story of the relevant part of Columbus' life in the order that the events occurred. Then in the last paragraph the writer might state which actions were rational and which irrational or partly rational.

Chronological ordering is, of course, a common way for novelists and historians to organize their material. But always there has to emerge some larger kind of pattern, idea, or feeling. If not, the listing of events can be boring and meaningless. Time-ordering, while it is used by almost everyone, is just a superficial device. The novelist uses it, but his real purpose is to recreate human experience in some full and rich sense. Look again, for example, at Carson McCullers' passage on p. 57. Look also at the student narratives in Chapter 1. All of these use a chronological technique.

When you use chronological order in your own writing, make sure that the events you write about are linked not only in a time sequence but in other ways as well. Perhaps the events illustrate a tendency, or show a contrast, or set up a causal link. When you write a paper about a novel or a play, it is especially important to make sure that you select details illustrating what you have to say rather than details which summarize the plot of the work studied. (See our notes on plot summarizing under *Irrelevance*, p. 10.)

Here is a legitimate use of a chronological technique to describe a whole cycle:

> Scientific knowledge of any group of related phenomena goes through a regular pattern. *First* there is a period of fact-gathering. *Then* appears a variety of different interpretations of some of the data. *Eventually* one of the interpretations is likely to become predominant; usually it drives the others into obscurity. *The next stage* is the concentration of nearly all scientific activity in this field within the framework of the victorious interpretation. *When, usually much later,* results are found which don't fit into the established framework, some scientists seek to revise or extend the framework. Others may challenge its basic principles and seek to establish newer and quite different modes of investigation.—student, on Thomas Kuhn's *The Structure of Scientific Revolutions*

EXERCISE

We stated earlier that events in a time sequence should also have
some unifying principle or idea. What is communicated in the following passage? What is the effect of the time sequence? What
would be lost if these details were arranged in some other way?

> The explosion did not come until February. In December the
> police arrested several hundred "agitators". In January fifty mem-
> bers of the parliament were placed under house arrest for an un-
> determined period. On February 3, police armed with automatic
> rifles surrounded a public meeting in Parliament Square and or-
> dered the crowd to disperse. Someone threw a firecracker, and
> immediately a shouted order led to a rattle of automatic firing.
> When the frightened crowd had disappeared, thirty-four bodies lay
> on the pavement, some of them children. On February 4, a state
> of martial law was imposed and tanks patrolled the streets of the
> city. On the fifth, the civil guard burst into Aguilla's apartment be-
> fore dawn, dragged him out into the street, beating him fero-
> ciously, and threw him into an armored van. Two hours later, as
> Maria Aguilla led a procession of women protesting the seizure,
> members of the guard again fired, killing three. By noon the city
> was in an uproar. A mob had gathered at Villanella Park and was
> marching toward the palace, armed with shotguns, pitchforks, and
> axes. For once the militia retreated. At 12:15 two squads sent to
> stop the protesters refused to fire and joined the marchers. At
> 1:10 General Ibanez issued a statement raising the state of martial
> law and restoring constitutional liberties. But by 2:30 Ibanez lay
> in the Fuego prison while a battered but smiling Carlos Aguilla
> proclaimed from the palace balcony a new era of universal
> suffrage, individual liberty, and freedom from foreign domination.

Idea Development Through Definition and Classification

It is often necessary to define a term or a concept prior to using it.
One favored method is a logical definition, which first puts the
thing being defined into the context of a larger class with which

the reader is presumed to be familiar. Thus, William James began
"Psychology is the science . . ." The second step is to identify
the characteristic of the particular thing that differentiates it from
the other members of the larger class. William James' definition
did this quite briefly:

> Psychology is the science of mental life.

Unfortunately some of the most boring student writing begins with
formal definitions of this sort. In any case, a random examination
of professional writing reveals few examples of development by
formal definition. What is more common is a working definition,
one that enables the writer to get on with his topic.

> The meaning of the term "conceptual thinking" must ultimately be conveyed by
> exemplification.—Stephen Körner, *Conceptual Thinking*

> Economics is about the everyday things of life; how we get our living and why
> sometimes we get more and sometimes less.
>   —Gertrude Williams, *Economics of Everyday Life*

Sometimes a form of classification is used instead of the definition. The writer breaks up one large concept or class of things
into two or more smaller ones:

> Roughly speaking there are two kinds of human thinking. There is *creative* think-
> ing, based on imagination and insight . . . This kind of thinking follows unpre-
> dictable channels, and follows no fixed rules. There is also *routine* thinking, that
> requires no special talent to carry it out. It proceeds according to fixed rules and
> along a course that is easily foreseen.—Irving Adler, *Thinking Machines*

This can sometimes be both easier to write and easier to read than
formal definition. Avoid the statement of personal inadequacy:

> "Imagination" is a very hard word to define. One of its meanings is the ability
> to bring an image into your mind.
>   —Alan Harris and Jack Cross, *The Language of Ideas*

Such a statement all too often suggests that the writer has not
given enough thought as to how he will present his ideas to the
reader.

Definitions, whether formal ones or working ones, are rarely
truly objective. They reveal certain biases characterizing the writer's

view of his subject. When in the nineteenth century William James wrote his excellent text, *Psychology,* the subject was hardly a science in the sense that physics or biology now is. His definition of psychology as the "science of mental life" reflects some wishful thinking.

In general, the writer who needs to define a topic or term prior to discussion would do well to use a working definition. Such a definition is most commonly used to clear the ground of any entrapping ambiguities and to set forth the area to be investigated. This student, for example, gives a working definition of "reality."

Reality in Films

Phrases like "stark reality," "real brutality," and "authentic!" appear in many advertisements for movies, both in newspapers and on marquees. But obviously *reality* means different things to different people, and here it must mean part of whatever it is that makes a film attractive to large groups of people. It is apparently not the kind of reality associated with documentary films. *Stark* reality would not likely be found in a film of an actual battle, an actual signing of a peace treaty, an actual marriage. It would not be found in a personal account of a flood by an actual eye-witness. Nor would this kind of reality be found in a re-creation of an actual event, in "The Last Days of Hitler," for example, which shows actors performing in what looks like a documentary film.

The kind of reality that draws crowds and creates excitement may be found in *The Godfather,* the story of a real underworld gangleader, both violent and tender, who was given a fictitious name—or in *Soldier Blue,* the story of a wild-west massacre of Indians by Yankee soldiers, which was also based on an actual account. Both of these films have some claim to historical accuracy, but it was probably the aspect of violence rather than accuracy which made them popular. Further, it was the explicitness of the violence which made them "real." The important questions for creating *stark* reality are not: Is there evidence that this happened? Were you there to see it? Have you got a film of it happening? Was this a likely or probable occurrence? The important questions are these: "Did it *show* the wound, *show* the needle, *show* the bullet, *show* the body?"—student

EXERCISE

Give working definitions for:

1. freedom of the press

2. conflict in a novel or play
3. culturally disadvantaged
4. group dynamics

Idea Development Using Cause and Effect

Organizing your material in terms of cause and effect is a useful way to develop ideas, especially for pieces of writing longer, say, than 500 words. This approach can be exploited in two basic ways.

A writer can explore causes or give reasons. How did something come about? Why? What reasons have other people given for what happened? Do you agree with their conclusions? What are your reasons, and how would you defend them?

Alternatively, a writer might ask himself the question: What are the logical results of the situation I have just described?

The following long passage shows how natural this kind of organization can be. First, the writer describes a lake and shows how it is being destroyed. (He breaks this part of the passage into four very short paragraphs.) And then with the phrase, "The trouble began innocently enough . . ." he turns to the deep-lying causes of the situation, going back into time and tracing events, one by one, to the present.

> *In a territory later called Nevada, a tribe of Indians—the Paiutes—owned a lake. The name was Pyramid Lake.*
>
> It was beautiful—much larger and more scenic than its famous neighbor, Lake Tahoe. Captain John Fremont "discovered" it "set like a gem in the mountains" in 1844, when the waters and banks were prosperous with fish and wildlife. Anaho Island off the northern shore served as a pelican rookery. Geysers, hot springs and rare oolitic sands were nearby, and the last of a species of prehistoric fish, the *Cui-ui*, swam unmolested.
>
> Pyramid Lake was deeded to the Paiutes, a conquered people, in 1859. The white man had no need for the lake, and the land around it appeared worthless.
>
> *Today, Pyramid Lake is in danger of disappearing from the earth. The Paiutes are fighting both for its survival and their own.*
>
> The trouble began innocently enough. Control over Indian affairs shifted from the War Department to the Department of the Interior in 1859. In the early

1900's a new philosophy of conservation became Governmental policy. Interior was charged with special responsibility for conserving our country's precious natural resources and its scenic wonders. In the name of conservation, strange things started to happen. But they did not become visible immediately.

Irrigation was gaining use in the Western U.S. during the same period, and in the early 1900's, Interior dammed the Truckee River just above Pyramid Lake to divert water for the Newlands irrigation project. It was supposed to make cultivable some 287,000 dry acres, but in 65 years it has accomplished only a fourth of that—and the acreage proved to be inferior for farming and ranching. It takes twice as much water as is legally permissible to serve the land, largely because the irrigation ditches are unlined and 65 per cent of the water leaks out or seeps away.

Around 1930, the Indians found there were no more trout in Pyramid Lake. Water from the river had been diverted so that trout no longer could swim upstream to spawn. The tribe began legal efforts to regain the water, which had been diverted or appropriated without consultation. A few BIA officials sympathized and tried to assist the Paiutes but were fired or "promoted" away from Nevada.

—Edgar S. Cahn, ed., *Our Brother's Keeper: The Indian in White America*

The writer must make it clear to the reader that something is the cause of something else, or the effect of it, but usually this is not difficult. For instance, in each of the following sentences two things are happening, and it is clear that the first is the cause of the second:

When a neutron hits a chunk of fissionable material larger than the critical size, the chunk develops a chain reaction releasing enormous amounts of energy.

A drop in dollar spending and a fall in farm prices is likely to be followed by pressure on the government to increase subsidies and absorb surpluses.

A woman who is mercilessly exploited by her husband may take refuge in a neurosis if her disposition admits of it.

But occasionally it is better to use certain linking words to put a more explicit emphasis on cause:

This collision *causes* the release of enormous amounts of energy.

Because of the drop in farm prices, pressure was exerted on the administration to absorb surpluses.

His merciless exploitation of his wife *led her to* (or *made her*) take refuge in a neurosis.

Sometimes the focus is on the second event, the effect or result rather than the cause:

The major event was Johnson's resignation. *Consequently* the already disunited party was shattered into four or five competing fragments. The *result,* Republican victory, was inevitable.

Three events—the resignation, the shattering, and the Republican victory—are linked by a cause-effect chain. But the focus is more on the *effect* of the earlier event rather than on which events caused what. Linking words which focus on effect include:

result	It follows that
consequence	necessarily
effect	therefore

Your own feel for words must tell you whether such words are best included or omitted in any given situation.

EXERCISE

For each of the following name two possible causes.

1. Demonstrations became more violent (or less common).
2. Foreign cars became more popular.
3. She became even more shy in the presence of men.
4. The President became very popular with students and workers, but big business remained hostile.
5. Private schools became more common, while public education decayed.

For each of the following name two possible effects.

1. Legislation was passed forbidding the emission of any harmful gases.
2. Each year the universities poured forth thousands of graduates for whom there were no jobs.
3. Educators had to guarantee in advance specific results that their students would achieve.
4. Drugs shown to be physically harmless were legalized.
5. Fish, meat, fruit, cereal crops, and vegetables provided a steadily diminishing proportion of the human diet.

Idea Development Using Comparison and Contrast

One excellent way to develop an idea is to set up a comparison between two things. Ask yourself, "What property do two things share? In what way are two things different?" (Comparison refers to similarities, contrast to differences. But *compare,* when used without *contrast,* frequently refers to both similarities and differences.) Comparing and contrasting may be used on practically any level. A comparison can work inside a single sentence, it can be the structuring device for a paragraph, or it can be the unifying idea of a whole paper.

Here are examples of comparison and contrast inside sentences and inside a paragraph:

My brother is not only cleverer than I am, but also he has many more friends. He must, then, be out of my way before the old king dies.—student

Like the American Indian the Australian aborigine lost his culture and lands under the overwhelming impact of the aggressive white invader.—student

The Maoris were more fortunate in retaining land-ownership rights than their Australian cousins were.—student

In his book, *Slavery,* Stanley Elkins reports that for the black child the plantation offered no really satisfactory father-image other than that of the master. In the vastly more horrifying German concentration camps of World War II many of the inmates did not hate the SS. In fact, they often sought to persuade themselves that the guards were hiding benevolence under the mask of a cruel father. The

camp inmates, dependent on the guards for life, food, warmth, and security took on the role of children, and were prepared to be loyal, docile, lazy, playful and silly, just as children are. Likewise, a full-grown black man was a "boy" until he was sufficiently aged to be labeled "uncle."—student

Note that in his comparison, Elkins is not reported as claiming that the American plantation was basically the same as a Nazi concentration camp. Instead, as he himself wrote, the concentration camp was "a special and highly perverted instance of human slavery."

Comparison and contrast can be an excellent way to define informally and to emphasize a particular characteristic. The writer of the following piece, for example, emphasizes a particular aspect of children's play by skillfully combining two sets of contrasts. The first contrast is between two types of children's street play in London. One is accepted by adults, the other strongly discouraged. But an outside event, a world war, causes a change in adult attitudes. The second contrast is between the way people used to feel about so-called "dangerous" play and the way people feel about it now.

[Children's games in prewar London] presented us with opportunities to help and play a part in the work of the community. It was play for us to shop for neighbors, to help the milkman on his rounds by leading his horse-drawn milkcart or pushing his float and measuring the milk from the huge churns. And it was play, for those of us fortunate enough to be on good terms with a shopkeeper, to make paper twists or funnels and sell broken biscuits from large crumb-filled boxes.

Some other forms of street play were not looked at in such an approving way by our elders. Floating bits of wood along rain-filled gutters, playing in derelict houses, lighting fires and building dens on vacant sites were regarded, perhaps rightly, as undesirable and to be stopped. They presented hazards, could be dangerous—and adult society, in its wisdom, did its best to interfere and discourage us. What was not recognized then was that, like children everywhere, we were imitating what adults did, and preparing ourselves for a social existence in a way that would have been impossible had we been confined to 'safe' play. But this was before the war.

The bombing of our cities during the war provided the next generation of children with exciting but even more dangerous sites on which to play. Fortunately the time had produced a new generation of parents, too; at least some of

whom were enlightened enough to realize that this sort of risk-taking but basically creative play was not only more enjoyable to a child but also rather more encouraging of development than any of the 'safe' play they could so easily have imposed. Out of their permissiveness and the still undeveloped ideas of a few 'cranks' who had taken the trouble to think about the place of play in children's lives was born the adventure-playground movement.

—Joe Benjamin, ''Children at Play,'' *The Listener*

The children's games during and after the war did not differ crucially from the prewar ones. Here the writer has focused on the likenesses. But now the attitudes of parents towards children's games are very different; therein lies the contrast.

Below is another example of comparison and contrast, taken from a sample paper in Chapter 1. The student first points out the likeness, even if it is superficial, between characters in a play of Brecht's. Galileo the astronomer looks up at the skies, and so do the dockworkers, he notices. But the student who wrote the following comment perceives that what is important is not the actions compared but the motives behind them. Thus, at a deeper level, Galileo is quite different from the dockworkers.

Galileo and His Countrymen

In the beginning of the play Galileo is excited by the social context of his research. He sees his discoveries, which challenge antiquated beliefs, as part of a social movement by which both workers and intellectuals will benefit. ''At last,'' he says, ''everybody is getting nosy. I predict that in our time astronomy will become the gossip of the market place and the sons of fishwives will pack the schools.'' He relates himself to the workers; like him they have discovered that there are contradictions between their observations of the universe and the ecclesiastical concept of the order of the universe. He tells the monks that even unread sailors and carpenters, not afraid to use their eyes, are discovering new ways of doing things.

But Galileo fails to consider that behind their similar discoveries there is different motivation. Curiosity motivated Galileo to study the sky, whereas the dockyard workers have jobs in which they are forced to take note of the sky. Whereas Galileo seeks to find the knowledge he acquires, the workers receive it without seeking. Galileo, excited by the fact that they have arrived at similar observations, falsely concludes that the workers are motivated by the same driving curiosity which motivates him—''that same high curiosity which was the true glory of ancient Greece.''—student

Below are suggestions for ways to use comparison and contrast in your own writing. These are especially useful when your task calls for "analysis." Where we say "compare," we could easily add "and contrast."

1. Contrast what is true with what is not true.
2. Contrast appearances, behavior, attitudes.
3. Contrast different methods of attaining the same result.
4. Contrast the apparent with the real, or the superficial with the deep, the fake with the genuine.
5. Compare motives. The same motive might result in different acts, one perhaps subtle and another crude. Or different motives might produce similar behavior.
6. Compare your own view of something with someone else's view of the same thing.
7. Compare the present with the past, one place with another.
8. Contrast a person's specific goal with the means he uses to attain it.
9. Contrast the potential and the actual. (Contrast, for example, what might have happened with what is happening, or contrast a man's intentions with his deeds.)
10. Contrast the severity, the extent, or the degree of two things.
11. Compare the conclusions reached by two different people. Compare the evidence they used. Compare the values or basic assumptions underlying their arguments. Have they used the same evidence but arrived at different conclusions? Are their conclusions the same in spite of different evidence? Examine the reasons for such discrepancies.

EXERCISE

A. Give examples of the way comparison or contrast could be used to develop the following topics:

1. the fairness (or unfairness) of our education system in meeting the needs of different Americans

2. a discussion of two works by the same poet, playwright, or novelist

B. Look back at the passage about the book *Slavery* by Stanley Elkins. Find the points of comparison or contrast: Who is the black child like? Who is the plantation master like? What is the plantation like? What difference does the writer take note of? What general point is being made?

C. Do the two passages below say the same thing or something different? Explain.

1. (About the city) A basic consideration has to be total number of people as well as open space. In other words, there should be less density allowed in all directions.

2. What are the facts about our city that people don't want to face? More than 21,000 hotel rooms and about 9500 residential units are here now, and present zoning would permit a boost in each category—in hotel rooms, to an astronomical figure of 68,000.

D. Do the two passages below say the same thing or something different? Explain.

1. If urban landowners note tighter restrictions (on building) coming, they will quickly make plans to build, thereby fueling a boom that adds to the area's problems. That's what happened when the County Zoning Law came in a few years ago.

2. If there should ever be a promise (threat?) to implement new zoning regulations, without a "moratorium" on building, there would be such a rush to get new projects under the wire that we could say goodbye to any hope of the area remaining even a reasonably pleasant, reasonably dense urban area.

E. Do the two passages below say the same thing or something different? (A more complex problem. Try to find two or three points of agreement and/or disagreement.)

1. Everyone senses the corrupting power of money, but few grasp the power of secrecy to subvert the public process. Secrecy is fatal to accountability—and accountability is the central ingredient of free self-government. What citizens don't know, they can't object to.
   —John Gardner, Common Cause, 1974

2. Have you ever wondered who can look at that tax dossier, or your medical history or job record, credit or military files, test scores or insurance appli-

cations? The sad truth is that many "private" or "secret" records are available upon request to Federal authorities, commerical firms and private investigators. . . . There are risks lurking in this ever-increasing collection of personal data. As information accumulates, an individual's computerized dossier appears more reliable and its content is treated as gospel, making an independent evaluation of him less likely. Not surprisingly, therefore, many people have come to feel that their success or failure in life ultimately may turn on what other people put in their file, . . .

—Arthur R. Miller, *Los Angeles Times Service,* 1974

F. On what points do the two writers below agree and/or disagree? (Try to find three or four points.)

1. The history books of every nation justify its wars as brave, righteous and honorable. This glorification is charged with overtones of patriotism and love of country. Virtues such as heroism and courage are regarded as being "manly" and are traditionally associated with waging war. Conversely, the avoidance of war or the pursuit of peace is generally regarded as "effeminate," passive, cowardly, weak, dishonorable or subversive. The brutal realities, even of traditional war, are glamorized and obscured by countless tales of heroism and glory, and the warnings of an occasional General Sherman that "war is hell (and) its glory all moonshine" are disregarded. It is by glamorizing war that it is made an acceptable institution. In fact, I agree with those who say that the obstacles to the elimination of war are mainly psychological ones of this kind and include, for example, the proliferation of military toys and war games, which prepare the mind for an acceptance of war and violence. But nevertheless these obstacles are not insurmountable; they are the creation of human minds and as such can be overcome by human intelligence. Human beings, if they work at it, can abolish war.

   —Adapted from *On Aggression* by Konrad Lorenz, quoting J. Marmac

2. War is the ultimate way we have of settling questions of right and wrong. We can ask all countries to do right, to remain within their borders, to cease violent attacks on neighboring countries, and to treat their own citizens in a humane way. We can ask; we can threaten; we can boycott. But if none of these means can stop a greedy, cruel, or ruthless government from imposing its will on helpless individuals or weaker neighboring countries, then war is the only alternative. War is awful, but the evil of war is less than the evil of tyranny. Given the innately selfish character of man and the limited resources of the earth, it is inevitable that rulers will continue to disobey international law. Other nations of the world must be pre-

pared to punish such disobedience. Thus, unfortunately, war as an institution must continue as long as man inhabits the earth.

Paragraphs That Take Note of Counterarguments

Writers should not argue both sides of a question. One should argue for something or against it. Note what happens below, for example, when a student writer is trying to sit on the fence. The first sentence argues for a national health plan, and the second against it.

> A national health plan would thus improve the general health of the population without really adding much more expense than the present unfair system. Government regulation could lead to too much red tape and doctors would strongly oppose government "interference."

This paragraph, the instructor will say, lacks a sense of conviction. It is all right to be impartial, but one should not change his mind in the middle of a piece of writing, as the student writer above seemed to be doing.

What the writer frequently has to do to preserve his own point of view throughout the paper is to show that the counterarguments are outweighed by other evidence. While conceding that certain things are true, he shows that these are less important than other facts. The writer in favor of capital punishment (Chapter 1) *conceded* that innocent people might be put to death, but *emphasized* that this would be rare, and furthermore that many lives would be saved since the threat of capital punishment would deter others from committing murder.

In the sentences below notice that there are two parts—the part considered by the writer less important and that considered more important. The first part he concedes, the second he asserts.

(1) Although he was pale and sickly, he could be aggressively courageous when courage was needed.

(2) Despite their shortcomings with respect to enforcement, the

consumer protection laws played the major role in undermin-
ing the old let-the-buyer-beware attitude.

(3) His self-respect and pride no doubt prevented Ishi from ac-
quiring a more rapid and facile command of English . . . But
these character traits seemed not to have seriously cut him
off from the people and activities he valued . . .

—Theodore Kroeber, *Ishi*

Notice that some words serve to subordinate an idea, to make it
the part which the writer concedes, words like *although, despite,
even though, in spite of,* and *admittedly.* Other words serve to emphasize the stronger idea: *but, however, nevertheless,* and *yet.*

On a larger scale the concession relationship may be exploited,
often quite effectively, as an argumentative technique. The writer
first "concedes" all the major counterarguments against the argument he wishes to support. If he is dishonest or negligent, he may
omit some of the most crucial counterarguments, but this lays him
open to devastating refutation. This counterargument stage might
be called the "although" section.

Then, in what might be termed the "nevertheless" section,
the writer marshalls his own arguments and perhaps undermines a
few of the "although" counterarguments.

For example, in a paper seeking to present in a more favorable light the Castro regime in Cuba, a student began by describing
the stream of refugees leaving Cuba weekly, the one-party system,
the mass executions at the onset of the revolution, the inefficiency
of many parts of the administration, the decay of industries which
had once flourished, the stifling of dissent among the peasants as
well as among poets and artists. This was his "although" section.

Then he went on to place all the aforementioned in a "proper
perspective," as he saw it. He described even worse conditions
under earlier regimes supported by the United States—executions
without trial by secret police and right-wing vigilante groups, mas-
sive corruption, starvation, disease, and a deliberate use of irrational terror to render the population more submissive. The industries which had once flourished had exported most of their profits

to the United States and were now languishing under an American-sponsored boycott. The peasants, though hardly overfed, no longer had to fear starvation or irrational terror. Corruption was rare, and people felt they had a voice in the future. The writer detailed further improvements and explained that earlier excesses had not continued. He concluded with a plea for our under-standing and sympathy, combined with a condemnation of those who preach against left-wing dictatorships in Cuba while arming and financing right-wing regimes elsewhere in the Americas and in Asia.

EXERCISE

A. Join each pair of sentences together, subordinating one and thus emphasizing the other. Then reverse the procedure, rewrit-ing the sentences so that the emphasis is reversed.

1. Many Americans are poor. The U.S. is the richest country in the world.
2. This novel deals with social issues. It is about the emotional development of a family.
3. The atom is tiny. It contains enormous power.
4. Carrot juice contains little or no protein. It is rich in vita-mins.

Take the two sentences you have written for (1), (2), (3), or (4) above. Examine the two carefully and think about their meaning. Then describe topics for which: (1) your first sen-tence of the pair would be a more appropriate opening than the second, and (2) your second sentence would be a more appropriate opening than the first.

B. Below are arguments and evidence that you can assume are true for purposes of this exercise. Suppose you want to show that Malthus was correct in predicting that the bulk of the world's population would, sooner or later, be forced to live at near-starvation levels. Which of the items below would be pro, and which would be con? Write a paragraph arguing that

Malthus was correct. Bring in all the items in the list, whether pro or con, yet stick to your point of view throughout.

1. Population is presently increasing faster than the food supply.
2. Food productivity is increasing since the introduction of hybrid strains of rice and wheat.
3. Fertilizers necessary for high-yielding crops are not plentiful because they are the by-product of oil or require large amounts of other energy sources for their production.
4. Improved health care has helped people live longer and has reduced infant mortality.
5. Presently tens of millions, a sizable portion of the world's people, are living close to the starvation level.
6. The population growth rate (number of births per 100,000 people) is going down in the wealthier countries.
7. Modern wars have taken great numbers of human lives.
8. We cannot predict. There may yet be other amazing scientific advances affecting food supplies.

Idea Linking and Linking Words

This chapter has been concerned with strengthening an idea by supporting it with detail. The reader must understand the link between the idea and the detail; otherwise the detail is useless and even harmful. If the reader does not see the point of the detail, the writer has failed to communicate.

The next chapter provides practice in tracking idea links through whole paragraphs, but it may be useful to note here that we make use of clue words for the purpose of linking. Think about *because of, for example, by contrast,* and *however.* Most speakers use these words without being conscious of their purpose in doing so, but the writer may have to become more conscious of them since he cannot depend on tone of voice or body language for making his point understood. He should think about when to use

them and when to omit them. The purpose of this exercise is to show students how linking words determine in part what can follow or precede a particular sentence.

Use your logical sense and imagination to write sentences that could have *preceded* each of the following. The first is done for you.

1. This was in spite of the fact that the little fish already had his mouth full with the juicy hindquarter of a worm. (Clue words: *in spite of, already*) (A possible sentence: With a sudden motion, he sucked up the remaining bit of floating food before his bigger rival could reach it.)
2. He was also something of a bore. (Clue word: *also*)
3. On the other hand, it was hardly fair to put them in jail when their superiors, who encouraged the plot, remained completely free. (Clue words: *on the other hand*)
4. They found, for example, crude stone implements and fragments of human skulls. (Clue words: *for example.* What could the findings be an example of?)
5. So, as soon as they could, they shifted the conversation to the topic of Henry's acquaintance with the late Mr. White's widow. (Clue word: *so*)
6. The result has been that some former college level mathematics courses are now introduced in high school, high school math has moved down to junior high school with a consequent revision of grade school courses. (Clue words: *result, consequent*)
7. It is not Edgar but the evil-hearted Edmund that one remembers long after seeing the play. (Clue words: *evil-hearted* must show contrast?)
8. There were, however, just enough votes in favor of the measure to allow its passage. (Clue word: *however*)

Mapping: A Way to Check Your Organization and Coherence

In an earlier discussion of *Incoherence,* p. 15, we used a student paragraph on Zuñi customs. The writer, explaining how a Zuñi woman arranges a divorce, suddenly introduced an apparently different topic. In fact there was a close link, but the writer had not taken the trouble to explain what the link was. So the reader, following along the logical line of the writer's thinking, came suddenly to a break in the logic.

The mapping procedure on the next page is a way of finding breaks, if there are any, in your own paragraphs. It is a way of checking your work. It requires, first, that you work out the main idea and, second, that you show what each sentence does in the paragraph: Does it describe? Illustrate? Give a cause or reason?

Show contrast? If you can work this out, you will have shown that there are idea links, which a reader should understand, between one sentence and the next and between each sentence and the whole. If you cannot, then it is likely that something is wrong with part of the paragraph. Maybe a sentence should be left out, or perhaps rephrased, to make the idea link more obvious to the reader.

We illustrate the mapping with seven idea links:

description	cause (or reason) and effect
example or illustration	comparison and contrast
definition or classification	concession
time/space sequencing	

You are free to modify these or add your own terms. Invent terms of your own if these will help you think, really think, about the logical connection between your sentences.

To make the map, work out first the main idea of the paragraph, which might be stated in Sentence 1, or Sentence 2, or implied by the paragraph as a whole but not stated.

1. Write out the main idea in your own words, even if you have to oversimplify.
2. Then look at the first sentence and decide how it is linked to the main idea: Does it describe it, illustrate it? Is it a contrasting idea? Is it a reason or cause connected with the main idea?
3. Do the same with the second sentence. How is it linked to the main idea? Is it linked to Sentence 1 in some way? (See example below.)
4. Draw arrows to show the links, as suggested by the example below.

The paragraph on the following page was taken from the middle of a student paper on the topic of civil service examinations in China. The question raised about the topic was rather interesting because it involved general questions about all tests:

Do you think the old Chinese examinations were a good way of finding able and competent civil servants?

The student's general response, her unifying idea, was

No, they were *not*.

> ¹ The exam was a test of irrelevant kinds of knowledge and skills. ² It covered a person's knowledge of the Confucian classics. ³ Often the writing of poetry was also an important item on the examinations. ⁴ While possessing this knowledge certainly never hurt anyone, it seems strange that matters such as economics, accounting, and general administrative procedures never appeared on the tests. ⁵ A comparable procedure would be to test Americans on all of Shakespeare's writing before putting them in charge of our Post Office system, or perhaps before making them judges. ⁶ In China, as a consequence of knowing little or nothing about practical matters of business and law, the magistrates and other officials were forced to rely upon their secretaries, clerks, and servants in order to accomplish their jobs. ⁷ This would sometimes lead to further corruption in the system if one of these people decided to work things for his own personal gain.—student

Main idea: The examinations were not a good way of finding able and competent civil servants.

Cause: ¹ Exams tested for irrelevant skills.   (This is why examinations were not a good test.)

    Examples: ² Confucian classics   (Examples of irrelevant
            ³ poetry writing   skills and knowledge.)

      Contrast: ⁴ Knowledge of economics,   (Relevant skills,
        accounting, general adminis-   contrasting with
        trative procedures   irrelevant skills.)

    Comparison: ⁵ Testing Americans on   (Irrelevant skills, like
    Shakespeare before making them   the ones above.)
    post office administrators or
    judges

Effect: ⁶ Magistrates forced to rely on   (An effect of possessing
subordinates.   only irrelevant skills.)

  Effect: ⁷ Subordinates could indulge in   (An effect of having
  corruption.   no skilled supervision.)

The diagram or map is one way of showing the idea relationships of the paragraph. The drawing of the arrows and the naming of the parts, as well as the degree of complexity, may vary slightly from one person to the next, but the process is the same for all: finding the idea relationships between sentences and between each sentence and the whole paragraph. Once you can accomplish this kind of task with other people's prose, and especially with your own, your reader should be able to follow you easily from one sentence to the next. When you do longer pieces of writing, it will be helpful to work out the links not between every sentence but between paragraphs.

You can also use mapping to help you read complicated articles or textbooks: find the links between paragraphs, or between one group of paragraphs and another, and decide how each part is linked to the main idea. By doing so, you can grasp the structure of the article. As a consequence, the material of the article will be much easier to remember.

EXERCISE

Another paragraph is mapped out below, this one a narrative paragraph. As the map is worked out here, it shows not the superficial time sequence but rather the underlying causes and effects. This is one version of the map; other versions are possible.

Study this map, and then work out in similar fashion a map for each of the paragraphs which follow it.

---

¹ When we first moved into our house seven years ago, there were only about eight families on the block. ² The area had originally been a tomato patch, but now it was a new subdivision with new houses and the realtor had said that we were a safe distance from Logan Heights, the black area. ³ In the next couple of years most of the houses on our block were sold. ⁴ Then it happened. ⁵ A black family moved into the neighborhood. ⁶ Panic immediately struck the neighboring families, including ours.

⁷ Until then, I had never come into contact with a black person. ⁸ All I knew was what white people had told me about them. ⁹ And as a kid I had soaked every word of it up. ¹⁰ So, before ever

knowing a black person, I already had in my mind an opinion that he was a no good so and so, and that he would slit my throat if I didn't stay away from him. [11] This, I'm sure, was the feeling of many of the white families on the street. [12] In the eyes of the whites, this one family of blacks made the neighborhood a black town, and their property values would drop. [13] So, what did they do? [14] The whites moved out and the neighborhood got blacker and blacker. [15] Pretty soon, our family really got scared. [16] We didn't go outside at night for fear that we would be jumped by one of them.—student

Main idea: Our all-white suburban neighborhood was afraid of the idea of black families moving in.

Description: [1,2,3] The new subdivision seemed "safely" white—just a few houses, far from crowded city and the black area.

(Describes the whiteness of the area.)

Contrast: [4,5] But a black family moves in.

(A contrast with the white neighborhood.)

Effect: [6] Panic

(The fear is a result.)

Reasons for (or examples of) panic: [7,8,9,10,11,12] Writer had never known a black person, believed the distortions he had heard

(Cause for the fear of both the young writer and other whites.)

Examples:

a black person might slit his throat

property values were sure to drop

Effect: [13,14,15,16] Whites moved out, more blacks moved in, his family became even more frightened, perhaps needlessly.

(Results of the panic, or illustration of the panic.)

1. I'd like to mention here that it is unwise to expect your company meals to look precisely like the company meals you see in the full-color food spreads everywhere. In this connection, I have news for you: food photographers do not play fair and square. It was once my privilege to watch a beef stew being photographed in the studio of a major food photographer. It was a superb stew—the gravy glistening richly, the beef chunks brown and succulent and in beautiful juxtaposition to the bright carrots and the pearly onions. I can make a respectable beef stew myself, but my gravy is never that gorgeous, and my onions invariably sink as though torpedoed. I inquired about this and discovered that the gravy had been dyed, and the onions had been propped up on toothpicks! Moreover, that very same morning, they told me, they'd had to lacquer a lobster. —Peg Bracken, *The I Hate to Cook Book*

2. "The great object of life," Byron wrote, "is sensation—to feel that we exist, even though in pain. It is this 'craving void,' which drives us to gaming—to battle, to travel—to intemperate, but keenly felt, pursuits of any description, whose principal attraction is to the agitation inseparable from their accomplishment." And Stendhal confirmed him when he said that an age of revolutions and wars gives a "continual thirst for strong emotions. When they subside for a while, boredom follows until they rise again." We are enough in the same situation today to make an interest in Byron revive. —V. S. Pritchett, "The Craving Void"

3. A poll of students will show that they are not very sure about what their own family incomes really are. Usually it turns out they have a slightly exaggerated notion of their fathers' earnings. And despite the recent (quite justified) claim of a prominent clubwoman that "women spend 70 per cent of the national income, and we soon hope to get hold of the rest," an astonishing number of wives have no conception of their husbands' paychecks. In addition, there are some people so inept at keeping records and with such variable earnings that they do not themselves know how much they make. Even where income is known within the family, there is a quite natural reticence to reveal it to outsiders; thus investigators who made a 1939 survey of the birth-control habits of native white Protestants of Indianapolis often found it harder to get financial data than intimate personal information. —Paul A. Samuelson, *Economics*

4. Now it may seem paradoxical and illogical, but I make a distinction between lying and being dishonest. You can be honest and yet a liar—that is, you can be honest about the big things in life although sometimes dishonest about the lesser things. Thus many of our lies are meant to save others pain. Truth-telling would become an evil if it impelled me to write, "Dear Sir, your letter was so long and dull that I could not be bothered reading it all." Or if

it forced you to say to a would-be musician: "Thank you for playing, but you murdered that Etude." Adults' lying is generally altruistic, but children's lying is always local and personal. The best way to make a child a liar for life is to insist that he speak the truth and nothing but the truth. . . .

I have never consciously told a lie to my pupils in thirty-eight years, and indeed never had any desire to. But that is not quite correct, for I told a big lie one term. A girl, whose unhappy history I knew, stole a pound. The theft committee—three boys—saw her spend money on ice cream and cigarettes, and they cross-examined her. "I got the pound from Neill," she told them, and they brought her to me, asking, "Did you give Liz a quid?" Hastily sensing the situation, I replied blandly, "Why, yes, I did." Had I given her away, I knew that forever afterward she would have no trust in me. Her symbolic stealing of love in the form of money would have received another hostile setback. I had to prove that I was on her side all the way. I know that if her home had been honest and free, such a situation would never have arisen. I lied with a purpose—a *curative* purpose—but in all other circumstances, I dare not lie.—A. S. Neill, *Summerhill*

5. That sandwich man I'd replaced had little chance of getting his job back. I went bellowing up and down those train aisles. I sold sandwiches, coffee, candy, cake, and ice cream as fast as the railroad's commissary department could supply them. It didn't take me a week to learn that all you had to do was give white people a show and they'd buy anything you offered them. It was like popping your shoeshine rag. The dining car waiters and Pullman porters knew it too, and they faked their Uncle Tomming to get bigger tips. We were in that world of Negroes who are both servants and psychologists, aware that white people are so obsessed with their own importance that they will pay liberally, even dearly, for the impression of being catered to and entertained

—Malcolm X, with the assistance of Alex Haley,
The Autobiography of Malcolm X

Criticisms to Anticipate in Writing a Paper

Writers of articles and papers want to produce prose that is trim, logical, and to the point, that says something original in a well-thought-out way, and gets on with the job. Editors, writing instructors, and bosses on the job use a fairly standard set of comments to show where the writing is *not* trim, logical, or to the point. The comment is a signal to change something, or to strengthen it, and almost always it has something to do with the content of your paper, not its form or mechanical correctness. The purpose of this chapter is to explain by example what these comments mean, to show how to rewrite the faulty part (if possible), and to help writers avoid the problem in the first place.

Vagueness

A writer who takes too little time to think through his subject matter is apt to present his ideas in a vague prose that all too often characterizes political speeches, as in the following paragraph:

> The problem of pollution is serious. Efforts have to be made to overcome it or the results will be dangerous. Because of our failure at all levels to come to grips with the problem and to meet it head on, its menace has grown. What is needed is a major effort to conquer it or life as we know it will cease to exist on this planet. Such an effort must take into consideration economic and human needs, but it must be put into effect without delay—student

The passage above repeats common slogans without any attempt to particularize them by referring, say, to particular rivers, sewage projects, or automobile exhaust restrictions. In the last sentence the writer gives himself a way out with his reference to unspecified "economic and human needs." The following paragraph is more detailed and more persuasive:

> The Mississippi River has been described as an open sewer, Lake Huron is a dead body of water, and orange trees wilt under the poisons hovering in the Los Angeles air. Yet Industrial lobbying groups in the state legislatures repeatedly succeed in turning back the most reasonable attempts to remedy the problems. The 1972 campaign over Proposition Nine in California shows all the forces and counter forces in action.—student revision

Vagueness does not always represent a deliberate attempt to withhold information. Sometimes it occurs simply as a result of laziness. For example:

> Basically Henry's whole character and way of speaking involve a hypocritical type attitude to the responsibilities of power. Sir William Bradshaw is really the same kind of person although he is a psychiatrist and Henry is a king. So both show hypocrisy is typical in power.—student

The writer has not bothered to specify the evidence for his characterization of Henry and Bradshaw. What had these men done or

said to make him think they were hypocritical? More detail of this kind would have given depth to the characterization, and it would probably have made the writer think of more intelligent things to say. At the moment the concluding sentence "So both show hypocrisy is typical in power" is unjustified. The word *so* is a claim by the writer that he has proved his point, when in fact he has offered no evidence for it.

Repetitiousness

College writing is often repetitious when the writer has failed to think out his ideas adequately before writing his first draft. He is doing some of the thinking as he writes. We use a student example here which is difficult to read, almost incomprehensible.

Explain the importance of Marshall McLuhan's ideas.

There is a vast gap between the scientific technology and the educational process of today. There is a well-established case for the proposition that our electrical technology has resulted in a radical discontinuity in our society. The discontinuity exists because scientific technology of today is advancing with greater speed than the educational process. With this discrepancy in the educational process, there exists a discontinuity within the environment. I agree with McLuhan's position about the electrical technology of today.—student

The writer asserts that there is a gap or discontinuity of some unspecified nature caused by the fact that technology has advanced faster than education. The vagueness and repetitiveness reflect a general lack of control over the prose that results from the author's apparent unwillingness to think for himself, to really think about McLuhan's ideas. The writer did, in fact, after thinking a little more, develop the idea that schools are preparing children for adult life in a society which no longer exists. The discrepancy between their expectations as fostered by the schools and their experience outside the classroom has led to a feeling of being lost and helpless in a land of strange monsters. This, the writer said, was what he believed McLuhan was saying. Then, after some further explanation of the ideas, the writer provided examples of the prob-

lems McLuhan was describing and showed that McLuhan was indicating what might be done to modify education so as to prepare people more adequately.

Here in a longer piece of writing is the same problem that we saw just now. The writer repeats the same general idea without giving specific detail. The idea, even though it might be a good one for a paper, remains shallow.

> Man was created and had dominion over all living things which inhabit the earth. But the pollution which he has made and his spoilage of nature raise the question of whether man has been just with regard to his control over living things. The necessity that man be able to control himself along with all other living things is immediate if he is going to be able to continue his and all other species.
>
> Man's lack of control has led to much contamination of the earth, its waters and atmosphere. Nowhere on earth is there someplace which has not been affected or will not be affected by this contamination which he has produced. This contamination has caused the extinction of much wildlife and the ruin of an ecological balance in the environments of living things.
>
> The extent of this contamination has caused an awareness of man's lack of control, and various campaigns have been started in an attempt to try and check this contamination. "Earth Day" and "Friends for a Better Environment" are just two such examples.
>
> It is my belief that these campaigns have helped increase the awareness of the contamination. They have set up "reclamation centers" for the re-cycling of certain materials, which might otherwise add to the pollution. But with each day that passes, more pollution is contributed to the already plentiful supply. Because of this fact, man will eventually impose certain controls on himself for the sake of survival. Studies have been started and are still continuing into possible ways of stopping pollution.—student

Irrelevance

IRRELEVANT PHRASES

There are some phrases, familiar to most teachers of composition, which are almost always irrelevant or unnecessary:

> I enjoyed the story very much. It kept me reading at a fast pace.
> I agree with the quote above.

> What I want to bring out . . .
> Thus I have proved/shown that . . .
> In this paper I will show that . . .
> Now I have given three examples of . . .
> Next is an explanation of . . .
> I am now going to prove that . . .—students

IRRELEVANT MATERIAL

The phrases above are irrelevant only in a superficial way. Usually the problem is more complex. "Irrelevant" usually means that part of the material is not pertinent to the argument being presented. The writer in some way has failed to see the relationship, or show the relationship, between some part of the paper and the main idea of the paper. It is quite common for an irrelevant sentence to seem perfectly relevant to the writer because he has other pertinent information in his mind that he has not written on the paper. But once the writer is aware that for his reader certain material is irrelevant, he should either remove it or revise it so that it does bear on the argument at hand.

The phrases above, such as "Now I am going to prove that . . . ," are often intended to assure the reader that the writer knows where he is going. But such assurances should be unnecessary if the paper is unified and the development orderly and logical. Normally, student writers are faced with a title or topic within which fairly limited goals are set:

> What does Margaret Mead mean by "culture"?
>
> "The problem of the cities." Discuss.
>
> Evaluate the contribution of Durkheim to sociological theory.
>
> Discuss the adequacy of the Copernican view of the universe.
>
> Compare the attitudes towards nature of the Hopi Indians with those of the white pioneers.
>
> "The current conservation craze is dangerous from the long-term point of view." Discuss.

The goal of a paper for a literature course might be to discuss one particular idea, "power" for example:

Assignment: Both the play *Henry IV, Parts 1 and 2,* and the novel *Mrs. Dalloway* present interesting notions of power although they are quite different. Compare these notions.

Suppose that these passages are parts of such an essay. How effective do they seem to you? Which are relevant and which irrelevant? See if your judgment concurs with ours.

Passage A: Shakespeare has justifiably been called the greatest of all playwrights while Virginia Woolf is one of the most sensitive women novelists of this century.—student

(True perhaps but probably irrelevant, even as part of the introduction.)

Passage B: "Power" is one of the key words in modern thought as it has been throughout the ages. Both Shakespeare in *Henry IV, Parts 1 and 2* and Virginia Woolf in *Mrs. Dalloway* deal with the effects of power, but their treatment is very different. In this paper I shall try to examine the differences between their notions of power.—student

Relevant but says little. Repeats the ideas already stated in the assignment.

Passage C: Before I examine the notions of power in these two books, it is first necessary to go into their subject-matter. *Mrs. Dalloway* is about a woman who is waiting for the return of a man whom she almost married, Peter Walsh. He had been the one she really loved. Instead she had married Richard Dalloway, a British member of Parliament, and they now have a grown-up daughter Elizabeth. The book tells her thoughts about what she has done and about her meeting with Walsh. There is also a subplot about an ex-First World War soldier who still suffers from shell-shock.—student

Irrelevant. A plot summary, while it may be useful for understanding a difficult novel, is distracting in a course paper. The writing that people do about literature should be a response to it, a personal response, just as the remarks one makes to another per-

son about a neighborhood fire are personal when both have been witnesses to the fire. Your audience, you can assume, has already experienced the literary work.

> **Passage D:** Power, according to Webster's *New World Dictionary*, is 1. ability to do; capacity to act; capability of performing or producing; 2. a specific ability or faculty; 3. great ability to do, act, or affect strongly; 4.a) the ability to control others; b) legal ability or authority; c) a document giving it. The parts of the definition relating to this part are 3 and 4a with 4b also being important. King Henry has the ability to act and to control others and he also has some legal authority although his right to be king is not a firm one since he seized power from the previous king. In Virginia Woolf's novel, the psychiatrist, Sir William Bradshaw, has power but it is not really legal authority. Mrs. Dalloway has little power of any kind and does not really want it.—student

Quoting from the dictionary is of little use here. The object of the paper is to define ''power,'' not in a dictionary sense but in a descriptive sense. The writer should describe what power consisted of and the way it functioned in the two literary works.

> **Passage E:** Like the poet Sylvia Plath, Virginia Woolf killed herself. Her interests were very different from those of William Shakespeare.
> —student

Details about the life of the author usually are irrelevant in an essay about the novels, plays, or poetry of that person. In this case the link is very strained, indeed, between the suicide of Virginia Woolf, the suicide of Sylvia Plath, and the notion of power in works by Shakespeare and Virginia Woolf.

> **Passage F:** In both the play and the novel, ''power'' is presented as control over human beings by other human beings. For Virginia Woolf, power is horrifying. The psychiatrist, Sir William Bradshaw, who is really power-crazy, tries to control the shell-shocked Septimus Smith and eventually drives him to his death. Mrs. Dalloway herself, by refusing to marry Walsh who might have controlled her, has kept her freedom and her ability to live her own life as a human being, not a puppet. Shakespeare accepts

power as not only inevitable but desirable if it is exercised with a sense of responsibility towards those controlled. Without authority and legitimate power, man does not know his place within the universe, and the kind of anarchy represented by Falstaff occurs. Virginia Woolf looks at power from within, from an individual mind seeking freedom from fear and interruption. Power is thus likely to be a menace. But Shakespeare looks at power from outside. He looks at the whole society of men and concludes that power, as manifested in legitimate authority, is necessary if men are to live harmoniously together.

Thus it has been shown that the notions of power are quite different in the two works discussed. Virginia Woolf sees power from the viewpoint of a person's inner consciousness—power is a dangerous force. Shakespeare sees power from the viewpoint of the society of men—power is a necessary force.—student

Relevant, but the last paragraph is unnecessary because it repeats the preceding one.

Passage G: I agree that both *Henry IV, Parts 1 and 2* and *Mrs. Dalloway* present interesting notions of power although they are quite different. It is not surprising that they are different because the works were written by two very different people. I think that Virginia Woolf, as a married woman, is naturally concerned about the repressive power that a husband can have over a wife. Shakespeare, however, does not come to grips with the corrupting power of the marriage bond in our civilization, probably because he wishes to maintain it.—student

Unnecessary first sentence. There's no need to inform the reader of your agreement. The rest is irrelevant because you are supposed to compare the notions, not to speculate about the personal opinions and lives of the writers.

Passage H: Although Virginia Woolf is a twentieth century writer, she is sometimes harder to understand than Shakespeare, who wrote in the sixteenth century.—student

Irrelevant.

Passage I: Shakespeare and Virginia Woolf are both concerned with the effects of power, but only Shakespeare is really concerned with the nature of power.—student

Good.

Passage J: Many Americans today are concerned about the power that others have over us. This power is not always properly managed or democratic. Shakespeare too, along with Virginia Woolf, writes about power.—student

First two sentences have not been *made* relevant, and the third really does very little to achieve the goals of the paper.

Incoherence (relevance in the paragraph)

A sentence within a paragraph may sound completely irrelevant or out of place. To the reader it seems totally unconnected, in any logical way, with the sentence that came before it.

To correct this, the writer has to remove the sentence to some more appropriate place or rewrite the sentence, making it fit the logic and ideas of the paragraph.

A paper on Zuñi marriage customs may quite validly include descriptions of the attitude towards adultery and of divorce procedures; but notice, however, that some of the sentences below interrupt the flow of ideas:

(1a)   Ending a marriage is not a very complicated matter. Adultery is not uncommon in Zuñi society. If a Zuñi wife is unhappy with her husband, she goes to a ceremonial feast in search of a new one. When she is sure she has a suitable husband, the old one will find all of his belongings on the doorsill. The rejected husband takes his things and goes back to his mother's house. Unfaithfulness usually does not break up a marriage. It is considered part of married life.—student

The sentence beginning "Adultery is not . . ." and the last two sentences have not been made relevant to the "ending-the-marriage" theme. The writer has not thought about the link between part of the material in the paragraph and the whole paragraph. The remarks about adultery could, for example, be tied in by grouping them together and linking them to the rest with a *but*. The result is a concession relationship conveying the idea,

Adultery may not cause divorce, but unhappiness may. The paragraph is more unified, more coherent as follows:

(1b) Adultery is not uncommon in Zuñi society, and even continued unfaithfulness usually does not break up a marriage. It is considered part of married life. But if for some other reason the Zuñi wife is unhappy with her husband, ending the marriage is not a very complicated matter. She goes to a ceremonial feast in search of a new one. When she is sure she has a suitable husband, the old one will find all of his belongings on the doorsill. The rejected husband takes his things and goes back to his mother's house.—student revision

In the following sentence the writer has focused on the words "not new":

The imposition of a wage freeze was not a new phenomenon to the growers.

The reader should expect the next sentence to explain why it was not new. But the student writing the paper wrote this:

(2a) The imposition of a wage freeze was not a new phenomenon to the growers. Now they could save on wages while charging as much as they could get for their output. This was because the price freeze applied only to processed goods, not to agricultural produce.—student

The first sentence hardly fits in with the other two. They give a good reason for the planters to have been pleased with the wage freeze. The paragraph will cohere, or hold together, better if the first sentence is changed:

(2b) The imposition of a wage freeze was not an *unwelcome* phenomenon to the growers. Now the growers could save on wages while charging as much as they could get for their output. This was because the price freeze applies only to processed goods, not to agricultural produce.
                                                        —student revision

Had the writer wished to keep the emphasis on the fact that such a freeze was not *new,* she might have written something like this, which is also coherent:

(2c) The imposition of a wage freeze was not a *new* phenomenon to the growers. A similar freeze had been imposed during the Korean War and

a much longer one during the Second World War. But this one was
more advantageous to the growers.—student revision

Overgeneralization

Generalizing is a legitimate part of the thinking process, but over-
generalizing is not. It is sometimes hard to determine just where
the boundary lies between the two. Certainly the subject is worthy
of discussion. If you are asked to criticize someone else's writing,
for example, or to write a critical paper on a political argument in
a news column, you might do well to examine the writer's generalizations. Is the evidence for them fair and representative, or does
it consist of an arbitrary collection of isolated incidents? Does it ignore large numbers of people or important pieces of evidence?

A writer overgeneralizes if he says, ''All textbooks are dull,''
because surely he cannot know about all textbooks. He knows
only certain textbooks—those he has read or heard about from
friends or even read about in other books. Omitting the word ''all''
is not much safer because

> Textbooks are dull.

really means to the reader that *all* textbooks are dull.

The same is true of phrases like *people in the North, the people of Switzerland,* or *blue-collar workers.* A writer cannot legiti-
mately say

> Swiss people are friendlier than Americans.

However, he can say:

> The Swiss of my experience. . . .
> Most Swiss that I have heard about. . . .
> Very often I have found that. . . .

There is meaning to

> A little over 33% of blue-collar workers vote a straight Democratic
> ticket every time they vote.

so long as it is clear what a blue-collar worker is. Such a statement has presumably come out of a statistical study in which a little over 33% of those interviewed said, "I vote a straight Democratic ticket when I vote." On the other hand, one can't really say:

> Seven out of ten Swiss are friendlier than Americans.

Friendliness is not the sort of concept which lends itself to statistical studies.

It is legitimate to make tentative generalizations so long as it is clear to the reader that the generalization is a tentative one.

> College students, I *suspect,* are no longer interested in knowledge as a reservoir of facts.

or

> College students are *probably* no longer interested in knowledge as a reservoir of facts.

But the credibility of this kind of statement will depend a lot on the context: Does the writer seem to know what he is talking about? Is there enough detail about these "college students" in his other sentences?

Writers frequently generalize by citing one example as typical of a whole class:

> Charles Harrison, living in a townhouse near the center of the city, knows he must lock and double-lock his front door. Living in the inner city all too often means living inside your own fortress.—student

But whether or not this is an overgeneralization depends on the circumstances. Some illustrations may not be representative. In such cases a hidden claim or premise is involved, one suggesting that such and such an event typifies a particular generalization when in fact this may not be so:

> Any elaborate welfare system is dishonest and self-defeating. We find a strong, healthy man preferring to live off of others instead of working to support him-

self. Welfare gives him a way to do this. If there were no welfare, he would have no choice but to work. We need to get rid of welfare except as a very temporary minimal subsistence system serving to bridge gaps in employment supply and demand.—student

The healthy man cited above may perhaps be typical, or perhaps his case is an isolated one. The writer has omitted the crucial evidence on this point. Some social scientists maintain that by far the largest number of welfare recipients are children, invalids, and the aged. They say that others are families whose major wage earner has lost his job, exhausted all unemployment benefits, and can still find no work. *If* this is so, the writer cannot honestly say the healthy man is the typical welfare recipient. *If* these social scientists are wrong, the writer has to show that they are.

In any case, a writer should not use a single illustration to distort the general picture or mislead the reader. The single illustration cited below is not enough to establish the general idea. The use of a name and location should not blind the reader into assuming that the illustration is as representative as the writer implies:

Students are graded not according to their competence but according to the political beliefs expressed in their papers. Stephen Crossland of UWM was given a C minus last December when he wrote a paper supporting our country's efforts in Southeast Asia. When he revised it and included a leftist condemnation of so-called atrocities, his grade was raised to an A minus. Moreover, all over the state new faculty are being hired on the basis of their answers to questions put by radical-liberal interviewers. I had one case of this less than a month ago at one of our most prestigious institutions. The situation in the universities is drastic, and drastic remedies are required.—adapted from a political speech

In the following paragraph the writer argues that Christianity is a religion less humane than the religion of the Aztecs. But notice that the evidence he chooses for comparison of the two religions is not really representative:

The Christian religion is far less humane even than the religion of the Aztecs. Crusading Christian knights righteously slew pagan men, women, and children

by the thousands. Fine upstanding Christian guards killed millions in concentration camps. The Aztecs only infrequently practiced human sacrifice. So it might be better for us all to adopt the ancient Aztec faith.—student

The writer has referred to only one cruel practice of the Aztecs, implying falsely that there were no others. The concentration camp example is weak; there is no evidence presented that the guards or their masters were following Christian tenets in their activities. More two-legged men have killed people than have one-legged men. This does not indicate that we all ought to give up one leg. If the writer is to make a good case for his initial generalization, he must show that the property of being Christian (rather than, say, the general property of political or religious fanaticism or of two-leggedness) is the one motivating the behavior he deplores. He might also seek to show that this motivation is not restricted to a specific historical period like the Middle Ages or World War II.

Oversimplification

Failure to think about details may lead to gross oversimplification of problems. A complicated set of events may be treated as if the events had but one cause, or as if there were two and only two sides to any dispute about them. For example:

> It is difficult for people like myself to realize what any type of racism is because I was raised with the idea that blacks, whites, reds, and yellows are all human beings. But many people must fight to conquer their discriminatory feelings.
> —student

In other words, the cure for racial prejudice is easy. Just raise your children so that they don't have it. An oversimplified problem is provided with an oversimple solution.

The author of the passage below has obviously thought little about the play he has to discuss. There are other facts about the play which should have shown the writer that his last two assertions are not only oversimplified but wrong.

> The basic problem presented in *Hamlet* is the hesitancy of the main character, Prince Hamlet. If Hamlet would take action without this unnecessary hesitation,

> the other problems in the play would give little trouble. Shakespeare's point is
> that some people are too hesitant.—student

A literary work, especially a major one, rarely has a single "basic"
point. Nor is a complex social problem likely to have one simple
answer. If you find only one, be sure to go back and look carefully
again. Have you considered all the facts? Have you provided a
"simple" solution which is really an impossibly complicated one?
Are you treating as bad guys or good guys people who are really
a puzzling mixture of good, bad, and morally neutral characteristics?

Confused Reasoning

A very frequent type of confused reasoning is the misuse of the
cause-effect relationship. Sometimes a rather strict causal relation
is implied between sentences, the writer claiming that something
causes something else. Sometimes the link is so obvious as not to
require evidence justifying it:

> The warm damp air rises to colder levels and therefore cools. The decreasing
> temperature of the rising air mass causes the vapor to condense into little drop-
> lets that may eventually become large enough to fall as rain.—student

> In that region the white churches reflected the racial values of the slave-owners
> supporting them, so that the blacks naturally preferred to form their own black
> churches.—student

But sometimes the link is not at all obvious:

> The growing interest in the environment has led to greater participation in
> snow-skiing and surfing. Consequently these activities have become the two
> most popular and enjoyable sports in the United States.—student

The first sentence claims a cause-effect relationship which is
far from obvious. There is increasing interest in the environment.
There is greater participation in the two sports. But the first phenomenon is not established as the cause of the second. Greater
participation in snow-skiing and surfing does not necessarily cause
them to become the most popular and enjoyable in the country.
And how could the last statement be verified?

Some cause-effect relations may be justifiable, yet may lack adequate justification by the writer:

> The whole has now become separate political units so separate that each considers itself distinct. This is why there is war between these units.—student

The explanation here is inadequate. The second statement does not follow from the first. Not every political unit considering itself distinct from other units goes to war with those other units. Additional facts must be considered. Here the student writer has added more details to justify the cause-effect linking:

> The whole has now become separate political units, so separate that each considers itself distinct. Yet there are still areas of industrial regulation and taxation where jurisdictions inevitably overlap. If one of the units succeeds in getting these responsibilities assigned to itself, it will surely end up by dominating the other units. This is why there is war between these units.—student revision

Without necessary additional evidence, the passages quoted above become examples of an unjustified hidden premise or claim:

> Greater participation leads to the greatest popularity and enjoyment.

and

> Political units considering themselves distinct will war against each other.

The invalid hidden claims should be clear to you in the following pieces of student writing:

> The Pharisees followed all rules scrupulously. As a result, they followed the letter of the law rather than the spirit of the law.—student

> The least violent of all physical activities is physical conditioning. Being least violent, it is the most popular and important form of athletics.—student

Unfortunately, a concealed claim and the corresponding lack of supporting detail can be quite harmful, and may arise from deliberate dishonesty:

> The economic growth of Red China and the consequent endangering of our own welfare and freedoms is beyond argument. Anyone who does not believe that China has expanded her economic growth immensely has only to look at the gross national product figures below. Obviously we must prepare for the even-

tual struggle by selectively stimulating those defense industries that will be
needed for conducting operations over huge land areas without adequate surface
transportation facilities.—student

In the above passage the writer has attempted to conceal within
his discussion the claim, unjustified by the passage itself, that
China's economic growth must inevitably lead to war with us. But
sometimes the hidden claims do not arise from deliberate dishonesty but from the substitution of slogans for rational thinking.
The slogans may even embody partial or complete truths, but the
user has not troubled to think them through or perhaps to verify
them.

Undefined Terms

Faulty definition is more than a problem of a word or two. The
writer quoted below should probably start over from the beginning:

Those who live in America, even though they may not discriminate, still have a
certain racist feeling because racism in America is institutional and has been
since the slaves were shipped over from Africa.—student

What is ''a certain racist feeling''? Does the writer intend to explain or define it? Does he really mean every person living in
America? What is ''institutional racism''? The term requires explanation if it is to be identified as the cause of the ''certain racist
feeling.'' Obviously the writer needs to explain what he means by
racism, to show how this racism has been institutionalized, and
then to show how such institutionalization conditions inhabitants of
America to have the racist feeling he refers to but does not describe. If he does this successfully, he will have isolated targets for
reform, replacement, or abolition. Having thought out the material
in this way, he can then begin to outline his paper.

There are also other problems with definition. If the writer
uses a term in a narrower or broader sense than the customary
definition allows, careful definition is even more important than

with little-known or little-understood terms. One surprisingly common problem is the use of a definition that runs quite counter to the way the defined term is normally used. The problem usually arises out of the writer's failure to consult a dictionary:

> The basic concept of Liberalism is trying to reestablish the values and morals of the past.—student

Perhaps the particular values and morals referred to are ones that fit in quite well with traditional definitions of Liberalism, perhaps not. More validly the example above could serve not as an ordinary definition but as a surprise paradoxical assertion or redefinition to be justified in the rest of the paper. Unfortunately the rest of the student's paper indicated that he intended the above to be a normal, informal definition of Liberalism. As such, it will not do.

Research Papers

In the course of your college work you are likely to have been assigned at least one research paper, resource paper, or library paper. There are two major purposes for such an assignment: (1) to allow for an in-depth study of a narrow topic, and (2) to teach students how to find relevant documents or other resources, how to document source material, and how to write an accurate and balanced account of the findings.

The purpose of this section is to illustrate the format of a research paper. For this reason much of our space is devoted to a sample research paper. Other aspects of the research process are treated very briefly.

Some Basic Rules About Research Papers

1. The topic you choose must interest you; perhaps it should be something that you have already done some reading or thinking about. Your research may confirm half-formed hunches, or it may, of course, undermine them.

2. The topic you choose must make use of your intelligence and judgment. The reader is interested in reading a research paper showing your own considered view of a certain large body of data.

3. As (2) suggests, you must organize your data and findings so that the paper is more than a patchwork of relevant quotations lacking any organizing principle.

4. As a researcher, you must consult an adequate number of sources. If there are far more sources than you have time to read, then you must narrow your topic and thus tell your reader what area you really have covered in depth. (If say, you have consulted only the *Encyclopaedia Brittannica*, you should entitle your paper "A Summary of What the *Encyclopaedia Brittannica* Says About X"—rather an absurd topic but at least an honest one. Notice how the sample research paper has handled this problem.)

5. You, as the researcher, are responsible for evaluating source material. An astrologer, who tries to interpret the effects of stars and planets on human affairs, is unlikely to be a reliable authority for a serious paper on astronomy. Serious and reputable scholars are generally more reliable than writers for popular magazines, or those who may have vested interests in particular points of view. But judgments of this kind depend in large part on the particular situation.

6. You must not pull source material out of its context in such a way that you distort the original meaning, or present a misleading account because important and relevant material is omitted.

7. In the paper you must give credit to the writers of books and articles that you have consulted. You must use appropriate forms in footnotes and bibliography, forms that will enable any other competent researcher to verify your documentation easily. (See *Footnotes* and *Bibliography* in the sample research paper and pp. 127–132.)

8. Using someone else's words or ideas without footnoting is re-

garded as plagiarism, or dishonesty in the use of source material. Every phrase taken from a book and used in your paper must be placed in quotation marks and footnoted. Every idea taken from a book, even if not directly quoted, must also be footnoted.

9. Do not let the mechanics of footnoting interfere with, or take the place of, the essential business of communicating. Quite often you can give the necessary information in parentheses in the text of the paper, without interrupting the flow of sentences and without the extra baggage of a footnote. (See the *Sample Research Paper* and *How to Footnote.*)

10. The writing should be as clear and interesting as other expository writing. It is important to say in simple language what the research means and, if possible, how it is related to the ordinary man. Some writers on very technical subjects include a description of their investigation which can be read without difficulty by the ordinary reader.

Guide to Punctuating Quotations

There are several conventions about the use of quotations and the appropriate way to footnote them.

1. When using your own words to tell what someone has said, do not use quotation marks:

> Alden and Magenis say that slavery was easy to abolish in the North as there were few slaves, but not so easy in the South where the plantation system depended on them.[1]

2. Some quotations are punctuated like conversation in a dialogue. The quoted material is a complete sentence in itself:

> The authors say, "They had little protection, however, from the occasional vicious owner."[1]

3. You can combine quoted and unquoted material in one sen-

tence so long as the sentence still reads smoothly and so long as the author's original meaning is not distorted:

> The closest this history comes to describing the slaves themselves is a brief mention that slaves, once working, were seldom cruelly treated "since it was to the interest of the master to keep them healthy and contented."[1]

4. Long quotations, three lines or more, should be written as a block, single spaced, and indented four spaces from the left margin. No quotation marks are used. Use a colon to introduce the quotation in most circumstances:

They describe the typical hardcore slave trader thus:

> He is not troubled evidently with a conscience, for although he habitually separates parents from child, brother from sister and husband from wife, he is yet one of the jolliest dogs alive, and never evinces the least sign of remorse. . . .[1]

5. You can use a row of three spaced dots to show that words have been left out (or four dots if one of them represents an omitted period):

> Hamm says "emancipation involved . . . serious consequences."[1]

6. You may insert in the quotation clarifying words of your own if you enclose them in brackets:

> Crèvecoeur points out that no one saw the "hardship of [the slave's] incessant toils."[1]

The Sample Research Paper

The writer of this sample research paper, a college freshman, chose to investigate the way American high school textbooks had portrayed life as a slave in America. He narrowed the field of in-

vestigation by choosing only books published between 1957 and 1971. Of these books he selected ten.

SAMPLE NOTE CARDS

After some preliminary reading in the ten books, the writer began to take notes on 4 x 6 cards. Here are samples of these cards, which illustrate

1. that note cards can contain paraphrases or direct quotations from the source material, as well as the researcher's own conclusions about the information;
2. that the researcher should put quotation marks around every word or phrase taken verbatim from the book;
3. that each card should contain just one bit of information to allow for easy separation and organization of material;
4. that each note card should be labeled with a sub-topic to show what aspect of the topic it concerns (of course, the label might have been added sometime after the note was written, at a time when the writer decided how he was going to organize his material);
5. that only the author's name, possibly an abbreviation of a book title, and page numbers are necessary on the note card;
6. that the information necessary for footnoting is provided by the smaller bibliography card (see sample bibliography card); [Since there are probably many note cards for a single source, the bibliography card will save time since it requires writing this information once instead of several times.]
7. that despite the best of preplanning, some cards have to be thrown away before the actual writing process because they turn out to be redundant or irrelevant.

Compare these cards with the source material and also with the research paper and its outline.

slavery – economic matter

This book seems to be explaining why
emancipation was gradual in the South.
"But since slaves were more numerous
in the South, emancipation involved serious
economic and social consequences."

Hamm, p. 270.

Note card 1. This card contains an exact quotation from the source and the student's comment. Note, comparing this with p. 3 of the sample paper, that the student was able to use the material exactly as he wrote it on the card and that he was careful to put quotation marks around what he took verbatim from the book. This helps prevent accidental plagiarism.

A footnote, or other means of crediting, was required in the paper. But since the bibliography card gives the full information necessary for footnoting, the student needed to write on this card only *Hamm* (the author's name) and the page number of the source. (If the writer had been using more than one book by Hamm, he would have had to give the title of the book from which the information came.)

Notice that the phrase at the top of the card, "slavery—economic matter," is a key-in to the outline (Part II-A-1). This card provides evidence for the point the student wanted to make in that part of the paper.

Fragments from Hamm's textbook, *From Colony to World Power*.

p. 270

Compare with Note card 1.

Gradual emancipation in the North. The eighteenth century was a century of enlightenment, in which the doctrine of equality was widely preached. Humanitarian ideas, and the fact that slavery was unprofitable in the North, caused the Northern states, in the last quarter of the eighteenth century, to abolish slavery. Some of the Northern states freed their slaves outright; others provided for gradual emancipation by decreeing that the children born to slave parents should be free.

> *slavery – treated as a matter affecting politics and legislation*
>
> Two long ¶s here. Many details given, describing Lincoln's Emancipation Proclamation and the political effects of it. Show that the Procl. may have won *some* friends and lost him the support of those who had believed that he was fighting merely to save the Union.
>
> Hamm, p. 342.

Note card 2. This card is keyed in to Part II-A-2 of the outline. Notice that this is a much-shortened paraphrase of the original source material, and notice that the student chooses to focus on only one part of the two-paragraph passage he refers to. (Examine the fragment of the original source.) When he used part of this information in writing the paper, he was required to use a footnote or some other means of crediting, *even though the reference to Hamm's material is brief and there is no direct quotation.*

The emancipation movement in the South. While the Northern states were freeing their slaves, the Southern states were sympathetically discussing the question of emancipation. But since slaves were more numerous in the South, emancipation involved serious economic and social consequences. Nearly all the Southern states had numerous anti-slavery societies. These organizations aided the American Colonization Society, which established the Negro republic of Liberia to which the emancipated American slaves could be transported.

p. 270

The Emancipation Proclamation. At the time this famous letter was published, Lincoln had already determined upon a course of action, but because the Union forces had met a long series of defeats, he did not think that the time was yet ripe to publish it to the world. In July he told his Cabinet of his intention to issue a proclamation freeing the slaves of the Confederate states, but at

p. 342

> *cultural life of the slave is ignored*
>
> "The English language, law customs, in-
> stitutions, and ideals, modified by a new en-
> vironment and influenced by other European
> peoples, were the foundations upon which
> the life and culture of the people of the
> U.S. were based."
> No mention of the base of the life and
> culture of the black people of the U.S.
>
> Hamm, p. 25.

Note card 3. This is a note card that was *not used* in the final writing, even though it was a helpful part of the research. (The phrase at the top of the card turned out to be not an aspect of the topic but rather the topic itself.) The words quoted here may have stimulated the student to think of what he wanted to say in the introduction or conclusion of his paper, but he did not use or borrow anyone else's material. Thus no foot note was necessary in the paper.

p. 342

Seward's suggestion he decided to wait until a Northern victory would make the proclamation seem more than empty words. In September, 1862, Lincoln considered Lee's defeat at Antietam an opportune time to announce that if the Confederate states had not laid down their arms by January 1, 1863, their slaves would be free. On January 1 he issued the final proclamation designating the states and parts of the states still controlled by the Confederacy. Since the Proclamation applied only to such territory, it could not immediately effect the freedom of a single slave. It was only a war measure. The Proclamation did not apply to the four slave states—Delaware, Maryland, Kentucky, and Missouri—which had not seceded, nor to those parts of the Confederacy which were already occupied by Northern troops.

Effect of the Proclamation on the purpose of the war. The Emancipation Proclamation made it plain to all that the war meant much more than the preser-

Compare with
Note card 2

vation of the Union and the exclusion of slaves from the federal territories. If the North were victorious, it would mean a new nation without slavery. Whether the Proclamation made more friends for the President in the United States than it cost him is hard to say. Lincoln had repeatedly stated that the war would go on until the Union was safe. Now he seemed to say that it would go on until the slaves were free. A popular bit of verse widely used by the Democrats in the Congressional campaign of 1862 stated:

> Honest Old Abe, when the war first began
> Denied abolition was part of his plan;
> Honest Old Abe has since made a decree,
> The war must go on till the slaves all are free.
> As both can't be honest, will someone tell how,
> If Honest Abe then, he is Honest Abe now?

It is impossible to say whether the losses sustained by the Republican party in the mid-term elections of 1862 were due to dislike for the Emancipation Proclamation or whether the Proclamation saved the party from complete defeat.

The transplanting of English institutions. The colonization of America meant the spread into a savage land of European modes of living, languages, ideals of life. In the Spanish and Portuguese colonies it meant a mingling with the natives, forming sometimes, as in Mexico and Brazil, a settlement practically native in appearance. In the English colonies, however, this was not the case, for wherever the English settled, they crowded the red men back into the interior. As a result, English civilization, as it spread into the American wilderness, remained predominantly English. The English language, law, customs, institutions, and ideals, modified by a new environment and influenced by other European peoples, were the foundations upon which the life and culture of the people of the United States were based.

p. 25
Compare with
Note card 3.

SAMPLE BIBLIOGRAPHY CARD

The bibliography card contains three kinds of information: the author, the title, and publication information (the place of publication, the publishing company, and the date). It is also convenient to list the library call number—in case the researcher wants to find the book for a second time—but this number does not go into the actual bibliography. At the time of typing the bibliography, the writer alphabetizes the cards by last name of the author and checks a sample bibliography for proper format.

Hamm, William A. *From Colony to World Power: A History of the United States* Lexington, Mass.: D. C. Heath, 1957.

Bibliography Card. In this case there was no library call number.

(See *The Bibliography,* p. 131, for ways of dealing with periodicals, anthologies, and so forth.)

AN ANALYSIS OF THE TREATMENT OF SLAVERY

IN SELECTED HIGH SCHOOL TEXTBOOKS

Alan Phillips
English Composition

An Analysis of the Treatment of Slavery

in Selected High School Textbooks

SENTENCE OUTLINE

This is the writer's unifying statement.

Thesis: Generally high school history textbooks discuss slavery only as it affected the white man with little or no mention of Negroes as people; better understanding of the black American today could be achieved by expanding texts to include this large minority.

Introduction

I. This paper demonstrates how little information there is in a selected number of high school history textbooks about the history of the black American.

II. For generations American history has been taught as it affected the white man, excluding almost completely the effect the history of the American Negro had on the developing states and on today's society.

    A. This is especially true of the earlier textbooks which, in general, cover only these areas:

        1. slavery and the economy

        2. laws about slavery

        3. the abolition movement

    B. These texts generally communicate the myth of the "happy" slave.

        1. They ignore the high mortality rate among slaves, the human rights denied Africans, the treatment of slaves on board ship and on the plantation, and what it was like to be a slave.

        2. They point out the "positive" aspects of slavery.

        3. Two texts, Planer-Neff and Wyman-Ridge, are possible exceptions.

        4. But none of these texts give the kind of description that Crèvecoeur gave his book published in 1782.

Outline - 2

III. The books examined of later publication date describe more objec-
tively the role of the Negro in the development of the United
States, but coverage still pertains mainly to the Negro as he
affects the white man.

   A. The text published in 1966, although dealing largely with the
   economic effects of slavery, does cover some of the evils of
   the slave trade and the Negroes' organized revolts.

   B. The text published in 1969 has an even more contemporary
   approach toward the inclusion of the Negro in United States
   history.

      1. It gives descriptions of the civilized communities in
      West Africa.

      2. It provides details on the high mortality rate and the
      low life expectancy on sugar plantations.

      3. There is also some attempt to describe the living and
      working conditions of the slaves.

      4. This text mentions the punishments for runaway Negroes
      and gives reasons for the white man's fear of the free
      black man.

   C. The last and most recent publication in 1970 shows pronounced
   changes in the treatment of Negroes by history textbooks.

      1. The description of the economic effects of slavery brings
      to light the false conceptions of the state of slavery in
      older textbooks.

      2. Included are comparative accounts of slave life by an
      English aristocrat and by an ex-slave.

IV. Good as they are, these modern books still fail to include dis-
cussions of much of what made up the life of the Negro slave.

V. History textbooks could be expanded to include more on the background of the Negro and would thus better educate every American
on the history of the United States, whatever his race.

**Concluding
paragraphs**

An Analysis of the Treatment of Slavery

in Selected High School Textbooks

Part I introduces the idea that history textbooks for high school students should portray the lives of black as well as white Americans. It poses the central question: have they done so?

Every year at Thanksgiving the exploits of some white men who landed in Massachusetts more than three centuries back are celebrated with considerable ceremony. Children have learned about them in history lessons for more than two centuries, for these Pilgrims are thought of as in some sense not just the founders of this nation but also as the ancestors of the American people today. Children have learned in school about the way the early white settlers lived, about the way Southern Belles entertained in their Southern mansions and about how rumbustious cowboys conquered the West, cowboys even now thought of as pure Caucasian. But approximately one in every eight Americans is black.[1]

[The writer footnoted this information because she found slightly different figures in different sources. The discrepancy was not important enough to comment on, however.]

How much have children learned about the ways of that American's ancestors? And is the situation changing? If understanding the history of this country is necessary for understanding American civilization today, then an almost complete ignorance of the past of a large segment of the population would hardly be an asset for understanding the thoughts and feelings of black Americans, or for black Americans to understand their own situation. Since the schools are the major instruments for passing on knowledge of the country's past, the books used in the school, particularly of course the history texts, should provide some answers to the questions posed above.

-2-

The textbooks discussed in this paper cover a period of thirteen years. The earliest book examined was published three years after the Supreme Court decision on the Brown vs. Board of Education of Topeka case (1954), which sparked a powerful civil rights movement and decreed that segregation has no place in the education system.[2]

The first section of books to be discussed were published between 1957 and 1964.

```
1957--Hamm, From Colony to World Power
1958--Bragdon and McCutchen, History of a Free People
1961--Craven and Johnson, American History
1962--Alden and Magenis, A History of the United States
1962--Planer and Neff, Freedom Under Law
1963--Steinberg, The United States--Story of a Free People
1964--Wyman and Ridge, The American Adventure
```

In these books the discussion of slaves and slavery up to the time of the Civil War is limited to the economic advantages of slavery, the legislation regarding the institution of slave labor, and the abolition movement.

The first mention of slavery in the Craven and Johnson book is in connection with the growth of agriculture; farms gave way to plantations, and "the number of servants and slaves in kitchens and fields grew."[3] These authors, as well as Steinberg, and Planer and Neff, all emphasize that slaves were a necessity in the cotton industry especially after the introduction of the cotton gin.[4] In the text written by Bragdon and McCutchen, the Negroes are seen as a sign of prosperity of Southern society rather than people in their own right.[5] The message is the same. Although they show that some plantation owners deplored the system of slavery, still their most detailed explanations are concerned with how difficult it was for the white

Part II in the original is seven to eight pages long. It gives a "no" answer to the question raised in the introduction-- i.e., "No, these books do not adequately portray the lives of black Americans." The purpose of this section is to show in what way this statement is true and to what extent it is true.

[Footnote 2 is necessary because the writer has paraphrased someone else's words. The original words were written by Earl Warren. "We conclude that in the field of public education the doctrine of 'separate but equal' has no place."]
Part II, A

-3-

man, in an economic sense, to free the slaves. Hamm, for example,
says, "since slaves were more numerous in the South, emancipation
involved serious economic and social consequences."6

This comes from Note card 1.

[The student then details the textbooks' coverage of laws regarding slavery and the abolition movement. After this he begins B of Part II, "the myth of the happy slave," of which we print a portion below.]

-8-

Other books in this group try to balance the negative aspects of
being a slave with its "positive" aspects. Alden and Magenis, while
they mention that slaves lived in huts, also state that they had
gardens in which to cultivate food. They say that some slaves "learned
to read and write" (Alden and Magenis, p. 198). Naturally they do not
fail to mention the inevitable "many planters who treated their slaves

Part II, B

well," and the fact that Andrew Jackson was fond of his slaves and always spoke of them as "the family." They point out that a very few
masters were cruel but otherwise imply that slaves were generally
happy. Yet at the same time they say, "Sometimes slaves tried to escape, and many owners lived in fear of slave revolt" (Alden and Magenis, p. 198). This appears to contradict the earlier implication of
the authors that most slaves were happy and contented.

Planer and Neff give more detail on the topic of escape. They
note that even the possibility of it was denied by the passing of the

Part II, B

fugitive slave law, which provided heavy penalties for helping fugi-
tives escape. But while their discussion is sympathetic in tone, they
give few details to show what it was to be a slave.

-9-

The most recent book in this category, Wyman and Ridge's <u>The American Adventure,</u> says more about the actual working conditions of slaves. It describes the old stereotypes of slave life—the slaves going happily about their work singing gaily in the fields—and emphasizes that the stereotypes are false (Wyman and Ridge, p. 254). There are fairly full descriptions of the selling of slaves. This text is the only one to report that family units had been broken up. The book quotes a contemporary account of the typical hardcore slave trader (Wyman and Ridge, p. 260):[10]

> He is not troubled evidently with a conscience,
> for although he habitually separates parents
> from child, brother from sister and husband from
> wife, he is yet one of the jolliest dogs alive,
> and never evinces the least sign of remorse . . .

Crèvecoeur had said much the same thing (Crèvecoeur, p. 156): "The daughter torn from her weeping mother, the child from the wretched parents, the wife from the loving husband . . ."

Of the authors mentioned, Crèvecoeur alone emphasizes the pitiful position of the black people. Even though they might have Sundays off, they were obliged to look after their own bits of land to feed themselves and their families. Many slaves had nothing to make up for their miseries, neither good food nor kindness, but only fear of the whip and death (Crèvecoeur, pp. 159–160).

> . . . they are obliged to devote their lives,
> their limbs, their will, and every vital exertion
> to swell the wealth of the masters; who look not
> upon them with half the kindness and affection
> with which they consider their dogs and horses. (p. 156)

The second category of books to be discussed, those of more recent publication, contains titles published in 1966, 1969, and 1970, respectively.

Here the writer begins Part III of the paper. He demonstrates that the newer

books give more coverage to the history of black Americans. As in Part II, he shows in what way this is true and to what extent.

Part III

Part III, C

-10-

1966--Link and Muzzey, <u>Our</u> <u>American</u> <u>Republic</u>
1969--Bartlett and others, <u>A</u> <u>New</u> <u>History</u> <u>of</u> <u>the</u> <u>United</u> <u>States</u>
1970--Freidel and Drewry, <u>America--A</u> <u>Modern</u> <u>History</u> <u>of</u> <u>the</u>
                <u>United</u> <u>States</u>

These histories illustrate the more modern trends towards recognizing for the black a more important role in the development of the United States than that of a possession, economic entity, or instrument of the white man's progress. However, they still tend to allocate far greater coverage to the economic advantages of the slave and to the abolition movement than to the slave himself, his living and working conditions, and his family life--where it existed.

-13-

A typical example of the remarkable change in modern textbooks is Freidel and Drewry's <u>A</u> <u>Modern</u> <u>History</u> <u>of</u> <u>the</u> <u>United</u> <u>States</u>, published in 1970.[13] This text describes the economic effects of slavery on Southern society in a manner which points out to the reader the possible flaws in older textbooks. The authors say, for example, "The plantation owners sometimes convinced outsiders that they were indeed the benefactors of the slaves" (Freidel and Drewry, p. 253). There is a detailed account by an African kidnapped from his native land, where he was a member of an aristocratic family. He describes in his own words conditons on the boat and finally his sale as a slave. This man, Olaudah Equiano, was fortunate in his purchaser. He became educated and finally a free man, and thus able to write about his

-14-

adventures (Freidel and Drewry, p. 253). The book also provides two
different perspectives on plantation slave life, which should give the
student a fair idea of how the picture of living conditions can be dis-   **Part III, C**
torted. One is a description by Sir Charles Lyell, an English geolo-
gist and aristocrat, and a guest of the plantation owner. The second
is an account written by an ex-slave, Solomon Northrup, who himself
experiences life as a slave on this same plantation (Freidel and
Drewry, pp. 254-255). This marked contrast reveals that most textbook
historians in the past had a tendency to ignore the slave's side of
the story and to choose descriptions biased in favor of the white
man's view of slavery.

Good as they are, these more modern books still fail to include   **This corresponds
much of what made up the life of the Negro either as a slave or as   to Part IV of the
a free man. There is nothing to imply that any form of African   outline, though it
culture was brought with them, yet these Africans obviously must have   could have been
held on to certain traditions which may have influenced the modern   part of III or the
generations of black people.   beginning of V.**

A reasonable understanding of this black background could better   **This is the
be achieved if the history textbooks were expanded to describe the   concluding ¶, or
black music, the black family units, the folk tales and other cultural   Part V of the
traditions which the blacks still held onto either as slaves or as   outline.**
free men. Such knowledge should form part of every American's educational background, whatever his race. He should not have to wait
for a college course in "Black Studies."

[The writer used footnotes only for the <u>first</u> reference to a source. For all subsequent references he used parentheses in the body of the paper. Thus the reader did not have to interrupt his reading more than necessary. Giving the publisher and place of publication is permissible but not absolutely necessary since this information is included in the Bibliography.]

-15-

FOOTNOTES

[1]Stephen J. Wright, "The Status of the Negro in America." in <u>The World Almanac, 1971</u>, ed. Luham H. Long (New York: World Almanac, 1970), p. 45.

[2]Samuel Eliot Morison, <u>The Oxford History of the American People</u> (New York: Oxford University Press, 1965), p. 1086.

[3]Avery O. Craven and Walter Johnson, <u>American History</u> (Lexington, Mass.: Ginn, 1961), p. 41.

[4]See Craven and Johnson, pp. 228-229; Mabel C. Planer and William L. Neff, <u>Freedom Under Law</u> (Milwaukee: Bruce Publishing Company, 1962), p. 240; Samuel Steinberg, <u>The United States--Story of a Free People</u> (Boston: Allyn and Bacon, 1963), p. 228.

[5]Henry W. Bragdon and Samuel P. McCutohon, <u>History of a Free People</u> (New York: Macmillan, 1958), p. 64.

[6]William A. Hamm, <u>From Colony to World Power</u> (Lexington, Mass.: D. C. Heath, 1957), p. 270.

[7]John R. Alden and Alice Magenis, <u>A History of the United States</u> (New York: American Book Company, 1962), p. 85.

[8]Walter D. Wyman and Martin Ridge, <u>The American Adventure</u> (Chicago: Lyons and Carnahan, 1964), p. 258.

[9]Michel-Guillaume Jean de Crèvecoeur, <u>Letters from an American Farmer</u> (1782; rpt. New York: E. P. Dutton, 1957), p. 155.

[10]The original source for this quotation is not given.

[11]Arthur S. Link and David S. Muzzey, <u>Our American Republic</u> (Lexington, Mass.: Ginn, 1966), p. 48.

[12]Irving Bartlett, et al., <u>A New History of the United States</u> (New York: Holt Rinehart and Winston, 1969), p. 35.

[13]Frank Freidel and Henry N. Drewry, <u>America--A Modern History of the United States</u> (Lexington, Mass.: D. C. Heath, 1970), p. 253.

-16-

BIBLIOGRAPHY

Alden, John R., and Alice Magenis. A History of the United States.
    New York: American Book Company, 1962.

Bartlett, Irving, Edwin Fenton, David Fowler and Seymour Mandelbaum.
    A New History of the United States. New York: Holt Rinehart
    and Winston, 1969.

Bragdon, Henry W., and Samuel P. McCutchen. History of a Free People.
    New York: Macmillan, 1958.

Craven, Avery O., and Walter Johnson. American History. Lexington,
    Mass.: Ginn, 1961.

de Crèvecoeur, Michel-Guillaume Jean. Letters from an American
    Farmer. 1782; rpt. New York: E. P. Dutton, 1957.

Freidel, Frank, and Henry N. Drewry. America--A Modern History of the
    United States. Lexington, Mass.: D. C. Heath, 1970.

Hamm, William A. From Colony to World Power. Lexington, Mass.:
    D. C. Heath, 1957.

Link, Arthur S., and David S. Muzzey. Our American Republic.
    Lexington, Mass.: Ginn, 1966.

Long, Luman H., ed. The World Almanac, 1971. New York: Newspaper
    Enterprise Association, Inc., 1970.

Morison, Samuel Eliot. The Oxford History of the American People.
    New York: Oxford University Press, 1965.

Planer, Mabel G., and William L. Neff. Freedom Under Law.
    Milwaukee: Bruce Publishing Company, 1962.

Steinberg, Samuel. The United States--Story of a Free People.
    Boston: Allyn and Bacon, 1963.

Todd, Lewis P., and Merle Curti. Rise of the American Nation.
    New York: Harcourt Brace Jovanovich, 1961.

Wyman, Walker D., and Martin Ridge. The American Adventure.
    Chicago: Lyons and Carnahan, 1964.

This paper reveals careful consideration of a complex and interesting topic. It is well organized; your own conclusions are clearly stated, carefully documented. Narrowing your topic to a few textbooks was a good thing to do since the narrowing cut down on the amount of material you assumed responsibility for. You should probably have given the criteria for selecting <u>these</u> ten rather than another ten. This is because there is always the possibility that these ten are quite different from the group as a whole. If you chose the books simply because they were the only ones you found in the library, then you should probably have said so. If these ten were the only ones in wide use over the country during the time period you mention, then that fact would have made your paper even more persuasive. Your writing on the whole is clear and interesting, and I think it would interest a large audience.

Footnotes

WHEN TO FOOTNOTE OR GIVE CREDIT TO A SOURCE

Footnotes indicate the precise source of your information. They allow the interested reader to verify the information and find out more detail.

1. Source material is often simply background reading done by the researcher. As such it will not appear in the footnotes, but it may appear in the bibliography.
2. Sometimes the writer uses an idea suggested to him by a particular passage in a book or magazine, by something he has read in the course of the investigation. This idea should be footnoted. (Sometimes people doing scholarly or scientific writing will even footnote ideas given to them by friends in conversation.)
3. If an idea or a fact is *not* new or original—or if it is something the researcher read quite a long time ago and he has since read it in other places—then it is part of a general pool of knowledge or ideas; it really does not belong to anyone in particular. Such ideas are *not* footnoted. For example, one would not footnote the fact that the Great Wall of China was 1500 miles long if he was fairly sure that this was an undisputed piece of information. He would, however, footnote such information if he had found another source saying the Wall was 1800 miles long. The footnote would be used for pointing out the discrepancy. Information about how an abacus works or what a sea anemone eats would not be footnoted because such information is generally available from many sources including major encyclopedias.
4. The writer can paraphrase, or put into his own words, material from books and magazines. In this case footnoting is necessary. (Note paraphrases in the Sample Research Paper. These were used instead of direct quotations to make for smoother, easier reading.)

5. Many items can be credited without a footnote. Use parentheses in cases where the inserted material does not seriously impede the reader. The Sample Research Paper was able to omit nearly thirty footnotes in this way.

HOW TO FOOTNOTE

Footnotes give readers all the information they would need for finding the original sources:

name of the author in full
name of the work
name of the magazine or anthology it appears in, if necessary, and
     its volume or series number
name of the editor or translator
name of the publishing company (necessary for ordering a book)
date of publication (to let the reader know when the work was
     written, as well as to indicate whether or not it might still be in
     print. Include the date of *original* publication as well as the date
     of the reprint you may be using.)

TYPING. Recent style manuals suggest typing all footnotes at the end of the paper. Single-space all lines of the footnote and double-space between the notes. Indent the first line five spaces, type the footnote number slightly above the line, and skip a space before the first word. Type the note as you would a sentence, using a capital letter at the beginning, a period at the end, commas and parentheses for separation of the various parts. Type the name of the author in normal order, first name first. (Study the *Sample Footnotes.*)

Footnotes may be typed in the same way at the bottom of the page. If so, they are single-spaced with a double space between each footnote. These footnotes should be numbered consecutively, not by pages, to avoid confusion in typing the paper or having it printed.

SECOND REFERENCES. Your first reference to a source should be fully footnoted, but later references can be given credit in a simpler way. A second reference to a play by Shakespeare or a book by Isaac Asimov might be given in parentheses in the body of the paper:

(*Romeo and Juliet,* Act III)

(3. 2. 22–24) or (III, ii, 22–24)   to show the act, scene, and lines of a play

(Asimov, p. 413)
(Asimov, *Guide,* p. 413)   to show the distinction, say, between two books by Asimov, both referred to in your paper

Inserting second references into the body of the paper, as recommended by the *Style Sheet* of the Modern Language Association, saves the reader the trouble of looking for footnotes more often than is necessary. Second references can also be given in brief footnotes, instead of parentheses, especially if these footnotes appear at the bottom of the page rather than at the end of the paper.

[1] Asimov, p. 413.

[2] Reeves, p. 92.

[3] Miller, *Psychology,* p. 3.   to differentiate from another work by Miller referred to in your paper

Some writers still use *ibid.,* meaning ''the same source as cited in the last footnote,'' or *op. cit.,* meaning ''in the work already cited, though not necessarily in the footnote just before this one.'' But in your own writing it is best to avoid the Latin phrases, since they are more difficult than English for most people to understand.

SAMPLE FOOTNOTES

Book with one author

    [1] Felix Greene, *Let There Be a World* (Palo Alto, California; Fulton Publishing, 1963), p. 62.

Book with two authors

    [2] Stephen Toulmin and June Goodfield, *The Fabric of the Heavens* (New York: Harper & Row, 1061), p. 33.

Book with more than one relevant date

    [3] Michel-Guillaume Jean de Crèvecoeur, *Letters from an American Farmer* (1782; rpt. New York: E. P. Dutton, 1957), p. 155.

Book with a translator or editor

    [4] Schoolboys of Barbiana, *Letter to a Teacher,* trans. Nora Rossi and Tom Cole (New York: Random House, Vintage Books, 1971), p. 154.

Short work in a collection

    [5] Ronald Gross, "Now It's Pepsi," *Pop Poems* (New York: Simon and Schuster, 1967), p. 15.

Newspaper editorial or article with a byline

    [6] James J. Kilpatrick, "Public Employees, Unions, and the Right to Work," *Los Angeles Times,* 20 March 1972, Part II, p. 7, Col. 5

Newspaper article without author

    [7] "Navy Pulls Out Secret Porpoise Team That Guarded Viet Harbor," (UPI news service, dateline Saigon) *Los Angeles Times,* 19 March 1972, p. 1, col. 5.

    [When the author is unnamed, it is useful to name the news service.]

Magazine article without author

    [8] "What Price Disney World?" *Consumer Reports,* March 1972, p. 173.

    [This magazine has a volume number and an issue number, but the date is sufficient for a magazine so readily available in most libraries. No comma is needed when a question mark already divides one element from the next.]

Article with volume number

    [9] Randall H. Waldron, "The Naked, The Dead, and The Machine: A New Look at Norman Mailer's First Novel," *PMLA,* 87

(March 1972), 272.

    [*PMLA* stands for *Publications of the Modern Language Association,* a journal published bi-monthly. This article appears in Volume 87 on p. 272 of the March 1972 issue. The volume number is given directly after the title in Arabic numerals (5 rather than V) and without the abbreviation vol. or v. The date, when it follows a volume number, is enclosed in parentheses and page numbers are written without p. or pp.]

The Bibliography

The bibliography provides in one convenient place a list of the materials used by the writer. It includes all the publication details necessary to anyone looking for the book, magazine, or recording. The publisher's name is included primarily to help anyone wishing to buy a copy.

    You should type items in alphabetical order by the last name of the author. Indent the second, third, and fourth lines to make the author's name in the first line stand out. Single-space every line and leave a double space between entries. Include all subtitles and the complete names of authors. Punctuate by separating with periods the three main divisions: author, title, and publishing information.

Article with anonymous author	Anon. "Navy Pulls Out Secret Porpoise Team That Guarded Viet Harbor." UPI news service, *Los Angeles Times,* 19 March 1972, p. 1, col. 5.
Book with more than one relevant date	de Crèvecoeur, Michel-Guillaume Jean. *Letters From an American Farmer.* 1782; rpt. New York: E. P. Dutton, 1957.
Book with one author	Greene, Felix. *Let There Be a World.* Palo Alto, California: Fulton Publishing, 1963.

Book with two authors	Jacobs, Roderick A., and Peter S. Rosenbaum. *Transformations, Style, and Meaning.* Lexington, Mass.: Xerox College Publishing, 1971. [The name of the second author is typed in normal order, first name first.]
Short work in a collection	Nash, Ogden. "The Sniffle" in *Poems to Enjoy,* ed. Dorothy Petitt. London: Macmillan, 1967, p. 24.
Book with translator or editor	Schoolboys of Barbiana. *Letter to a Teacher,* trans. Nora Rossi and Tom Cole. New York: Random House, Vintage Books, 1971.
Article with volume number	Waldron, Randall H. "The Naked, the Dead, and the Machine: A New Look at Norman Mailer's First Novel." *PMLA,* 87 (March 1972), 271–277.

[Volume numbers, like 87 above, are written without the abbreviations vol. or v. Following a volume number, dates are enclosed in parentheses and page numbers are written without the letters pp. or p.]

Standard References In the Library

Guide to Reference Books by Constance M. Wincholl

This is an index of indexes, or one large book which will tell you the names of dictionaries, bibliographies, and other indexes. This entry on electronic music, for example, tells where to find an extended list of books on the topic. All abbreviations are explained in the front of the reference.

The Humanities | Music

Electronic music

Cross, Lowell M., comp. A bibliography of electronic music. [Toronto], Univ. of Toronto Pr., [1967]. 126pp. $5. 67–2573.   **2BH25**

More than 1,500 entries; author listing with subject index.
   Rev.: *CH* 4:636.

Davies, Hugh. Répertoire international des musiques électroacoustiques. International electronic music catalog. Cambridge, Mass., distr. by M.I.T. Pr., [1968]. 330pp. $10. 68–20151.   **2BH26**
   Intends as far as possible "to document all the electronic music ever composed in the almost twenty years since composers first began to work in this medium."—*Compiler's Pref.* Listing is by country, then by city and studio.

The Encyclopaedia Brittanica

This is a helpful start for many topics. Consult the bibliography at the end of the article.

The Reader's Guide to Periodical Literature

Look up authors, subjects of any kind, or titles of articles which you believe may be included in magazines from the present back to 1890. (Another guide, *Poole's Index,* will take you back even further.)

The Social Sciences and Humanities Index

Consult this index for material likely to appear in more scholarly journals.

A special paperback guide that you might want to purchase is *Reference Books: How to Select and Use Them* by Saul Galin and Peter Spielberg, Vintage Book V–561. This guide also has helpful hints on library research and documentation.

Suggested Topics

The following suggestions may help you find a topic that you would like to pursue. Almost all of them are much too broad and would have to be narrowed according to your interests and the material available.

African tribes and the growth of nationalism

Alphabets

The American Revolution from the point of view of the English
   Parliament and King

Animals: the recent history of a particular species of animal—
   involving the conflict of human interests (for example, the deer,
   otter, seal, snail, prairie dog, eagle, leopard)

Breast cancer

Children's games, learned from peers and passed from generation
   to generation

Children's language

China: the role of Chiang Kai-shek in the development of modern
   China

Creation of the solar system: rival theories

Dams: the Aswan Dam

Dams: controversies over the U.S. Corps of Engineers

Disarmament conferences

Earthquakes in America

Energy: disagreements over the "energy crisis"

Farming: the small farm

Free schools

Guatemala: contemporary events in Guatemala (or another small
   Central or South American country)

Hemingway, from the point of view of other writers and artists

Human Behavior: human control of human behavior

Instruction for bilingual children

Jazz in the 30's, as contrasted with jazz in another time period

Job prospects for graduating seniors

Justice: poor people and the courts

Language and aphasia

Language and thought (To what extent does language determine
   what we think?)

Martian canals

Mass transit: developments in your locality

Medical care: differing approaches to medical care in England, Sweden, Japan, the U.S.

Music: two kinds of music or two kinds of instruments

Old people and their political clout

Picasso: late work and early work (or the work of another artist)

Poets: comparison of the subject matter of three or four contemporary poets

Pollution of Lake Erie (or another body of water)

Pollution: public attitudes toward pollution in the last ten years

The Presidency: public attitudes toward any past U.S. president during his office

Science and moral responsibility (in a particular context)

Solar energy

Strikes: attitudes toward strikes as a negotiating tool

Students and police

Students and the public

Textbooks: attitudes toward a particular minority in selected history textbooks

Textbooks: presentation of another country (countries) in elementary geography books

TV and education: How effective is TV?

TV: freedom of the press and network TV

The Vitamin C controversy

War: public attitudes at the time toward the War of 1812 and the Spanish-American War

Women: their role in selected children's stories

A Writer's Grammar

Grammar and Syntax

A grammar of a language is a description of how the FORMS of a language—sentences, phrases, words, sounds—are matched to the MEANINGS expressed. For the writer, the most useful part of a grammar is likely to be SYNTAX, the rules we follow, usually unconsciously, when we form sentences. Break these rules and the result will not only be ungrammatical, but also, often, an incoherent string of words:

> What architecture is if you disregard the technical points of designing buildings and town planning, and then you must concern yourself with creating environments for every scale of human association.

However, merely following the syntactic rules does not necessarily guarantee that you have found the best way to express your

137

meaning. The full meaning of a sentence depends on the meanings of each word and also on the ways the words are arranged and grouped together in a sentence. Different groupings are likely to result in different emphases, even though the basic meanings are the same. The following sentence

> Creating environments for every scale of human association, not just designing buildings or planning towns must be the concern of architects.

is a good one. It has the same basic meaning as this sentence:

> Architects must be concerned not just with building design or town planning but with the creation of environments for every scale of human association.

But the second version places more emphasis on the role of architects by mentioning them at the very beginning. At the same time, the important final position is used for "the creation of environments for . . ." While the first sentence ends a little flatly, the second builds up to a climax. Try saying them aloud. You as a writer have to arrange forms in the way that seems to express most accurately and clearly what you want to say.

Dialects and Speech

Each speaker of English speaks it in a slightly different way. But certain general characteristics of pronunciation, vocabulary, and syntax mark off groups of speakers as belonging to a certain location, class, age group, or other kind of speech community. The language of each of these groups is known as a dialect. Differing degrees of social prestige are assigned to these groups of dialects. Certain vowel sounds or sentence forms are frequently regarded as "pure," "correct," "educated," or "standard," while others are condemned as "impure," "incorrect," "ignorant," "substandard" (or more charitably, "nonstandard"). In England a native speaker who fails to pronounce the *h* in "herb" may be labeled "unedu-

cated'' though, of course, he must omit the *h* sound for ''honest.'' Such a valuation arises from economic and psychological stresses in a society rather than any sound linguistic criteria. In that speaker's dialect, dropping *h* is a general and logical rule. Similarly speakers, both black and white, of some American dialects don't pronounce the final *t* in words like ''accept'' or ''insist.'' But although such speakers may follow this pronunciation rule rigorously, they are still apt to be told by speakers of more prestigious dialects that their English is ''incorrect.''

Written Dialects

Although some dialect differences are carried over from spoken English to written English and even, in the case of Black English, used as the basis for a written literary language, no one's written English is the same as his spoken English. Say aloud the sentences of this paragraph and you will be very conscious of how hard it would be to make them sound like part of a natural conversation. An examination of newspaper articles, scientific reports, student papers, personal letters, and automobile warranties will soon show that written English varies more according to the conventions or ''style'' expected for each such activity and the readers to whom the writing is addressed. Written English is learned later in life than spoken language and is acquired with more difficulty.

Grammaticality and Correctness

All dialects of English, written or spoken, share certain ways of arranging subjects and objects, prepositions and nouns, and the like. They have a common vocabulary of English words whose meanings remain for the most part constant for all dialects, especially the written ones. Certain grammatical restrictions arise from some meanings. Whether you are writing in London, England, or Jackson, Mississippi, or Wellington, New Zealand, you must still obey such

restrictions as the following if your writing is to be recognized as a normal and comprehensible sample of English prose:

1. The verbs "hope," "hate," and "admire" cannot have the noun "walls" as their LOGICAL subject, i.e., walls cannot hope, hate, or admire except in works of fantasy. It is, however, possible to make "walls" the GRAMMATICAL subject for verbs like these:

   Walls are hated and abominated by prisoners and children.

   Here, as in all passive sentences, the LOGICAL subject ("prisoners and children") is not the GRAMMATICAL subject. However, for almost every such passive sentence there is an active one with basically the same meaning, for example,

   Prisoners and children hate and abominate walls.

2. The verb "elapse" cannot have an object.
3. The phrase "on account of" cannot be followed immediately by the verb "sings."

Breaking rules like these will result in incorrect sentences in any English dialect (except for certain kinds of experimental English found in some literary works). For instance, the following sentences collected from real speakers and writers are wrong in a similar way, though less obviously so, and they would be wrong in any dialect.

   I really want to impart upon you just how big our used car sale is.

(The speaker probably meant "impress" rather than "impart." "Impart" requires different prepositions and objects after it.)

   War is the lesser of two evils. It will inhabit the earth as long as man does.

(Man can inhabit the earth, but war cannot inhabit anything. The logical subject of "inhabit" has to be an animate noun, one referring to people or animals.)

> There I was, standing in front of a crowd of people in this sparse turquoise negligee.

(A negligee can be thin, transparent, or polka-dotted, but it cannot be "sparse." Only collective nouns like "population" and "vegetation," which refer to something that can be broken up and scattered around, can be sparse.)

EXERCISE: GRAMMAR AND RULES

The explanations in parentheses above are statements about rules of English. Make similar statements about the sentences below, explaining what rules have been violated. This is to help you grasp what a *rule* is.

1. The administration's intervention deteriorated the situation gravely.
2. So remembered was the Cid that his story was written fifty years after his death.
3. It is advisable that the mines will be closed down immediately.
4. He sailed to the west coast of Africa with the hope to reach India.
5. The Romans however avoided to cross the Rhine.

Subjects and Predicates

Basically an English sentence consists of two parts, one serving as the subject, the other as the predicate.

The subject of a sentence is often described as the *topic,* what the writer or speaker is going to make some *comment* on. Thus the subject of the sentences below, *the black overseers,* marks what the writer is making a comment about:

a. *The black overseers* had to protect their people and simultaneously represent the interests of their masters.
b. *The black overseers* had therefore to be diplomats.

The *comment* part of sentences (a) and (b):

(a) had to protect their people and simultaneously represent the interests of their masters
(b) had therefore to be diplomats

is usually known as the *predicate.*

EXERCISE: SUBJECTS AND PREDICATES

A. Copy each of the subject forms below and add a predicate to it to make a full sentence.

1. Politics
2. Mondale
3. Several singers
4. Modern politics
5. The article in the latest issue of the *New York Review*
6. The very handsome old Moore house that once stood on the corner

B. Provide each predicate below with a subject and write out the full sentence.

1. is small, with a few booths, a few tables and a squat counter, all peach, plastic wood and yellow.
2. uses two-thirds of its funds for secret activities.
3. had rented a shabby but expensive apartment on Riverside Drive.
4. reproduce works by artists in the Revelle collection.
5. will be given to graduates with a major in English or linguistics.
6. would have meant that rice production would have to be limited despite the world food shortage.
7. failed to satisfy his critics.

Predicates, Finite Verbs, and Fragments

The most essential part of a predicate is usually the verb. Verbs are usually the first words in a predicate. Look back at the predi-. cates in B in the last exercise. The verbs are:

B. 1. is
   2. uses
   3. had rented
   4. reproduce
   5. will be given
   6. would have meant
   7. failed to satisfy

Some of these are one-word forms; some contain several words. But they are all what grammarians call FINITE. A *finite* verb begins with either an auxiliary verb like *will, would, did, might,* or the simple verb in the present or past tense, like *uses* or *failed.*

Apart from exclamations and command sentences, no group of words can be a full sentence unless it has a finite verb.

EXERCISE: SENTENCE FRAGMENTS 1

The following contain verbs but not *finite* verbs. Therefore (1) to (7) are not sentences. They are called *sentence fragments.* When you read them aloud, your own language sense will tell you they are incomplete. Rewrite each of them, making the verb finite so that the string of words is a full sentence.

1. the visitors standing at the gate (Change "standing" to *stand, stood, are standing, will stand, have stood,* or *had stood,* etc.)
2. people in the audience to stand up to cheer
3. several falling from a great height
4. *Residence on Earth* remaining the greatest of Neruda's books
5. the new process synthesizing oil from several still unidentified chemical elements

6. important problems analyzed by Rochefort
7. their fathers having left their families to seek work

Sentence fragments like those in the exercise above must not be used as full sentences. However, such fragments can occur as parts of full sentences. So the fragment

> a politician speaking at a rally

can serve as the subject of a sentence:

> A politician speaking at a rally once claimed that only women are sane enough to vote.

In fact, perfectly good sentences like

> A security guard was standing nearby.
>
> The treaty was proposed by Metternich.

can be reduced to fragments like this:

> a security guard standing nearby
>
> the treaty proposed by Metternich

which can then be included as parts of other sentences:

> Meigs attracted the attention of *a security guard standing nearby.*
>
> *The treaty proposed by Metternich* stipulated a gradual reduction in wheat tariffs, leading to their eventual abolition.

EXERCISE: SENTENCE FRAGMENTS 2

Convert the following sentences into fragments. The first one is done for you.

1. The driver had rigged up an emergency operating light for the doctor.
   (The driver, having rigged up an emergency operating light for the doctor, . . .)

2. The ministers were appointed by the king.
3. Construction workers were grumbling about the growing unemployment in their industry.
4. Those companies were doubling or tripling their profits during the crisis.
5. Dr. Fujii's wife was sitting motionless on a bench near the wall.

EXERCISE: COMPLEX SENTENCES

Write five sentences, each containing one of the fragments that you created for the previous exercise. The first one is done for you.

1. The driver, having rigged up an emergency operating light for the doctor, found there was little else he could do.

Dangling Modifiers

It is all too easy to misuse such fragments by treating them as if they were full sentences with finite verbs. But even when the fragments *are* in a good sentence, writers must take care that it is clear what or who the fragments refer to. Here is an example:

> Government lawyers, *denying any misconduct on the part of federal investigators,* requested that the wiretap information be included in the jury exhibit.

In this sentence, the fragment, *denying any misconduct on the part of federal investigators,* is used to modify, or add further information about, ''government lawyers.''

One interesting kind of variation is produced when the modifier is brought up to the beginning of the sentence:

> *Denying any misconduct on the part of federal investigators,* the government lawyers requested that the wiretap information be included in the jury exhibit.

It is still clear from this sentence that the government lawyers

were doing the denying. However, such "modifier preposing," as the process is called, is not always a good idea. Take the sentences

A. The three injured men, *staggering along very unsteadily,* saw two drunks with pink carnations in their lapels.

B. The three injured men saw two drunks with pink carnations in their lapels *staggering along very unsteadily.*

It is clear from A that it was the three injured men who were staggering along. And it is clear from B that it was the two drunks with pink carnations in their lapels who were staggering along. Both sentences are quite clear and unambiguous. Yet if the modifier, *staggering along very unsteadily,* is preposed in each sentence, the resulting sentences are:

A. *Staggering along very unsteadily,* the three injured men saw two drunks with pink carnations in their lapels.

B. *Staggering along very unsteadily,* the three injured men saw two drunks with pink carnations in their lapels.

Once the modifiers have been preposed, A and B turn out to be the same! The reader cannot tell who is actually staggering along. The sentence is now unclear, ambiguous. When it is unclear who or what the modifier refers to, the modifier is said to be *dangling. Dangling modifiers* are an occupational risk for writers seeking to vary their style.

Sometimes dangling modifiers appear to refer to nothing else mentioned in the sentence:

Walking along unsteadily, the trees looked like gray, dripping mourners.

If the trees are walking, then of course the modifier has not been left dangling. The reader mentally attaches the modifier to the subject of the sentence, *the trees.* (*The trees, walking along unstead-*

ily, . . .) But if the modifier refers, say, to someone mentioned in a previous sentence, or to the writer, then the modifier is dangling and has to be repaired:

> As I walked along unsteadily, the trees looked to me like gray, dripping mourners.

EXERCISE: DANGLING MODIFIERS

Write out the six sentences below with the italicized modifiers pre-posed. If the resulting sentence is ambiguous, write "Dangling Modifier." If the meaning of the new sentence is clear but different from that of the original, explain what the difference in meaning is.

1. Lord Robbins, *a cigar dangling under the left side of his waxed moustache,* advanced toward the surprised spectators.
2. The small boy watched him advance, *a cigar dangling under the left side of his waxed moustache.*
3. The tall guardsman bowed low to an elderly lady *startled by the loud explosions.*
4. The policy of the new administration, *looked at more closely,* differs hardly at all from that of the Ford administration.
5. The Brigade, *advancing rapidly towards Bremerhaven,* sighted Marshall Foch.
6. The public network, *already suffering from previous budget reductions,* was now forced to cut back its cultural programs.

Pronouns and Reference

Similar problems can arise with pronouns. These can also dangle without any obvious reference, especially when they are forms like *this* or *which.* These forms may refer to a particular person or thing mentioned elsewhere in a piece of writing or to a general situation or event represented perhaps by a whole clause or sentence.

EXERCISE: PRONOUN REFERENCE

Explain the reference of the italicized pronoun forms below. Pay particular attention to those forms whose reference is unclear or ambiguous.

1. The king immediately issued a new decree, *one which* allowed the victims to defend *themselves.*
2. The king immediately issued a new decree *which* forbade any *such* attacks on *him.*
3. The king issued a new decree. *This* intensely irritated Haiman's followers.
4. The king told Haiman to have Mordecai ride before *him* through the city, *which* made *him* very despondent.
5. Esther was frightened to go before the king. But *her* father said even Queen Vashti would have done *that* for *her* people. *It* would be selfish for Esther to refuse.

For other pronoun problems and further details about this exercise, see "Pronoun and Antecedent" on pp. 200 to 204 of the Mechanics section.

Preposing

Subjects were described earlier in this section as *topics,* what the writer (or speaker) is going to make some *comment* on. In fact, the subject of a sentence is not always the topic of the sentence. The sentence below is quite an ordinary one:

> Bickerton discusses this experiment in more detail when he considers the aftereffects of hypnosis.

Here the object, *the experiment* that Bickerton discusses, can become the topic if it is brought up to the front of the sentence, or PREPOSED.

> *This experiment* Bickerton discusses in more detail when he considers the aftereffects of hypnosis.

The topic of the sentence is now *this experiment.* The rest of the sentence serves as a *comment* on the topic.

Preposing is a very useful device. If the writer wishes to give greater prominence to Bickerton's consideration of the aftereffects of hypnosis, he may prepose the whole *when* clause so that the content of that clause becomes the topic:

> *When he considers the aftereffects of hypnosis,* Bickerton discusses this experiment in more detail.

EXERCISE: PREPOSING

For each pair of examples, (a) does changing the order make a difference, and if so, what is it? (b) Construct your own pair of examples similar to each of these. The first one is done for you.

A. 1. Guests should be sure to return the keys before they leave.
   2. Before they leave, guests should be sure to return the keys.
   (a) Sentence A2 places more emphasis on the time when guests should return the keys than Sentence A1 does.
   (b) 1. Cadets must sign the blue register book whenever they return after midnight.
       2. Whenever they return after midnight, cadets must sign the blue register book.
B. 1. Hemingway would have made Nick less likable if he had made the boy less sensitive.
   2. If he had made the boy less sensitive, Hemingway would have made Nick less likable.
C. 1. McKeever gently yet ruthlessly probed the defendant for further details of the agreement.
   2. Gently yet ruthlessly McKeever probed the defendant for further details of the agreement.
D. 1. The baron became quite a different creature after sunset however.
   2. After sunset however, the baron became quite a different creature.

Subordination and Finite Verbs

It was claimed earlier that, with certain minor exceptions, no group of words lacking a finite verb can be a full sentence. However, this does not mean that a finite verb necessarily makes a group of words a full sentence. Look at the following, for example. They all include a finite verb, yet they are not complete sentences.

1. after he *comes*
2. although they *had denied* the reports earlier
3. in order that his son Henry *might succeed* to the throne
4. because the shortages *had driven up* prices
5. despite the fact that the solution *contained* sodium phosphate
6. whatever the schools *need*
7. which *reveals* the whole argument to be fallacious
8. that the incident *had* ever *happened*

The eight nonsentences above are known as *subordinate clauses.* Clauses in English are groups of words that include a finite verb or verb phrase. While clauses can be complete sentences, the addition of certain words like *after, although, because, who,* and *that* will make them subordinate clauses. For example, the sentence

He had felt nauseous that night.

consists of a single clause with a finite verb. It is a complete sentence, asserting the main information the speaker or writer desires to communicate. The writer is asserting that someone had felt nauseous at a particular time. But if the writer attaches "because" to the front, making the sentence into a subordinate clause, he is no longer asserting anything.

because he had felt nauseous that night . . .

Now the writer will use the *because* clause to cast light on some other information contained in a main clause.

Because he had felt nauseous that night, he refused to play for the Queen.

| subordinate clause | main clause |

EXERCISE: SUBORDINATE CLAUSES

Add main clauses to the eight subordinate clauses given above so that the result is eight good sentences.

EXERCISE: POSITION OF SUBORDINATE CLAUSES

For many of the sentences you wrote for the previous exercise, the subordinate clause could have been placed in a different position. Write out one alternative version for each sentence. Describe any meaning differences between the original and alternative versions.

Highlighting with IT

Writers can rearrange material so as to highlight or place emphasis on parts of it. The preposing process described earlier illustrates one kind of highlighting. But here is another, also usable for simple nouns or for whole subordinate clauses. In the table below, the element highlighted in the sentences on the right is italicized.

Regular	Highlighted
Roger Gray starred in that play.	It was *Roger Gray* who starred in that play
	It was in *that play* that Roger Gray starred.
Wars cause inflation because they stimulate nonproductive expenditures.	It is *because they stimulate nonproductive expenditures* that wars cause inflation.
	It is *wars* that cause inflation because they stimulate nonproductive expenditures.

EXERCISE: HIGHLIGHTING WITH IT

Using *it is* or *it was* as your highlighting device, highlight the italicized words in the sentences below:

1. *The mossy path* invited us to wander.
2. Metcalfe used *their gross national product* as the criterion for judging the worth of nations.
3. We can remain prosperous *only if the education system is geared toward economic productivity.*
4. The orbit of a meteor is defined *by its velocity and direction.*
5. Certain physicists, *to solve this paradox,* suggested that the latitude curve of the radiation owed its origin to the sun's magnetic field.
6. Local school boards will be looking at school bus transportation *with a view to recommending changes in safety procedures.*

Highlighting with WHAT

Contrast the sentences on the left with the highlighted versions on the right.

Regular	Highlighted
His condescending manner irritated me.	What irritated me was *his condescending manner.*
The bulldozer destroyed the cottage.	What destroyed the cottage was *the bulldozer.*
	What the bulldozer destroyed was *the cottage.*
	What the bulldozer did was *destroy the cottage.*
Many children now lack a feeling of security.	What many children now lack is *a feeling of security.*
Palmerston was a blustering bully.	What Palmerston was was *a blustering bully.*

Men, above all, want to be respected as individuals.

What men want, above all, is *to be respected as individuals.*

EXERCISE: HIGHLIGHTING WITH WHAT

Use *what is* or *what was* to highlight the italicized words in the following sentences.

1. *Technical training* is less valuable if too specialized.
2. Marconi concluded *that the Boers could not have obtained any of our instruments.*
3. .They shared *a common desire to be treated as people, not workers.*
4. Future experimenters must adjust for *lense distortion.*
5. Skinner wants to tell his contemporaries *that salvation lies in submitting to state control.*

EXERCISE: HIGHLIGHTING WITH "WHAT" OR "IT"

A. Choose from some article or book five consecutive sentences having no highlighting with WHAT or IT. Convert them into highlighted sentences. Underline the words highlighted.
B. Do the same for five sentences of your own writing.

Active and Passive

The various processes shifting parts of a sentence around do not change the most basic meaning of a sentence. The sentences below do not differ in basic meaning. They differ only in what is highlighted.

> Roger Gray starred in that play.
>
> It was Roger Gray who starred in that play.
>
> It was in that play that Roger Gray starred.

Such processes, which change sentence structure without

changing basic meaning, are called *transformations*. Perhaps the best-known of these is the *passive transformation*. This transformation converts the structure of these sentences:

(1a) Joseph welcomed the ambassador.

(2a) Some of our most prominent citizens planned this criminal attack on basic human rights.

into

(1b) The ambassador was welcomed by Joseph.

(2b) This criminal attack on basic human rights was planned by some of our most prominent citizens.

Like the other transformations discussed, the passive transformation is a way to rearrange the structure of a sentence so as to highlight particular parts of it. Neither the **a** active sentences nor the **b** passive sentences are better in themselves. But sometimes one of them "feels" better in a given context than the other. For example, you may feel (as we do) that the passive sentence **2b** is slightly preferable to the active sentence **2a** as the last sentence of the following paragraph:

> This conspiracy was not merely an attempt to sway a national vote. It was an attack on human rights. But this is not all. _____

The passive transformation makes "this criminal attack on basic human rights" the topic and shifts the old subject, "some of our most prominent citizens" to the end, converting this piece of new information into the climax of the sentence and of the paragraph. Putting material into the "by" phrase of a passive sentence is a good way to give the material extra emphasis. In suspense stories it gives the author a chance to use special theatrical effects:

> Andrew Fotheringay looked triumphantly at the pale guests. "Lady Murgatroyd, this murder, this almost perfect crime, was planned and executed by . . ."
> A shot rang out and Fotheringay lay crumpled on the marble staircase.

Passive sentences also allow the writer to emphasize what would otherwise be the object and to omit the logical subject, the one doing whatever-it-is. The sentence

$\begin{Bmatrix} \text{Someone} \\ \text{An executioner} \end{Bmatrix}$ beheaded Ann Boleyn on Tower Hill before a weeping crowd.

may seem less elegant than this one:

Ann Boleyn was beheaded on Tower Hill before a weeping crowd.

In this last sentence, the person who did the beheading is not mentioned. Ann Boleyn, the logical object, is now the topic. We are being told something important about her.

Many style handbooks recommend that writers avoid passive sentences. Active sentences are often thought to be simpler and more direct. However, this is not always the case. We suggest that you try out both forms. Then you can choose the one that sounds best to you. See p. 255 for practice in making this choice.

EXERCISE: PASSIVE TRANSFORMATION

Write the passive form of the following sentences. The first one is done for you.

1. Peter Piper picked a peck of pickled peppers.
   A peck of pickled peppers was picked by Peter Piper.
2. This author wrote *Ulysses.*
3. Corny Kelleher closed the long daybook.
4. The king summoned the spirits of the dead.
5. Nearsightedness handicapped Mr. Bloom.
6. A large-sized lady with perfect teeth addressed Stephen.
7. The fact that Molly loved him astonished Mr. Bloom.
8. Bloom carefully removed the saucepan from the stove.

EXERCISE: PASSIVES AND ACTIVES

1. Find the first sentence in the paragraph before the previous exercise. (*Many style handbooks recommend that writers avoid passive sentences.*) Convert this sentence to the passive (beginning with "That . . ."). Read the active and passive sentences aloud and then write a brief comment on how they sound.
2. Convert the second sentence of the same paragraph into an active sentence, (beginning "People often think . . ."). Read the active and passive versions of this sentence aloud and comment briefly on them.

"By" Phrases

By phrases allow the author to hold off giving important information until late in the sentence. This device may be used even in active sentences.

> Agamemnon's skillful maneuvering gave the Greeks more time.

If you need to emphasize the *how* part of Agamemnon's achievement you may shift the details into a *by* phrase:

> Agamemnon gave the Greeks more time by his skillful maneuvering.

EXERCISE: "BY" PHRASES

Transform the following rather clumsy sentences into sentences using *by* phrases. The first sentence is done for you.

1. Sternberg's shouting at the girl attracted a number of bystanders.
   Sternberg attracted a number of bystanders by shouting at the girl.
2. The producers' arguing vehemently changed the minds of the three senators.

3. The consumers' threat to boycott all meat products made farmers uneasy.
4. Henry's being aggressive startled everyone.

Sentence Embedding

Subjects can be words like *Henry* (*Henry was mean on Sundays*), or phrases like *the kid next-door* (*The kid next-door was his enemy*). Subjects can also be phrases such as

Henry's aggressiveness . . .

This last kind of phrase is a reduced version of the sentence ''Henry was aggressive.'' Two reduced versions of this sentence are possible:

Henry's being aggressive . . .

Henry's aggressiveness . . .

Either one could be the subject of a new sentence.

Henry's being aggressive startled everyone.

Henry's aggressiveness startled everyone.

So these last two sentences each have a reduced sentence embedded within them.

There are a number of other ways of embedding sentences. Suppose the sentence

Galahad had arrived late.

is to be embedded as the subject of another sentence:

(*something*)   surprised Lancelot.

One possibility is to convert the Galahad sentence into a nominal, or a kind of noun:

Galahad's late arrival surprised Lancelot.

Alternatively the -ING construction might be used:

> Galahad's having arrived late surprised Lancelot.

Note here the possessive ending on the subject and the *-ing* ending on the first part of the verb phrase.

But instead of embedding with *'s . . . -ing,* a writer could choose *infinitive embedding,* using *for* in front of the subject and *to* in front of the verb:

> *For* Galahad *to* have arrived late surprised Lancelot.

Or a writer might choose clause embedding, using the embedding word *that:*

> *That* Galahad had arrived late surprised Lancelot.

Use the invented term *embedder* for elements like *'s . . . -ing, for . . . to,* and *that,* which are used to embed one sentence structure inside another:

Gerundive Embedder: possessive . . . *-ing*

Infinitive Embedder: *for   to*

Clause Embedder: *that*

The Galahad sentences above differ little if at all in meaning. But this isn't always true:

> **(A)** She hated (*for*) Carl *to* cheat that man.
>
> **(B)** She hated Carl*'s* cheat*ing* that man.

The (*B*) sentence implies that Carl may really have cheated the man, whereas the (*A*) sentence allows more easily the possibility that Carl did not actually cheat him.

Not all verbs can be followed by all kinds of embedders. The verb *know* allows only the clause and infinitive embedding:

> I know you *to* be an honest man. (The *for* part of *for . . . to* often has to be deleted.)

I know *that* you are an honest man.

Ungrammatical: I know your being an honest man.

The sentence

That Galahad had arrived early surprised Lancelot.

is a little clumsy. The embedded sentence together with its embedder *that* may be moved out of its position to a place at the end of the sentence:

___surprised Lancelot *that Galahad had arrived early.*

Since *surprised* has no subject, a pronoun empty of meaning—*it*—has to be introduced. This *it* stands for the embedded sentence.

It surprised Lancelot *that Galahad had arrived early.*

The process of shifting an embedded sentence in this way is called *extraposition.* Extraposition is used for other kinds of embedded sentences:

INFINITIVE NOMINAL

For him to do that was unusual.   It was unusual *for him to do that.*

RELATIVE CLAUSE

A boy *who wanted to join the Peace Corps* came.   A boy came *who wanted to join the Peace Corps.*

Extraposition often makes a sentence more readable and easier to understand:

Not extraposed: *That Peer Gynt should have stood up to the Button-mender instead of evading him* now seems clear.

Extraposed: It now seems clear *that Peer Gynt should have stood up to the Button-mender instead of evading him.*

EXERCISE: EXTRAPOSITION

Try extraposing the following sentences. In which of these sentences does extraposing make for much greater clarity?

About the other sentences—those for which the different versions are almost equally clear—make some comments about any difference you notice in the focus of each version.

1. That the medieval community of scholars developed into the modern vocational schools for lawyers and schoolteachers seems strange. (Begin *It seems* . . .)
2. For the government to impose controls was unthinkable for those who had always believed that unbridled private enterprise would always be an essential part of American life. (Begin *It was* . . . . Then begin another version with *For those who* . . .)
3. That she was indeed guilty was not doubted by any state or federal law enforcement office although proofs were still lacking. (Begin *It was not* . . . . Then try to write a third version superior to both of these versions.)

Relative Clauses

Look at the following increasingly-more-specific set of items.

1. Someone
2. A soldier
3. The soldier
4. The stocky soldier
5. The stocky soldier who had earlier tried to frighten Oliver

Item five contains a relative clause beginning with *who.* Relative clauses are indeed useful ways to narrow down, to specify more precisely for the reader, what we are writing about. They usually begin with *who, whom, which, that,* or *whose,* all of them commonly known as relative pronouns.

EXERCISE: RELATIVE CLAUSES

Convert the second sentence of each pair below into a relative clause. The first one is done for you.

A. 1. The poet broke all the accepted rules.
   2. He dominated that period.
   The poet who dominated that period broke all the accepted rules.
B. 1. The critic was Samuel Johnson.
   2. His comments were most devastating. (Use ''whose.'')
C. 1. Several measures were repealed.
   2. They angered the middle classes.
D. 1. He met with a number of citizens.
   2. They had opposed the legislation.

Restrictive and Nonrestrictive Relative Clauses

Not all relative clauses are used to narrow down the reference of something or someone. Those that do are called *restrictive relative clauses.* Not too surprisingly, those that don't are sometimes called *nonrestrictive.* These are normally used to add new information rather than to further identify. Here are two examples of nonrestrictive clauses.

(1) King Henry then turned to Simon de Montfort, *who immediately denied that the Baron wanted to dethrone the king.*

(2) The 1974 recession, *which drove many smaller oil distributors out of the industry,* further strengthened the oil giants.

Although the author may use these nonrestrictive clauses for information new to the reader, he is deemphasizing or subordinating the information by putting it into a relative clause. Such relative clauses are usually pronounced with a slight pause between them and what they refer to:

Simon de Montfort PAUSE who immediately . . .

and, in written English, this pause is marked with a comma. If other material follows the clause, a comma marks the end of the clause. (For more discussion of the comma, when to use it and when not to use it for setting off relative clauses, see p. 222 under *Commas*.)

Relative Clauses and Clause Reduction

The sentence

> **(1a)** The one who was most offended at this lack of advance notification was de Gaulle.

contains a relative clause *who was most offended,* which can be reduced to a more compact phrase, as in

> **(1b)** The one most offended at this lack of advance notification was de Gaulle.

In fact, any relative clause beginning with the relative pronoun *who, which,* or *that* followed by a form of *be* (*is, are, was, were*) can be reduced to a phrase by deleting the relative pronoun and the *be* form. So,

> **(2a)** The doctor who was waiting in the garden . . .

becomes

> **(2b)** The doctor waiting in the garden . . .

Similarly the relative clause in

> **(3a)** This situation, which was more serious than Louis had expected, frightened the French leaders.

can be reduced to the phrase in

> **(3b)** This situation, more serious than Louis had expected, frightened the French leaders.

A clause, remember, contains a subject nominal and a finite verb phrase. The subject nominal in relative clauses may be the relative pronoun itself (*who, which, that*), or a possessive relative pronoun with a noun:

> **(4a)** Marlborough, *whose armies* were already menacing Paris . . .

These are reduced differently. The possessive relative pronoun *whose* loses its "relativeness" and becomes the ordinary possessive, *his.* The form of *be* (*were*) is deleted in the usual way:

> **(4b)** Marlborough, his armies already menacing Paris . . .

In addition to Relative Clause Reduction, another transformation is needed when the relative clause has only an adjective after *be.* This so-called Adjective Transformation shifts an adjective to the position in front of the noun in the main clause. Thus, by Relative Clause Reduction, we transform:

> **(5a)** I saw a general who was furious storming towards me.

into the ungrammatical

> **(5b)** I saw a general furious storming towards me.

which has to become, by the Adjective Transformation:

> **(5c)** I saw a furious general storming towards me.

Useful as Relative Clause Reduction is in making prose more compact, it often has another effect. The content of the clause is pushed a little further into the background when the clause is reduced. Look back at (2*a*), (3*a*), (4*a*), and (5*a*) and compare them with (2*b*), (3*b*), (4*b*), and (5*c*).

EXERCISE: RELATIVE CLAUSE REDUCTION

Copy out the following passage after you have reduced the italicized relative clauses into smaller phrases:

They ate in groups of four at small square tables of synthetic marble, *which had been purchased cheaply* from a cafeteria that was *discarding them.* The rain, *which was falling across the windows,* had the effect of sealing in light and noise. Hook made haste to be among the first group *which was entering their common sitting room,* Andrews's old livingroom, *which had been furnished in black leather* and equipped with a vast cold fireplace.

—after John Updike, *The Poorhouse Fair*

A Final Note of Caution: Monster Sentences

The various transformations described in this section are techniques that the writer uses to revise his first draft rather than to create a first draft. An awareness of the grammatical resources of his language should be invaluable for the writer. The writer revising his own writing is faced with a number of choices as to form. The choice is the writer's and he is judged, in part, by his choices. Obviously, an unnecessarily complicated sentence is worse than several separate simple ones. At one extreme is the overuse of short, jerky sentences not clearly related to each other. At the other extreme are monster sentences like this:

That Bertolucci is aware of the fact that the equation of politics with sex is extremely complex is apparent in his having changed the Moravia ending in such a way that the entire film is ultimately modified by ambiguity. It is also apparent in Bertolucci's cinematic style, which is so rich, poetic and baroque that it is simply incapable of meaning only what it says—and which is, I think, a decided improvement over Moravia's sometimes tiresomely lean prose.

—Vincent Canby, "Film: 'The Conformist'"

EXERCISE: MONSTER SENTENCES

Make the following sentences more readable and clear:

1. By believing a just and moral cause, such as the eradication of war, justifies the denial of opportunities to participate in war research and ROTC on college campuses, the protestors against war research fall into just the trap Nietzsche warned of, for

they take on the old practice of denying basic freedoms when those freedoms come in conflict with the aims of society.

2. Even if the government refused to use its mechanical systems solely for the national defense, the government is maintaining an army which is disproportionate to its need to defend itself, since we are not under attack or at war, or its responsibility to other nations as agreed upon as a result of the myriad of post-World War II defense treaties.

Word Choice

Student writers often find it very difficult to choose words that are right for what they have to say. This section is intended to help you choose words which clarify your message rather than distort it. Traditional rules of usage are given here in simplified form. This section is also intended to show how complex many other rules of usage are, rules that rarely appear in any dictionary or grammar text.

One of the difficulties is that many writers falsely believe that even out of context some words are better than others.

1. Descriptive or vivid words like *gallop, trudge,* or *charge* are better than plain words like *go*. [This is oversimplified partly because it is difficult to say just what descriptive words are. Adjectives of taste or color or sound can make dull writing come alive, but used without reason they can, of course, detract from the writer's intended meaning.]

167

2. Long words and abstract words like *elucidate* or *inasmuch* give a paper a certain dignity so that the paper may be taken seriously. They also create a necessary distance between the writer and his message. [This is not always true. Simple clear words may also lend dignity to a piece of writing. Language should be clear, direct, and as simple as the message will allow. A writer rarely needs to create distance between himself and what he says. Except for specialized kinds of scientific or legal writing, simple, noncolloquial words are preferable.]

When choosing words try not to rely on such laws and formulas, but concentrate instead on the context of your writing. Be aware that one word is never the same as another in every respect.

Words and Implication

If you describe a man as *accusing* another of some action, you are taking it for granted that the accuser believes the action to be bad. Thus if you change the following sentence

>Lawyers *said* that Smith controlled the airline.

to

>Lawyers *accused* Smith of controlling the airline.

you have implied something quite different in the second sentence from what you have implied in the first. Compare the two versions below:

>(A) Lawyers *claimed* that Smith controlled the airline.
>(B) Lawyers *realized* that Smith controlled the airline.

It is clear that in the two sentences the lawyers are "doing" something different. In (*A*) they *claimed*. In (*B*) they *realized*. But now turn your attention to the writer of these sentences, some unknown person. From what he has written, does it appear that he assumes that Smith controlled the airline, or is he unsure about this? Read the sentences again. In (*A*) the writer does *not* reveal

any belief of his own that Smith really did control the airline. But
(*B*) does communicate such a belief. In (*B*) it is not just the lawyers who believe that Smith controlled the airline—the writer of
the sentence believes it too.

The point may be clearer if you think of the verb "know"
(similar to "realize") and what it implies about the person who
uses the word in speech or writing. Can you say

> Irma knew that Columbus sailed to America in 1967.

—not unless you put quotation marks around "knew," or not unless there is some modern figure named Columbus. If you use
"know" in the ordinary sense, you—the speaker or writer—are
assuming that what is *known,* by Harry, or Irma, or any other subject, is true. If you did not assume this, you would not use the
verb "know," but some other verb like "thought" or "supposed."
The interesting point about all of this is the light it can shed on a
writer. If someone writes:

> Sister Carrie found out that the big city uses human beings and in
> the end destroys them.

he, the writer, implies by the use of "found out" that he also believes in the destructiveness of the big city. By changing the verb
to "came to believe" he would not imply that he necessarily
shared the belief.

EXERCISE

Point out the differences, if any, between the (*a*) and (*b*) sentences
below:

1a. Kennan understands that we must deal promptly with aggression.
1b. Kennan believes that we must deal promptly with aggression.
2a. She perceived that Roger had already reported the accident.
2b. She believed that Roger had already reported the accident.
3a. An analysis of Plato's theories of education shows that they

have played a major role in the development of modern educational theory.

3b. An analysis of Plato's theories of education suggests that they have played a major role in the development of modern educational theory.

4a. He had noticed that the memorandum had been forged.

4b. He had asserted that the memorandum had been forged.

Jargon

Words and phrases like *intrasystemic feedback, inferiority complex, median income, logical inference, imperialism, recession, depression, reinforcement of behavior* have fairly precise meanings within the technical disciplines to which they belong. But they can be unclear and misleading in more general use.

A jargon is a vocabulary of words and phrases used by specialists to make technical discussion in their specialization more compact and precise. Unfortunately, such a jargon may also be used as a way to shut off outsiders from a discipline or to impress. The following is a legitimate use of jargon:

> If morphemes are defined in terms of phonemes, and, simultaneously, morphological considerations are considered relevant to phonemic analysis, then linguistic theory may be nullified by a real circularity.
> —Noam Chomsky, *Syntactic Structures*

In the context in which it appeared—a technical linguistic discussion of how to formulate grammars—this is compact, precise, and understandable to linguists.

But the same cannot be said for the following public report on foreign language training by the government. The writer was trying to report that some supervisors thought instructors' comments should be included with both major examination results and minor quizzes. Apparently not everyone had agreed:

> It was observed that there was a dichotomy of opinion with regard to tabulation of macro-success levels discernible at higher administrational levels concerned with implementation of the aforementioned evaluation

procedures. It was felt by some that although anecdotative as well as quantitative data had been purposefully incorporated into micro-success level reporting, such data were also desirable if the less micro-task oriented evaluations were to have meaningful dimensions.

The language here is an inflated jargon designed to impress rather than to communicate real information about language testing procedures.

Such an abuse of jargon is often labeled ''gobbledygook'' or occasionally ''officialese,'' but public officials are not the only ones who use it. You will easily recognize it from its official, impersonal, even dehumanized tone, its complicated sentences, and its overuse of long words.

Euphemisms

A euphemism is an expression used as a substitute for words that might be distasteful or embarrassing. In 1793 a decapitation was called a ''shorn crown.'' Today a prison is a ''correctional institution.'' A bombing attack can be a ''protective reaction strike'' and stealing by employees has been called ''inventory leakage.''

Such words are an attempt, conscious or unconscious, to protect both writers and readers from some part of the reality. If a friend ''passes on,'' the implication is that he has not really *died* but has merely gone to another existence. *Sleeping pills* suggest drugs—possible addiction, possible overdose, possible death—but ''nighttime medication'' is almost free of such unpleasant suggestions. And ''ripping off'' implies that there is no victim, as there would be if somebody had been *robbing* or *burglarizing*. The phrase suggests that the original owner (frequently an institution) had no real need for the item which was ''ripped off.''

Occasionally a euphemism is so ingrained in the language that it is impossible to avoid. You should try, however, to become aware of euphemisms, and, where possible, to seek more exact, more direct words which will better fit the context of your writing.

Pompous Words

Certain old pompous phrases like "the rewards of virtue," "the path of knowledge," "on the highway of life" are not likely to be produced nowadays. But there is a modern equivalent which almost everyone produces at some time or another. The sentences below were written by a freshman student who was describing his efforts to compose some experimental music. The translations are the student's explanations.

> The instruments I employed in my piece were difficult to choose because I truly had no conception of my musical production.

Translation: It was difficult to choose the instruments because I had no idea how I wanted my musical production to sound.

> The project was nebulous and my understanding was even more unformulated.

Translation: I did not understand what I was supposed to do.

> My *modus operandi* was quite unusual and unique.

Translation: My approach was unique.

> I desired that an enhancing characteristic of my piece would be style and continuity.

Translation: I wanted my piece to have style and continuity.

The existence of the translations should make it easier for the student to evaluate the content of his writing. He may decide to change several of the sentences still further.

In a desire to sound professional, many writers lose control of their language. Not only do the big fancy words sound pompous but many of them are used wrongly as well. The following ungrammatical sentences were written by sane and sensible native speakers of the language who simply lost hold of what they wanted to say:

I for one believe the Bible should be read with an objective point of view and believe certain things to be questionable as factual.

Student Revision: Parts of the Bible are not literally true.

It is a well known fact that early man signified natural phenomena with something invisible or intangible to his knowledge.

Student Revision: Early man invented invisible spirits or gods to explain the occurrence of mysterious natural phenomena like lightning.

The fact that I was learning to speak Spanish created quite an impressive experience for me.

Student Revision: I was pleased to be learning how to speak Spanish.

It is drama that shows how some situations are incapable of being avoided by tragedy.

Student Revision: Drama shows that in some situations tragedy is unavoidable.

Man is a product of his own destruction.

Student Revision: Some men have destroyed themselves.

Ordinarily the cure for such word use is simply to read the whole paper aloud, spot the strange-sounding sentence, and rephrase it. If, however, a sentence like one of those above does not sound strange to him, the writer is probably not familiar enough with the words to know how they can and cannot be used in particular contexts. The next section explains how grammatical context limits one's choice of words.

Words and Grammatical Context

Each word learned by a speaker of a language carries with it many little rules, and while such rules are hardly ever written down, they are nevertheless in effect. For example, people say

> She composed a symphony.

but some semantic rule prevents them from saying

> She composed a novel.

even though ''compose'' can mean *to write* and one can *write a novel*. The existence of such rules explains why synonyms in a dictionary or in a thesaurus are not always interchangeable. *Develop* and *evolve* are sometimes synonyms but only *develop* can go in the blank here:

> Hemingway was able to _____ a clean, uncluttered style.

As for *evolve:* man *evolved,* a theory can *evolve,* and the British Constitution *evolved* from centuries of court precedents. *Develop* can be used wherever *evolve* is used—man *evolved* or man *developed*—but *evolve* cannot be used everywhere that *develop* is used. The verb *evolve* does not allow an object—''Hemingway evolved a style'' is wrong—but *develop* can be used with or without an object. (A theory can *develop,* or scientists can *develop a theory*.)

Consider also the synonyms *aggravated* and *worsened.* Only *worsened* will fit in the blank below:

> Mrs. Hale's condition _____ daily.

whereas *aggravated* might be used in the following context:

> The damp air _____ Mrs. Hale's condition.

The verb *worsen* cannot take an object. It is ungrammatical to say ''The doctor worsened my illness.'' *Aggravate,* on the other hand, cannot be used *without* an object. ''My lumbago aggravated everyday'' is wrong. So is ''The tension in the office aggravated.''

Such examples show that some verbs do not allow objects; other verbs require an object; and still others allow an object but do not require it.

A larger dictionary sometimes supplies this kind of information

about context by means of example sentences, but dictionary space is limited. The larger the dictionary, the more sentences can be provided, and so the closer it can come to giving a complete picture of the contexts in which the word is used.

There are occasions when a word is wrong, and an educated native speaker senses that it is wrong. But he may have difficulty seeing why the word is wrong. Here are a few examples illustrating rules that, if violated, make a sentence "sound wrong."

Example 1: The boycott method was proven in a strike organized by Chavez and the Farm Workers Union.

Correction: The boycott method $\begin{Bmatrix} \text{was proven} \\ \text{was proved} \end{Bmatrix}$ effective in a strike organized by Chavez and the Farm Workers Union.

Probable Rule: This usage of *prove* requires a statement of what is proved. You cannot *prove* a thing, only a statement about a thing.

Example 2: a. The purpose of the Inquisition was to investigate heresy, contended to be brought about by contacts with non-Christians.

b. Kissinger did not contend the glorification of war.

Correction: a. The purpose of the Inquisition was to investigate heresy, which, the Inquisition contended, had been brought about by contacts with non-Christians.

b. Kissinger did not contend that war was glorious.

Probable Rule: The verb *contend* is often used to mean "advance an opinion in an argument." It must normally be followed by *that,* not a noun [or nominalization, as

in (*b*)], and not an infinitive with *to,* as in (*a*). In complicated sentences like (*a*) it is easy for a writer to lose his language feel. You can use *argue* instead. The strangeness of this sentence might have been more evident had it been read aloud.

Example 3:	The nature of the soul in Plato's *Republic* is a secondary but vital aspect in his discussion of justice.
Correction:	The nature of the soul in Plato's *Republic* is a secondary but vital theme in his discussion of justice.
Probable Rule:	The word *aspect* normally takes the preposition *of: an aspect of Plato's thought.* However, this word is frequently used wrongly as a general term meaning *topic, theme,* or *concern.*

Many of these abstract words are easily misused by student writers. The usage rules are complicated and different for each word. Thus *insight* can be *given* only to a human being. But it has to be *contributed* to a problem. You cannot hope to learn all such rules. Familiarity with them comes from much reading. In the meantime, if you are unsure about them, use more specific terms and rephrase your sentences. A more specific statement may well be superior to one with *aspect* or *insight* used correctly.

EXERCISE

Each of the following sentences should "sound wrong" to a native speaker of English. Rewrite the sentence and write a probable rule for each, in the manner of the boxed-in examples. If any of these do not sound wrong, then your own internal grammar of English is, to some slight degree, incomplete. Consult a big dictionary or a verbal friend. Try to find out which words "sound wrong."

1. That suit becomes her constantly.
2. Hotspur's intervention deteriorated the situation considerably.
3. The atmosphere ameliorated slightly when the presents were brought in.
4. The poet relates a part of human nature familiar to everyone.

Prepositions

When you revise a paper, look for prepositions like *in, on, with, from,* and *to* which sound strange when the work is read aloud. The sentence

> The writer deals on the idea of free choice.

should be changed to

> The writer deals *with* the idea of free choice.

The phrase

> interested with people

should be

> interested *in* people

With phrases as familiar as these, your own language intuition should enable you to spot the mistakes and correct them. In cases where you are not sure, or if you find a preposition circled on your paper, then look up the whole phrase in a dictionary. *Analogy,* for example, can take *with:*

> He was the first to make the *analogy* of earth *with* a spaceship.

but *analogous* takes *to:*

> Earth is *analogous to* a spaceship in several respects.

(At this point the writer should consider whether *analogous to* is better than *like* in the context of the piece of writing.)

Prepositions in some cases can change the whole character of a sentence. Think of the verb *treat,* for example, and the ways in which different prepositions will change its meaning:

treat *with:* The doctor *treated* the sickness *with* aspirin and penicillin.

The poor shepherd *treated* him *with* great kindness.

He was accused of *treating with* the enemy during a war.

treat *of:* (usually in a scholarly context) This article *treats of* the three types of argumentation.

treat *for:* The doctor *treated* him *for* measles, chicken pox, and scarlet fever all at once.

treat *to:* I *treated* my entire family *to* a double-dip rocky-road ice-cream cone.

Below is a list of idiomatic phrases containing prepositions which are commonly the source of mistakes. Read through the list to make yourself more aware of these words. However, do not try to memorize such lists. Become familiar with their use by listening, talking, and reading.

accordance with:	in accordance with company policy
accountable for:	accountable for her own conduct
accountable to:	accountable to no one but himself
acquiesce in:	acquiesce in a plan to execute the dictator
acquit of:	acquitted of all misdemeanor charges
adhere to:	adhered to the strictest rules of conduct
analogous to:	analogous to a spaceship
analogy with:	his analogy of earth with a spaceship
aspire to:	aspires to the Presidency
attribute to:	abnormal behavior which can be attributed to brain damage
characteristic of:	characteristic of those who have hardening of the arteries
charge with:	charged with murder; charged with safekeeping the company's records

compatible with:	a policy not compatible with the aim of world peace
concerned about:	concerned about her poor health
concerned for:	concerned for the innocent victims
concerned with:	a matter concerned with the use of our funds
concerns himself with:	concerns himself with the affairs of others
concur in:	to concur in this decision
concur with:	the U.S. concurring with the British on this issue
consistent with:	behavior consistent with his past record
contribute to:	contribute to the eradication of disease
deprived of:	deprived of home and security
different from:	different from the previous ruler
distinct from:	"enjoyment" as distinct from "happiness"
distinguish between:	distinguish between the laws of science and the laws of ethics
distinguish from:	distinguish these laws from those laws
divide between:	money divided *between* his aunt and his niece, money divided *among* his five nephews. (However, *between* is occasionally used for more than two, especially in informal situations.)
endowed with:	endowed with a million dollars
implicit in:	consent not given in so many words but implicit in his remarks about personal responsibility
implied by:	consent implied by his remarks
inconsistent with:	a philosophy inconsistent with controls
infer from:	can infer from her speech that she opposes such freedom
liable for:	liable for medical claims that may be brought against her
liable to:	(informal for *likely to*)
objective of:	objective of the mission

peculiar to:	a custom peculiar to this religious sect
pertinent to:	laws not pertinent to juvenile crime
prohibit from:	prohibited from trespassing
succeeded in (or succeeded at):	succeeded in guessing his name
succeeded to:	succeeded to the throne
tendency to:	tendency to become violent
tendency toward:	tendency toward laziness

Pairs of Words Commonly Confused

Use this list in the way most helpful to you. Consult particular words when directed to do so. If you are already quite confident with words, then read through the list to make sure you are aware of all of these distinctions.

An asterisk (*) is used to show incorrect usage.

accept/except
Accept is the verb: She *accepted* the honor.
Except is the preposition akin to *exception: Except* for Harry, everyone was there. With the *exception* of Harry, everyone was there.

advice/advise
Advice is the noun: They give *advice.*
Advise is the verb: They have *advised* me to . . .

affect/effect
Affect is a verb: Will the drug *affect* his mind?
Effect, akin to *effective,* is usually a noun: We could see no such *effect.*
Effect can sometimes be a verb: The committee wants to *effect* (bring about) change.

all ready/already
All ready means "all prepared": The men are *all ready* to go.
Already refers to time: They are *already* briefed. They are *already* dressed.

all together/altogether
   All together means ''all in a group.''
   Altogether means ''completely'': They are *altogether* unreliable.
allusion/illusion/delusion/elusive
   Allusion means ''reference'': His *allusion to* Christ . . . He *al-
   luded to* Christ.
   Illusion, like ''hallucination'' or ''dream'' refers to something not
   really in existence or not really true: The apparent curve was
   an optical *illusion.*
   Delusion: If one is really deceived by a false impression, he is
   deluded by it; the false belief is a *delusion.*
   Elusive suggests something hard to catch, almost slippery: The
   criminal was *elusive;* he *eluded* all attempts at capture. The
   truth was *elusive.*
amount/number (less/fewer)
   Amount is used with mass nouns like ''sugar'' or ''flour'': a
   small *amount of sugar*
   Number is used with count nouns like ''people'' and ''countries'': ''Countries'' can be counted, but ''flour'' and ''sugar''
   cannot. Thus a *number of people* but not *a large amount of
   people,* nor *a large amount of countries.*
   Less and *fewer* observe the same restrictions. *Less* is restricted
   to mass nouns: *less food, less water, less sympathy.* Such
   phrases as *less people, *less countries* are not allowed. Count
   nouns require the word *fewer: fewer people* and *fewer countries.*
   (Notice that *more* applies to both count nouns and mass nouns:
   more people, more sugar, more sympathy, and *more countries.*)
approve of/approve
   Approve of refers to personal attitudes about something: I *approve of* her choice.
   Approve means to give official ratification: A President might approve a treaty, although he previously disapproved of it.
attribute/contribute
   Attribute: One *attributes* an effect *to* a cause; e.g., We can

attribute this broken window *to* last night's vandalism.
Contribute can mean "to cause" or "be part of a cause": Rising
costs *contributed to* the discomfort of the middle class.

choose/chose
Frequently a spelling mistake. *Chose,* which rhymes with *froze,*
is the past tense of *choose.*

cite/sight/site
Cite often means "set forth": to *cite* evidence, *cite* statistics,
cite your own experience
Sight is the common word akin to *seeing.*
Site means "place."

complement/compliment
Complement is related to "complete." Together, two things
complement each other or make a whole: Bare wooden tim-
bers in a room *complement* rough-textured walls. Two jobs
can *complement* each other.
Compliment is related to "praise."

conscience/conscious
Conscience is the individual's knowledge of what is right and
wrong.
Conscious means "aware" or "awake."

continual/continuous
Continual means happening repeatedly over a period of time:
The phone rings *continually.*
Continuous suggests that there is no stopping and starting: The
water ran *continuously.*

council/counsel/consul
A *council* is a group of committee, like the President's *Council*
on Economic Affairs.
Counsel is advice. He gave good *counsel.*
A *consul* is an official, who often lives in a foreign city to look
after the commercial interests of the home country.

credible/credulous/creditable
> *Credible* means "believable." I found his story *credible*.
> *Credulous* applies to a person in a believing frame of mind, though not necessarily "gullible."
> *Creditable* applies to behavior which reflects credit on the persons involved.

disinterested/uninterested
> *Disinterested* is an appropriate attitude—impartial and unbiassed: Only disinterested persons may serve on juries.
> *Uninterested* refers to "lack of interest."

due to/because of
> *Because of* is favored by professional writers.
> *Due to* is more often found in bureaucratic prose and carries with it a bureaucratic flavor.

formally/formerly
> *Formally* means "in a formal way."
> *Formerly* refers to the past. He was *formerly* a senator but is now an ambassador.

human/humane
> *Human* refers to people as opposed to animals.
> *Humane* suggests decency and compassion: It was a *humane* act.

imply/infer
> *Imply* is what a writer does when he communicates meaning but not in an explicit way: He *implied* that I was a liar, even if he didn't say so.
> *Infer* is what the reader does when he puts two and two together as he reads. His inferences or conclusions may or may not be justified, of course: I *inferred* from his letter that he was coming to meet me.

irrelevant/irreverent
> *Irrelevant* means "not pertinent": This data is irrelevant.
> *Irreverent* suggests disrespect.

its/it's
> *Its* is possessive: The cat drank *its* milk.
> *It's* is the contraction for "it is" or "it has."

judicial/judicious
> *Judicial* refers to judges, courts, and laws.
> *Judicious* suggests "wise," "prudent," or "cautious."

lead/led
> Frequently confused. *Lead,* when it rhymes with *led,* means the
> kind of *lead* in a pencil. The past tense of the verb *to lead* is
> spelled *led.*

lie/lay
> *Lie* means "to recline." She *lies down* after lunch every day.
> *Lay* is the past tense of "lie." She *lay down* after lunch, but
> now she's up again.
> *Lay,* in another sense, means "to put." Will you *lay* this on the
> table? I *laid* it on the table yesterday.

lose/loose
> A frequent spelling mistake. *Lose* is pronounced "looze."
> *Loose* is pronounced with a hissing *s.*

luxurious/luxuriant
> *Luxurious* is what new homes might be called: A *luxurious* home
> in an affluent suburb.
> *Luxuriant* means "thick" or "abundant" usually, but not always,
> in connection with plants: The *luxuriant* vegetation and the
> closeness of the air were almost unpleasant.

moral/morale
> *Moral* refers to right and wrong: He considered it a *moral* obliga-
> tion.
> *Morale* means "spirit" or "mood": the *morale* of the troops.

practical/practicable
> *Practical* is the opposite of theoretical: He was a brilliant man

but not very *practical.*

Practicable means "can be done" or "feasible:" They claimed
that mass transit was no longer *practicable.*

proceed/precede

Proceed means "go ahead": *Proceed* with the plan.

Precede means "to go in front of": The captain *preceded* his
troops into battle. Mr. Gray *preceded* me in this job.

principle/principal

Principle means "rule:" He knew the *principle* of navigation.

Principal is the "chief" or "main" part of something: She was
the *principal* source of ideas.

prophecy/prophesy

Prophecy is the noun: All were alarmed by his *prophecy.*

Prophesy (the last syllable rhymes with "pie") is the verb: He
was able to *prophesy* the coming of the Messiah.

respectfully/respectively

Respectfully means "in a respectful manner."

Respectively is used to show relationships or connections:
Seated left to right are Smith, Brown, and Gomez, the President, Vice-President, and Treasurer, *respectively.*

there/their

There refers to place.

Their is the possessive of *them: Their* ideas, *their* responsibility.

whose/who's

Whose is the possessive of *who:* I've discovered a writer *whose*
ideas are exciting and novel.

Who's means *who is* or *who has: Who's* coming now? *Who's*
arrived lately?

Metaphorical Words

Metaphorical language is used to show what something is like. A
town may *mushroom,* like the familiar fungus, or workers in a fac-

tory may scurry about like so many *ants in an anthill.* A crowd can *flow* (the crowd is like liquid), or ideas can *jell.* In every case two things are being compared to make the message clearer and more easily understood.

Theodora Kroeber describes the life of Ishi, a Yahi Indian who lived in the California hills, hiding from white men for many years. She says, ''The years of Ishi's total disconnection from history were most of the years of his life: a long interlude of stillness.''

> ''disconnected''—like a cord from an outlet
>
> ''interlude''—like a period of rest between two pieces of music or other activity

''The senses strain to understand what must have been the waking and sleeping of that time; and if Ishi could not light up for us its traumas and tragedies, he could and did describe and reenact for us something of its day to day living.''

> ''light up for us''—a clear image, better than the familiar ''shed light on''—from *Ishi In Two Worlds* by Theodora Kroeber, p. 99

But use metaphorical language sparingly. Never force it. As this writer continues, she turns to literal language because metaphors are unnecessary. The following passage is clear, simple, and eloquent.

> The hidden ones fished with the harpoon and the net, and hunted with the bow and arrow, and by setting snares—silent weapons all. They gathered acorns in the autumn, enough if possible to see them through the winter. They ate green clover in April, and brodiaea bulbs in early summer. In mid-summer they went to Waganupa, four nights' journey, to its cooler air and deeper shade and more abundant game.

There can be problems in the use of metaphorical language. Sometimes a writer produces visual confusions, like these:

> The groundswell of enthusiasm suddenly fizzled. (A groundswell can't fizzle, but it could flatten out.)
>
> I'm snowed under with work, but I'll struggle on to the end. (Maybe ''struggle up to the surface''?)

Here is an impossible one:

> The key to the solution, if we can unravel it, will dissolve all doubts. (A key can't dissolve anything, nor can a key be unraveled. A key would not open up a solution, though maybe it would open the door up to the problem and let the solution in?)

This sentence is beyond repair. The writer may be suggesting that there is a solution (only one), and once the solution is discovered, everyone will recognize it as the correct solution. If we accept such a statement, we must still recognize that it tells us very little.

Other such mixed-up metaphors can be repaired. This student writer intends to compare the Constitution to a building's foundation. But in his first sentence he says there is a foundation *under* the Constitution. Is the Constitution the upper part of the building, or is it the foundation?

> They laid down the foundation of the federal government under the Constitution. The Constitution was the foundation by which men consented to govern themselves.

And how do men govern themselves by a foundation? This will have to be made clear to the reader.

One possible rephrasing is this one:

> The Constitution was to be the foundation for the new federal government. It was the set of principles by which the citizens would govern themselves.

Clichés

Phrases like "in a nutshell," "well-rounded person" and "the American way of life" are ready-made metaphorical phrases. Such phrases are called *clichés* after an old printer's instrument. In an unthinking, mechanical way a writer can reproduce stock phrases in the same way that a printer could stamp an entire word or phrase on a sheet of paper—no trouble, no thinking, no originality involved. Unfortunately, the phrases communicate this staleness, lack of force, and evidence of shallowness to the reader.

Phrases like the following are typical:

building blocks of success	life is not a bowl of cherries
through thick and thin	(or bed of roses)
all walks of life	a ray of hope
taking the bull by the horns	

One problem with giving advice about clichés is that certain of them have become so embedded in the language that avoiding them may lead to more awkwardness than using them. When used in appropriate contexts "the tide turned," "(someone's) back to the wall," or "face to face" may be more communicative than paraphrases.

Certain ideas can be clichés, the ideas for example that the savage is childlike, that businessmen have ulcers, that women long to be mothers, that Scotsmen are penny-pinchers, that success comes to those who work hard. This is not to imply that such ideas are never true. They may indeed be true. The fault is to utter such notions when they are divorced from experience or data.

For example, the writer of the following introduction to a paper on modern art appears not to have thought beyond conventional and expected clichés about the subject:

> One of our modern problems of society is that in this world of white, middle-class values a person with unconventional ideas who is a little different is looked down on. You are not accepted unless you are a conformist. This is why modern art is not popular today.

A more determined and original approach to the subject might include a more detailed account of the "white, middle-class values" as contrasted with the values suggested by particular works of modern art. As it is, the writer's first paragraph provides little hope that he will say much of interest, drawn from his individual experience. This is the main problem with cliché—its use is likely to shut off genuine and productive communication.

Written Slang

Written slang, like its spoken counterpart, is a vigorous kind of language used in very informal situations. Personal letters to friends are the most obvious places where slang may be appropriate; it is almost never used in legal briefs, formal correspondence, or in academic writing.

Most readers would judge it inappropriate for someone to write on a job application:

> My credentials and qualifications are *pretty heavy* [i.e., *impressive*].

or to write in an academic report:

> Reports by Miller, 1967, and Harrison, 1972, suggest that such attempts at peer group identification are not *genuinely cool.*

Colloquial English

There are many kinds of written English, ranging from the sometimes stilted English of a presidential address to the everyday slang just discussed. Written English is a very conservative medium. The use of colloquial expressions in a piece of writing communicates an informal conversational manner. Such a manner is rarely appropriate for academic writing, where formality is often regarded as showing seriousness and informality is interpreted as revealing either frivolity or a lack of sensitivity to what is appropriate. Expressions like *fire* meaning "dismiss," *be floored* (by a problem), *fix* meaning "prepare food" are usually labeled as colloquialisms. If you are unsure about a particular expression, a large dictionary is a useful guide, although its use of the term *colloquialism* is likely to include slang and many clichés. Unfortunately what is colloquial for one reader may be quite acceptable to another equally scholarly person. You have considerable scope for your own judgment as to the suitability of language for the topic and audience.

Wordiness

Say simply and directly what you want to say. Scratch out words which add nothing to the meaning. A wordy sentence like this one:

> They all bear a distinct similarity in the fact that they are eloquent.

can be changed to a shorter one:

> They are all eloquent.

Not only does the writer save words and space, but he gains in forcefulness.

> If we look at the whole situation logically, we see a problem. For every problem there is a solution. In order for something to be solved, It must answer the problem in such a fashion that there are no other problems created. The problem of student demonstrations is a deep, involved problem, yet there is a solution. The solution does not lie with arresting or expelling. Where it hides is a secret not yet told.

A reduced version is better, clearer, and more forceful:

> Arresting or expelling those who participate in demonstrations will not solve the complex problem of student unrest.

It is useful to divide Wordiness into three categories.

Wordiness I, the most annoying, is the most long-winded, pretentious, or pompous. The writer appears not to have thought out what he wants to say. He has nothing very specific to say, and he thinks in great cloudy generalities. The rambling passage on student unrest is feeble.

Wordiness 2 (Redundancy) is less severe, less annoying. The writer has accidentally said the same thing twice or more.

> Violent death has now become a commonplace thing, a thing of everyday occurrence in life.

The remedy is to scratch out the unnecessary phrases so that the sentence reads

> Violent death has now become commonplace.

Occasionally, one idea is implied by an earlier one. Again, delete the unnecessary word.

> It was gray *in appearance*.

could just as well be

> It was gray.

since the word *gray* implies *in appearance*.

Wordiness 3 involves single words which should frequently be eliminated. Note the examples:

> War is regarded as (being) brave, righteous, and honorable.

> To a Benedictine monk (obtaining) peace of mind is not gained by reaching out and acquiring all the things that laymen crave.

EXERCISE

How could the following be rephrased to eliminate stuffy, wordy, pompous, and pretentious prose? For example, here is one way you can rephrase the first sentence:

> One difference is the student coach in English classes here. At Scarborough High School English classes do not have coaches.

1. One of the differences between the English classes in this school and those of Scarborough High School is that of a student coach in this school.
2. According to the author, it is obvious to him that military games and toys should be discontinued entirely.
3. Writer Y perceives that the selfish character of man and the nature of the earth make the institution of war an unending process and one which will continue as long as man exists.

4. We can, through generalizing the nature of the problem, see that the trouble appears to lie in our inability to grasp relationships.

5. This necessary effort is essential for the safety of the school children.

6. At a glance one can tell that these writers are of completely opposite differences of opinion.

7. The opening of the tape is more or less an introduction to prepare the listener for what is to come. It mostly says to have an open mind for what is to come. This opening is a song, "Listen," which informs the audience that it is important to listen and be aware.

8. But what I think is true is that because children are supposed to be so controlled with their releases that when the point comes to where they are supposed to give in to their impulses, the strain of the withholding will create guilt subterfuges, and situations which might have been avoided.

9. One has to be sure about beginning skiing because the cost of equipment is quite expensive.

10. I have not learned anything of value from these movies that will benefit me in the future.

11. Science, in its never-ending search for answers, continually demands new and innovative methods for solving the problems which constantly confront them.

Mechanics

Abbreviations

In special kinds of written forms such as legal documents, technical papers, footnotes, and addresses on post cards, abbreviations are used to save time and space. Since there is little need for that kind of economy in college writing, however, abbreviations should generally be avoided. Use abbreviations only when you think they will help the reader.

TITLES

Write out all titles except Mr., Messrs., Mrs., Mmes., Ms., Msgr., St., and Dr. If these titles are not followed by a proper name they too should be written out.

Incorrect: The Dr. was sued for malpractice.

Correct: Dr. Fry (or *The doctor*) was sued for malpractice.

193

Certain titles like Reverend, the Honorable, Colonel, President, are usually written out. They can be abbreviated only if the first name or initials are included.

Incorrect: Rev. Hayes, Hon. Blake.

Correct: Rev. Christopher Hayes, Hon. D. R. Blake.

DEGREES

Academic degrees are usually abbreviated: B.A., M.A., Ph.D., M.D., D.D.S. Use a title either before *or* after the name, but not both places.

Incorrect: Dr. J. W. Myer, Ph.D.

Correct: Dr. J. W. Myer, or J. W. Myer, Ph.D.

COUNTRIES, STATES, ETC.

Spell out names of countries, states, months, days of the week, and units of measure.

Incorrect: Victoria lost six lbo. between Mon. and Fri

Correct: Victoria lost six pounds between Monday and Friday.

In general writing, spell out words like *Avenue, Boulevard,* and *Company.*

Correct: Gunn's Trailer Company is situated between Claremont Road and Wyoming Boulevard.

FAMILIAR ABBREVIATIONS

You may use familiar abbreviations for organizations, government agencies, trade names, scientific words, and technical terms.

CIA	Central Intelligence Agency
ROTC	Reserve Officer Training Corps
RNA	Ribonucleic acid
Rh factor	Rhesus factor
OED	Oxford English Dictionary

UNFAMILIAR ABBREVIATIONS

If you plan to use repeatedly an abbreviation that is not commonly known, explain it the first time you use it.

> Stop Littering Our Bays and Beaches, an organization commonly known to San Diego residents as SLOBB, sent out fifty members to clean the Solana Beach coastline.

LATIN EXPRESSIONS

Commonly known Latin expressions may be used in abbreviated form, though many writers prefer to use the English equivalents.

cf.	*confer,* means *compare*
e.g.	*exempli grata,* means *for example*
i.e.	*id est,* means *that is*
etc.	*et cetera,* means *and so forth*

(NOTE: In general *etc.* should be avoided in college writing. Rephrase your list, introducing it with *such as* or *including*. The literal translation *and so forth* is only a little better than *etc.*)

Inappropriate: The intramural program consists of baseball, basketball, swimming, golf, etc.

Appropriate: The intramural program consists of sports such as baseball, basketball, swimming, and golf.

Appropriate: The intramural program includes baseball, basketball, swimming, and golf.

(NOTE: If an abbreviation comes at the end of a sentence, only one period is used.)

> Plato, the Greek philosopher, died in 347 A.D.

Agreement

SUBJECT AND VERB

Here are the rules for making verb endings agree with subjects. For practice in applying the rules, turn to *Passages for Editing,* p. 246.

Singular subjects require singular verbs; plural subjects require plural verbs.

> The baker decorates the cake.
> The bakers decorate_ the cake.

INTERVENING PHRASE. When the subject is followed immediately by the verb, as in the above examples, mistakes in agreement are rarely made. When there is an intervening phrase, however, some writers may make the verb agree with the nearest noun, rather than with the actual subject of the sentence.

> Gardiner, together with a number of less well-known associates, has formed a powerful and highly independent public lobby. (*Gardiner has,* not *a number have*)

> The bogus manuscripts, whose lack of authenticity was discovered by William Day, make interesting reading nevertheless. (*Manuscripts make,* not *William Day makes*)

INVERTED SENTENCE. When the word order of a sentence is inverted, agreement is sometimes difficult to establish. Be sure to identify the true subject of the sentence correctly, especially if it comes after the verb.

> Riding the horse were the two girls, Valerie and Therese. (*girls were,* not *horse was*)

> In the greenhouse grow many varieties of flowers. (*varieties grow,* not *greenhouse grows*)

COMPOUND SUBJECT. Two or more subjects joined by *and* take a plural verb.

Karate and judo *seem* to be increasing in popularity.

Rushing the passer and covering punts *are* the major deficiencies in the Chargers' defense.

(NOTE: When a compound subject refers to a single thing, the verb is singular.)

Blood, Sweat & Tears appeals to many age groups because of its effective combination of rock and jazz.

COMPOUND SUBJECT: *OR, NOR.* If two or more subjects are joined by *or, nor, either . . . or,* or *neither . . . nor,* the verb should agree with the nearer subject.

Neither oils nor *water colors have* been purchased by the Art Department.

Either the dogs or the *cat has* to go.

Either the dog or the *cats have* to go.

COLLECTIVE NOUNS.

1. A singular verb is used when the collective noun is regarded as a unit.

The *cast* of **Waiting for Godot** *is* a small one.

The archaeology *section is* planning a dig near Poway this summer.

2. A plural verb is used if the collective noun refers to the members of the group.

The *cast* of **Waiting for Godot** continually *miss* their cues.

The archaeology *section,* sitting apart from the rest, *were* drinking their chocolate milk and balancing their tuna sandwiches on their knees.

(NOTE: The last examples, though grammatically correct, have an awkward sound to them. For these and like sentences, it is often better to use a subject that is clearly plural.)

The members of the cast of **Waiting for Godot** continually miss their cues.

The archaeologists sat apart from the rest, drinking their chocolate milk and balancing their tuna sandwiches on their knees.

PRONOUNS AS SUBJECTS.   Note that the following pronouns are singular and therefore require singular verbs:

anybody	everybody	somebody	either	one
anyone	everyone	someone	neither	none
anything	everything	something	each	nobody

We believe that everyone who *has* visited this exhibit *has* left with a deeper understanding of urban problems.

Neither poet *writes* about the individual in crisis.

But although some purists insist that *none* can only be singular, the word is widely used as a plural:

None of the writers *has* captured the immigrant experience as eloquently as Elia Kazan. (Singular)

None of the writers *have* captured the immigrant experience as eloquently as Elia Kazan. (Plural)

NOUNS PLURAL IN FORM BUT SINGULAR IN MEANING.   Though a few nouns appear to be plural because they end in *s,* their meaning makes them singular. They take singular verbs.

Rabies is always fatal if not treated immediately.

Mathematics is required of all freshmen.

Economics has been added to the curriculum of the graduate school.

INTRODUCTORY *THERE* AND *IT*.   A sentence may begin with the introductory word *there* (sometimes called an "anticipating subject"). Whether the verb is singular or plural depends on the subject which follows the *there* or *it*.

There *are* numerous *cases* of heroin overdose not only in the inner city, but in the suburbs as well.

In my opinion, there *is* little *evidence* of criminal intent.

It always takes the singular *is,* even if a following noun is plural:

It is the mountains which I find so difficult to sketch.

SHIFTS IN TENSE AND PERSON

VERBS.   Avoid needless and confusing shifts of tenses.

Shift: Mill *stresses* the importance of originality as the catalyst for social progress and *insisted* that individuality must not be repressed.

Consistent: Mill *stresses* . . . and *insists*. . . .

Consistent: Mill *stressed* . . . and *insisted*. . . .

Shift: For months I *had admired* Susan Morange from afar, but I *haven't* the courage to ask her for a date.

Consistent: For months I *had admired* . . . but I *hadn't*. . . .

Consistent: For months I *have admired* . . . but I *haven't*. . . .

PRONOUNS (PERSON OF).   Avoid needless and confusing shifts of pronouns from one person to another. (First person: *I, we;* second person: *you;* third person: *he, she, it, one, they.*)

Shift: If *one* is to read Beckett's plays intelligently, *you* should first familiarize *yourself* with Beckett's novels. (A shift from third to second person.)

Consistent: If *one* is to read Beckett's plays intelligently, *he* should first familiarize *himself* with Beckett's novels.

Consistent: If you are to read Beckett's plays intelligently, *you* should first familiarize *yourself* with Beckett's novels.

Students often are in a quandary about the use of the first person *I* in a paper. There should be no hesitancy to use *I* if the

paper concerns a personal experience. However, if the paper is of a more general nature—comparing the outlooks of two historians, for example—the first person should be used sparingly. Because the student is expressing his own opinions, the *I* in such a paper is taken for granted even though it doesn't actually appear. To make the *I* explicit in such a sentence as "*I believe* Marx criticized the Industrial Revolution in his early works" is a waste of words. If there is an instance, however, when the writer makes a point contrary to someone else's, the use of *I* is vastly preferable to such tortured phrases as "This writer thinks" or "The author of this paper believes." In short, when a reference to yourself is necessary, feel free to use *I*.

PRONOUN AND ANTECEDENT

A pronoun should agree in number with its antecedent. A singular antecedent requires a singular pronoun; a plural antecedent requires a plural pronoun.

> *John* felt *he* deserved a raise. (*He* is the pronoun. *John* is the antecedent.)

> The *employees* felt *they* deserved raises.

INTERVENING PHRASE.   Mistakes in agreement generally occur when the pronoun is separated from its antecedent by an intervening phrase. Be sure to identify the correct antecedent.

> It is all too easy to get lost inside a complex sentence and to make grammatical *errors* which won't seem obvious at a *glance* but *which* impede<u>s</u> comprehension.

The relative pronoun *which* refers to "errors," not "glance," so the "which" is plural, not singular. Hence it takes the verb "impede," not "impedes."

ANTECEDENTS: COMPOUND NOUNS.   A pronoun referring to compound nouns joined by *and* is usually plural.

Even though *Chris* and *Tim* were expert swimmers, *they* were drowned in a dangerous rip tide.

Chris and *Tim* lost *their* lives.

A pronoun referring to compound nouns joined by *or, nor, either . . . or,* or *neither . . . nor* usually agrees with the nearer antecedent.

She took advantage of anyone or *anything which* could further her career.

She took advantage of anything or *anyone who* could further her career.

In sentences like the following, however, the plural pronoun is customary even when the second noun of the subject is singular:

Neither the father nor the sons have finished *their* household chores.

Neither the sons nor the father have finished *their* household chores.

ANTECEDENTS: COLLECTIVE NOUNS. A collective noun takes a singular pronoun if the noun is regarded as a unit.

The *jury* took *its* time in reaching a decision.

A collective noun takes a plural pronoun if the noun refers to the members of the group.

Deciding that *they* could reach no decision that night, the *jury* retired to *their* rooms to get some sleep.

(NOTE: To avoid awkwardness, it is sometimes better to add a subject that is clearly plural.)

The members of the jury, the jury members.

Deciding that they could reach no decision that night, *the jury members* retired to their rooms to get some sleep.

PROBLEMS WITH PRONOUN REFERENCE

Read the examples below and the comments following them.

1. The king immediately issued a new decree, *one which* allowed the victims to defend *themselves.*

   Comment: The words *one which* refer to the new decree, while *themselves* refers to the victims. It is clear to the reader what the pronouns refer to.

2. The king immediately issued a new decree *which* forbade any *such* attacks on *him.*

   Comment: The pronoun *which* clearly refers to "decree." The pronoun *him* may refer to the king or to some other male previously mentioned. In such a situation check the previous sentences. These may clearly show who the "him" is, so it may be that this sentence should be left unchanged. The only way to know is to look at the sentence in the larger context of the whole piece of writing. *Such* in "such attacks" is not, strictly speaking, a pronoun. Here it is really an abbreviation for "attacks such as these," and probably refers to attacks mentioned in an earlier sentence. Again the reference would probably be clear if we had the whole paragraph in front of us.

3. The king issued a new decree. *This* intensely irritated Haiman's followers.

   Comment: This is ambiguous in reference. The word could refer to the new decree. (*The new decree caused the irritation.*) Or *this* could refer to the whole event of the king issuing a new decree. It might be that Haiman's followers had no objection to the new decree itself but did object to the king, rather than someone else, *having issued* the decree. The writer needs to change (3) to avoid such confusion, to spell out what he really means.

4. The king told Haiman to have Mordecai ride before *him* through the city, *which* made *him* very despondent.

Comment: The first *him* could refer to the king or Haiman, the second *him* to Haiman or Mordecai. Or both could refer to someone else mentioned in an earlier sentence. The pronoun *which* is also unclear. Does it refer to everything earlier in the sentence—to the king telling Haiman to have Mordecai ride before him through the city—or just to Mordecai's riding through the city, or just to the city (unlikely), or to . . .? To let the reader know who rides behind Mordecai, who is despondent, and what *which* refers to, the writer should revise completely. More information will probably be necessary:

Haiman was told to arrange a procession in which Mordecai would ride in honor before the king. Haiman grew despondent at this command since he hated Mordecai.

5. Esther was frightened to go before the king. But *her* father said even Queen Vashti would have done *that* for *her* people. *It* would be selfish for Esther to refuse.

Comment: All of the pronouns here are clear; although the reference of three of the four is somewhat complicated. The first *her* clearly refers to Esther. The *that* (*would have done that*) refers to going before the king. Unlike the vague *which* and *this* found in some of the earlier examples, this pronoun clearly refers to the whole event—going before the king—and cannot refer to any part of the phrase. The second *her* would be linked to Queen Vashti in the minds of readers, and not to Esther, since a queen is thought of as "having people." The *it* (*it would be selfish*) is also clear. It refers forward to *for Esther to refuse.* (This introductory *it,* sometimes known as the expletive *it,* is further discussed on p. 198.)

PRONOUN FORMS: WHO OR WHOM, I OR ME

WHO, WHOM.   *Who* and *whoever* are normally subjects. *Whom* and *whomever* are objects of verbs or of prepositions.

Whoever arrives first should make the first speech.

It is irrelevant *who* did the damage.

Present the bill to *whoever* broke the window. (*Whoever* is the subject of its own clause.)

To *whom* did you give such poor advice?

Chisholm was the candidate *whom* we most admired.

(NOTE: *That* is also possible in the last example while *who* is increasingly acceptable.)

CLAUSES. When a pronoun is a subject of a clause, it takes the subject form even when the whole clause is the object of a verb or of a preposition.

Give this to *whoever* is wearing a red carnation. (*Whoever* is the subject of the clause *whoever is wearing a red carnation.*)

I condemn only those *who* are unwilling to forgive. (*Who* is the subject of the clause *who are unwilling to forgive.*)

AFTER PREPOSITIONS. Pronouns which follow prepositions take the object form.

He showed the experiment to *me.*

Mr. Szanto will probably divide the work between you and *me.*

APPOSITIVES. An appositive should be in the same case as the noun or pronoun it explains.

We, Bart and *I,* went to the Del Mar Racetrack.

The foreman shouted at both of us, Pete and *me,* before we had a chance to explain.

Capitals

There are two fundamental rules to remember: Capitalize the first word of a sentence. Capitalize proper nouns and adjectives.

Here are some other guidelines.

SENTENCES AND POETRY

1. Capitalize the first word of a sentence.
2. Capitalize the first word of each line of poetry when the poem is printed in the traditional way.

> Wind, bird, and tree,
> Water, grass, and light:
> In half of what I write
> Roughly or smoothly
> Year by impatient year,
> The same six words recur.
> —David Wagoner, "The Words"

3. Capitalize the first word of a direct quotation that is a complete sentence in itself

   Stan Mason says, "The finest automobile built today is the Ferrari."

   No capital is used if the quotation is a fragment.

   Stan Mason claims that he was "financially embarrassed."

4. Capitalize the first word after a colon only when the statement that follows the colon is lengthy or when you want to give the statement particular emphasis. When in doubt, use the lower case.

WORDS THAT ARE CAPITALIZED

1. The personal pronoun *I* and the exclamation *Oh*.
2. Words referring to the Deity and Holy Scripture.

   the Lord   the Koran
   the New Testament the power of His love

3. Days of the week, names of months, and calendar items. Names of seasons are *not* capitalized.

   Tuesday   Labor Day
   February winter

4. Official titles before (not after) the name of the bearer.

    He visited Governor Rockefeller.

    He visited Nelson Rockefeller, governor of our state.

5. Proper names of persons, places, and things, but not names of classes of persons, places, and things.

Capitalize	Do not capitalize
Sam	a man
Mr. Jones	a man
Florida	a southern state
People's Park	a park
Sather Gate	a monument
Notre Dame University	a midwest university
2015 Los Arbolos Court	a shady street
Literature 2B	a literature course

(NOTE: The Junior Prom, but, Jerry is a junior.)

6. Religious, racial, linguistic, national, and political groups.

Catholic	Polynesian	Communist
Negro	French	Spanish

(NOTE: At this point in history many writers capitalize *Black* just as they capitalize *Spanish* and *English*.)

7. Names of social and economic groups are not capitalized.

    the bourgeoisie   the aristocracy

8. Names denoting family relationships are capitalized when used with the person's name or when they stand for the name. They are not capitalized when preceded by a possessive.

My first mitt was given to me by Grandpa Brown.

My first mitt was given to me by Grandpa.

My first mitt was given to me by my grandpa.

9. Historical periods or events.

    the Iron Age   the Battle of Algiers

10. North, south, east, and west are capitalized only if they refer to a specific location.

    I was born in the Southwest.

    The map says we should travel further south.

11. In titles of books, articles, papers, and the like, capitalize the first and last word, important words, and prepositions of more than four letters. Do not capitalize articles (*a, an, the*) or conjunctions.

    King Kong Meets the Daughter of Frankenstein

    "Casey at the Bat"

    "My Life Before and After the War"

12. Names of trains, aircraft, and ships.

Hyphens

The hyphen is most often used to link two or more words which are considered as a single unit. However there is a growing tendency, especially with two-word combinations, to omit the hyphen and to write the combination as a single word. Moreover two-word combinations appear to go through three major stages. At first as nouns they appear as two separate words without a hyphen, as did *rail road;* then as adjectives preceding a noun as a hyphenated

combination, *rail-road;* and finally, some years after they become assimilated into common vocabulary, as a single word, *railroad.* Thus, we cannot give a set of cast-iron rules for inserting or omitting hyphens; we can only set some guidelines. For specific words, consult the most recent edition of a good dictionary.

1. Hyphenate words used as an adjective *in front* of a noun, as in

> The *well-known* playwright arrived in a *reddish-brown* convertible with a *freckle-faced, red-haired* child.

However, if the combination *follows* the noun, the hyphen is usually omitted:

> The playwright was *well known.*
>
> The convertible was *reddish brown.*
>
> The child was *freckle faced* and *red haired.*

The hyphen is also omitted if the first part of the combination is an *-ly* adverb, as in

> the gently swaying trees
>
> the irritatingly arrogant monarch

2. Use hyphens for other word combinations considered as a single unit, such as

> mother-in-law
> great-grandfather
> able-bodied
> letter-perfect

3. Use a hyphen after such prefixes as *pro-, ex-,* and *self-,* as in

pro-consul
ex-convict
self-made man

Here again there is considerable variation. For example, *premeditated* and *prehistoric* no longer have hyphens while *pre-industrial* still requires one.

4. Where a prefix ending in a vowel is combined with a word beginning with a vowel, a hyphen usually appears, as in

re-engage
anti-establishment

There is considerable variation for words beginning with *co-*

co-worker	cooperate
co-exist	coexist
co-conspirator	coincidence

5. Use a hyphen between prefixes and proper names.

pre-Christian
anti-American (but *antisocial*)
pro-Italian

6. Use a hyphen to prevent confusing one word with another word with the same spelling, such as

recreation	*and*	re-creation
resort	*and*	re-sort
recover	*and*	re-cover

7. Use a hyphen to separate written-out numbers *twenty-one* through *ninety-nine,* and to separate written-out fractions such as *three-eighths.* However, you may omit a hyphen from commonly used fractions such as *one half* and *two thirds.*

8. Use a hyphen to break words at the end of a line. See *Word Division.*

Italics

Where a printer uses italics, the typist uses underlining. The *New York Times* is the same as the <u>New York Times</u>. The following should be underlined in your writing:

1. Underline titles of books, magazines, plays, motion pictures, operas, long poems, and works of art.

   > <u>The Scarlet Letter</u> (novel)
   > <u>Time</u> (magazine)
   > <u>Who's Afraid of Virginia Woolf</u> (play)
   > <u>Godzilla Meets Dracula</u> (movie)
   > <u>La Bohème</u> (opera)
   > <u>Paradise Lost</u> (long poem)
   > <u>The Thinker</u> (statue)

   Do *not* underline titles of magazine or newspaper articles, songs, poems, or short stories.

   > "The Snows of Kilimanjaro" by Hemingway
   > "Alcoholism in America," reprinted in the <u>Chicago Sun Times</u>

2. Underline words referred to as words.

   > I notice in your paper you misspelled <u>expedient</u> twice. (You may use quotation marks instead of underlining.)

3. Underline names of ships, trains, and aircraft.
4. Underline scientific names.

   > <u>ursus terribilis</u> (grizzly bear)

5. Underline foreign phrases not yet naturalized into English. Refer to your dictionary to see which words are still thought of as foreign.

   > <u>quantum libet</u> (as much as you please)
   > <u>post cibum</u> (after meals)
   > <u>post facto</u> (after the fact)

   There is no need to underline a foreign expression if it is in

quotation marks. You must underline, however, if foreign and English words are mixed.

"Lo meteremos en un colegio," said Pablo.

"You are his sister, n'est-ce pas?" he asked.

Be sure to underline abbreviations of Latin words in footnotes such as ibid., op. cit.

UNDERLINING FOR EMPHASIS

Underlining is a crude way to show emphasis in expository writing. Instead of

Armando Rodriguez argued that difference is strength, not destruc- tion.

one can write

It was Armando Rodriguez who argued that difference is strength, not destruction.

or

Armando Rodriguez was the man who argued that difference is strength, not destruction.

But underlining is often used to good effect in the writing of dialogue because it accentuates the speaker's inflection and gives insight into the speaker's character.

I introduce him to all my friends. Let him clutter up the whole apartment with his horrible manuscript papers, and cigarette butts, and radishes, and what not."—J. D. Salinger, "Just Before the War with the Eskimos."

Numbers

The main question regarding numbers is whether to use only the figure or whether to write out the word. These rules describe the customary use of numbers.

WHEN TO USE WORDS TO REPRESENT NUMBERS

1. Isolated numbers under 100.

> I saw four killer whales.

(NOTE: In a series of numbers of which some are less than 100 and others more, be consistent. Normally you should use figures.)

> I saw 4 killer whales, 8 lady bugs, 13 giraffes, and 152 aardvarks.

2. Numbers at the beginning of sentences.

> Three hundred and eleven Cub Scouts attended the Jamboree.

(NOTE: Dates are an exception to this rule.)

> 1963 was a good year for Amalgamated Hinges.

3. Round numbers or indefinite expressions.

> I've told you a million times not to exaggerate!

> The Beatles drew forty or fifty thousand to their concert at Shea Stadium.

WHEN TO USE FIGURES TO REPRESENT NUMBERS

1. Most writers continue to write out numbers from one to a hundred. It is acceptable, however, to use figures for numbers of 10 or more.

> There are 43 more than expected.

> There are forty-three more than expected.

> There are 542 more than expected.

2. Dates.

> September 21, 1944

> She lived in Baltimore from August 5, 1938 to June 7, 1963.

(NOTE: Always write out in full the ordinal form for the day of the month: fifth, third, ninth.)

3. Street, room, and telephone numbers.

> Send my mail to 2354 North Sierra, Solana Beach, California, 92075.

4. Measurements.

> Please use 8½ by 11 paper for your assignments.
>
> The carton weighed 22 pounds, 11 ounces.

5. Money.

> $3.24, $18 apiece, $0.44, 44 cents.

6. Decimals and percentages.

> She owed 42 percent of the bill.
>
> The pole measured 42.8 feet.

7. Time of day when used with A.M. or P.M.

> 8:00 A.M., eight o'clock

8. Pages and divisions of a book.

> p. 4, Chapter 9, pp. 6–11, Act V, Scene II, line 29.

9. Use commas to separate the thousands from the hundreds. This is optional for round numbers.

> 2500 or 2,500; 4,311,248.

CARDINAL AND ORDINAL NUMBERS

Cardinal numbers indicate number only: 2, 3, 19.

Ordinal numbers indicate order: second, third, nineteenth. Ordinal numbers should not be abbreviated (2nd, 3rd, 19th) but written out.

PLURALS OF NUMBERS

Plurals of numbers are written either with *'s* or *s:*

> I need four 2 by 4's. (2 by 4s)
>
> In your list, I notice only three 6's (6s) and two 12's (12s).

Parallel Structure

Here the rule for parallel structure is given and illustrated. For practice in applying the rule, turn to *Passages for Editing*, p. 254.

The rule for constructing parallel forms is a simple one: express similar ideas in similar forms. Match nouns with nouns, verbs with verbs, infinitives with infinitives, prepositional phrases with prepositional phrases. If you mix constructions, the relationship between ideas is obscured, and the reader might be confused.

Some violations of parallel structure may not cause real misunderstanding:

> Steak and lobster are my favorite foods, and so is eating chicken.

But the following parallel sentence sounds better and makes more sense:

> Steak, lobster, and chicken are my favorite foods.

Sentences which lack parallel structure can be corrected in more than one way. Whichever grammatical construction you choose for your sentence, however, remember to use it consistently.

Not Parallel: Early to bed and rising early makes a man healthy, gives him wealth, and he will be wise.

Parallel: Early to bed and early to rise gives a man health, wealth, and wisdom.

Parallel: If a man goes to bed early and rises early, he will be healthy, wealthy, and wise.

Parallel: Early to bed and early to rise makes a man healthy, wealthy, and wise.

Parallel: Going to bed early and getting up early makes a man healthy, wealthy, and wise.

SERIES

Use a parallel construction to express a series of words, phrases or clauses.

Not Parallel: Automobile manufacturers are alleged to have tried to spy on critics, to conceal safety data, to restrain competition, and buying off influential legislators.

Parallel: Automobile manufacturers are alleged to have tried to spy on critics, to conceal safety data, to restrain competition, and to buy off influential legislators.

Parallel: Automobile manufacturers are alleged to have tried spying on critics, concealing safety data, restraining competition, and buying off influential legislators.

Not Parallel: The main character in Miller's play is conscientious, devoted, and he worked hard.

Parallel: The main character in Miller's play is conscientious, devoted, and hard-working.

CORRELATIVES

Be sure that correlatives (comparisons and contrasts like *either . . . or, neither . . . nor, not only . . . but also, both . . . and*) are followed by parallel forms.

Not Parallel: I quickly saw that my only alternatives were to run or staying and facing the consequences.

Parallel: I quickly saw that my only alternatives were to run or to stay and face the consequences.

Not Parallel: Sam was not so pleased by the huge, roaring red buses, nor even when he heard Big Ben chime the hour, as he was by one absurd little milk cart.

Parallel: Sam was not so pleased by the huge, roaring red buses, nor by Big Ben chiming the hour, as he was by one absurd little milk cart.

        —Adapted from *Dodsworth* by Sinclair Lewis

(NOTE: To make clear a parallel construction, it may be necessary to repeat an introductory word such as a preposition, an article, or the *to* of an infinitive.)

Awkward: At the used-book sale, I bought a physics text and literature handbook.

Better: At the used-book sale, I bought a physics text and a literature handbook.

Awkward: Joan is going to the bank, and the sandal shop, but not the university.

Better: Joan is going to the bank and the sandal shop, but not to the university.

Plurals

To form the plural add *s* to the singular (*books, chairs, lights*), if the plural makes an extra syllable, add *es* (*churches, boxes, presses, flashes*). These basic rules have a number of common exceptions, which are listed below.

1. When a noun ends in *y* preceded by a *vowel*, form the plural by adding *s*.

    boy   boys
    toy   toys
    tray   trays

When a noun ends in *y* preceded by a *consonant,* change the *y* to *i* and add *es.*

    filly   fillies
    travesty   travesties
    army   armies

2. If a noun ends in *o* preceded by a *vowel,* form the plural by adding *s.*

studio	studios
patio	patios

If a noun ends in *o* preceded by a *consonant,* add *es.* (A few such nouns take *s* only, and a few others can take either *s* or *es.* Consult a dictionary if you are unsure.)

Negro	Negroes
echo	echoes
potato	potatoes
tomato	tomatoes

soprano	sopranos
piano	pianos
zero	zeros *or* zeroes
cargo	cargos *or* cargoes

3. When a noun ends in *f,* change the *f* to *ve* and add *s.* (*fe* becomes *ves*)

knife	knives
leaf	leaves
half	halves
thief	thieves

Some nouns that end in *f* form the regular plural.

chief	chiefs
belief	beliefs
roof	roofs

4. Some nouns, usually names of animals, have the same form for singular and plural.

fish
sheep

trout
deer
salmon

5. Some nouns are singular but always end in *s*.

rabies	Rabies *is* still a killer.
physics	Physics *is* not so difficult.
economics	Economics *has* become difficult.
measles	Measles *has* not been eliminated.
mathematics	Mathematics *has* become popular.

6. Most compound words are made plural by adding *s* to the last word.

all-Americans
rear admirals
ex-convicts
judge advocates

When the first word is clearly more important, however, it usually takes the *s*.

sisters-in-law
fathers-in-law
governors-elect
attorneys-at-law

Nouns ending in *ful* normally take the standard plural form.

cupfuls
teaspoonfuls

7. Some words have a foreign plural as well as an Anglicized plural ending in *s* or *es*. The foreign plural is commonly used in technical or scientific writing. A few examples:

	Foreign Plural	Anglicized Plural
cactus	cacti	cactuses
formula	formulae	formulas

	Foreign Plural	Anglicized Plural
index	indices	indexes
radius	radii	radiuses
vertebra	vertebrae	vertebras

Certain nouns of Greek and Latin origin ending in *is* are made plural by changing *is* to *es*.

Singular	Plural
analysis	analyses
basis	bases
crisis	crises
diagnosis	diagnoses
neurosis	neuroses
parenthesis	parentheses
psychosis	psychoses
thesis	theses

Possessives

The possessive can be expressed either with an apostrophe (*Bill's, dog's, Superman's*) or with an *of* phrase (*of the book, of the building*).

POSITION OF THE APOSTROPHE

1. If the word does not end in *s*, add *'s* to make it possessive.

Jim	Jim's book
week	week's wages
friend	friend's mother
men	men's hats

2. If the word ends in *s*, add an apostrophe alone. (However *'s* is often added to singular nouns ending in *s*, and almost always to those ending in *ss*.)

Jesus	Jesus' disciples (or Jesus's disciples)
actress	the actress's gown
Mr. Jones	Mr. Jones' car (or Mr. Jones's car)
the cats	the cats' (plural) food

WHICH FORM OF THE POSSESSIVE TO USE

1. Traditionally, the *'s* construction is used with living things and the *of* phrase with inanimate things (*John's home, the dog's bark, the end of the story, the top floor of the building*). This rule is by no means inflexible. In many cases, either construction could be used (*at the end of the day, at day's end*). Some idiomatic expressions take only one form (*a day's pay, and the like*).

2. If a sentence is awkward or ambiguous because of an *'s* construction, use the *of* phrase instead:

    Very Awkward: The boy down the street's house burned down yesterday.

    Better: The house of the boy down the street burned down yesterday

    Somewhat Awkward: He could not explain the faculty and staff's motives.

    Better: He could not explain the motives of the faculty and staff

IT'S *AND* ITS

It's is a contraction for *it is* or *it has*.
Its is the possessive form of *it*. (No apostrophe.)

It's [It is] unusual for historians to confess their personal biases in their published works.

It's [It has] broken down three times already.

Its power [the power of it] is frightening.

Punctuation

APOSTROPHES

IN CONTRACTIONS. An apostrophe takes the place of one or more missing letters.

I'm (I am)	hasn't (has not)	we're (we are)
can't (cannot)	haven't (have not)	isn't (is not)
won't (will not)	it's (it is; it has)	weren't (were not)

Contractions were once thought to be inappropriate in college papers. However, there has been a recent, though certainly not universal, movement toward the acceptance of contractions. They are acceptable in all but the most formal of college papers.

IN POSSESSIVES. See *Possessives,* p. 219.

THE COLON

Do not confuse the purpose of the colon with the purpose of the semicolon. The semicolon, like the period, *separates* elements, whereas the colon is used to *introduce.*

1. Use the colon after a statement which indicates something is to follow.

    Toad had stocked his vehicle with everything he might need: sardines, playing cards, writing paper, bacon, dominoes, and canned lobster.

2. Use the colon to introduce a long quotation.

    The letter of Charles D. Cooper was published in the newspapers: "General Hamilton has come out decidedly against Burr; indeed when he was here he spoke of him as a dangerous man and ought not to be trusted. . . . I could detail to you a still more despicable opinion which General Hamilton has expressed of Burr."

3. Use the colon in the following special situations: after the salutation in a business letter; between title and subtitle of a book; between chapter and verse in a Biblical reference; between hour and minute.

    Dear Sir:
    The Driver Ant: Unrestrained Killer
    Psalms 1:11–14
    12:01 A.M.

COMMAS

(See also *Run-On Sentences* for run-ons or comma splices.)

1. Use commas between main clauses in a compound sentence.

> The collection contains a varied set of adolescent autobiographies, but it provides too little supplementary information about the children who wrote them.

> The use of amphetamines by professional football players is increasing, and it is feared that this practice is spreading to other sports.

Commas may be omitted if the clauses are short.

> The rain fell and the wind blew.

2. Use commas after long introductory clauses or phrases, or after short ones if necessary.

> Although the moon also raises tides in the atmosphere, their effect is so slight that they will not be discussed here.

> When Shakespeare found a ready-made plot, he often built a drama around it.

> To construct a house in the expensive suburban community, you have to be prepared to spend at least $25,000 for the lot alone.

> Investigating the problem, surgeon Valdez discovered a defective plastic valve in the aorta. (Note the possible misreading if the comma is omitted.)

> To many overworked and underpaid sharecroppers, Chavez was the first to offer real hope of change.

When the modifying phrase *follows* the main clause, no commas are used if the sentence reads smoothly.

> Chavez was the first to offer real hope of change to many overworked and underpaid sharecroppers.

> Atmospheric tides will not be discussed here although they also are caused by the moon.

3. Use commas with nonrestrictive modifiers. The discussion
    below will explain the difference between restrictive and non-
    restrictive clauses. These two sentences are similar but not the
    same:

Sentence 1: I saw the clown who was wearing red suspenders dis-
             appear into the crowd.

Sentence 2: I saw the clown, who was wearing red suspenders,
             disappear into the crowd.

The first contains a restrictive clause, or one which ''restricts''
the general class ''clown'' to one particular clown. The second
contains the same clause, but this time it is nonrestrictive, making the meaning of the sentence slightly different. Notice that
the sentences sound different when read aloud. The two sentences can be paraphrased in this way:

Sentence 1: I saw a number of clowns. One of the clowns was
             wearing red suspenders (the others were not). This
             clown disappeared into the crowd.

Sentence 2: I saw one clown. He happened to be wearing red sus-
             penders. He disappeared into the crowd.

To make the difference clearer, one might imagine a context for
each sentence:

Sentence 1: At the circus there were four clowns. I saw the clown
             who was wearing red suspenders disappear into the
             crowd.

Sentence 2: At the circus there was a fat lady and a clown. I saw
             the clown, who was wearing red suspenders, disappear
             into the crowd.

The ''who'' clause in the first sentence is a *restrictive clause*
(no commas). It is essential to the sentence because it distinguishes the clown who was wearing red suspenders from the
other clowns who weren't. It restricts the class of clowns to a
subject—one particular clown. In other words the clause tells

which clown. The clause in the second sentence is *nonrestrictive* (set off by commas). The purpose of the *nonrestrictive clause* is not to differentiate one clown from another (there is only one), but to supply incidental information about that clown. Since the information is incidental, the clause is a parenthetical element, set off by commas in the way all parenthetical elements are.

a. Clauses which begin with *that* are usually *restrictive* and require no commas.

   The message that you sent was incoherent.

b. Some nouns, because they are one of a kind, cannot be restricted any further. Thus, any clause which follows such a noun would be *nonrestrictive.*

   My father, who is a religious man, never fails to attend daily mass.

   Mr. Bill Thompson, who is our Dean of Students, is away in Europe for the summer.

   Our newest boat, which is painted red and white, took its maiden voyage last weekend.

c. *Appositives,* phrases which provide incidental information, have the same function as *nonrestrictive clauses.*

   Samuel Beckett, the Irish novelist and dramatist, recently received the Nobel Prize for literature.

d. A fairly accurate way to determine whether you should use commas or not use them is to read the sentence aloud. If you read through the sentence without pause and without lowering the pitch of your voice, the clause is probably restrictive. That is, no commas are needed. If you pause or lower your pitch, the clause is probably nonrestrictive.

4. Use commas to set off parenthetical expressions such as

however, for example, on the other hand, and *moreover*.

> The main operation, *however,* will be performed under general anesthetic.

> *Moreover,* the Democratic Party needs to solve its financial problems.

If single word parenthetical expressions cause no hesitation when read aloud, they are best not set off by commas.

> Faulkner's finest novel is perhaps *Light in August.*

> Children certainly make better recoveries than adults with the same brain injury.

5. Use commas to separate items in a series. (If no misinterpretation is possible, the comma between the last two items is optional.)

> Baldwin wrote novels, short stories, essays, and an occasional newspaper article. (Last comma is optional.)

> Before he would make any reference to the solar explosion, he insisted on evaluating theories about the moon's origin, criticizing predictions that the moon would move closer to the earth, and presenting arguments that the sun was slowing down the earth's rotation. (Last comma makes reading easier here.)

Coordinate adjectives modify the same noun. If the adjectives could be reversed, or joined by *and,* a comma should be used. If not, no comma should be used.

Also Possible:
He had a crafty, brilliant mind.
He had a brilliant, crafty mind.
He had a crafty and brilliant mind.

Impossible:
I couldn't understand the rapid African dialect.
I couldn't understand the African, rapid dialect.
I couldn't understand the African and rapid dialect.

6. The addition of a comma is sometimes necessary to prevent a momentary misreading of a sentence. For example, try reading the following phrase without the comma:

> In the eighteenth century, institutions such as orphanages. . . .

THE DASH

The dash is used to indicate a sudden change of thought or to set off a parenthetical expression. Use the dash instead of parentheses if you want to give emphasis to the parenthetical expression. The dash can be effective, but be aware that its overuse can produce a distracting, choppy effect.

The typewritten equivalent of the dash is two hyphens with no spaces before, between, or after.

PROPER USES OF THE DASH

> When I lit my candle and went up to my room that night there sat pop--his own self.--Mark Twain, The Adventures of Huckleberry Finn

> It seemed to him now that they were all just shapes like chessmen the negro, the sheriff, the money, all--unpredictable and without reason, . . . --William Faulkner, Light in August

> I know--rather I think I know--what you mean.

> The persons who remember the aftermath of the first encounter can only smile sadly--it had all happened before.

THE EXCLAMATION POINT

Exclamations like "Ouch!" and "My kingdom for a horse!" rarely appear, of course, in expository prose. Avoid using the exclamation mark to add artificial emphasis. The words themselves or extra detail should carry the emphasis.

Instead of

> He was stupid and vicious!

a writer can say

He was a stupid, vicious man, capable of sending his friends to the gallows and innocent children to prison.

PARENTHESES

Parentheses are used to enclose supplementary or explanatory material.

Each essay should range between three and five typewritten pages or their handwritten equivalent (roughly 700 to 1200 words), excluding the pages needed for footnotes and bibliography.

Don't allow parentheses to become stylistic crutches. Set off material with parentheses only when absolutely necessary. Sentences will look better and read easier if the material is integrated.

Awkward: Mr. Smith (Teddy's father) seemed to delight in scolding Teddy (even though Teddy rarely did anything wrong).

Better: Mr. Smith seemed to delight in scolding his son Teddy, even though the boy rarely did anything wrong.

PARENTHESES AND BRACKETS. Do not confuse the use of parentheses with the use of brackets. Parentheses are used for explanatory remarks in your own writing. Brackets are used for explanatory remarks you wish to insert in quoted material.

Of professional football players, Bartley Horwitz (in *Pro Football: Big Business*) says, ''Many [of the Green Bay Packers] have used their professional careers as stepping-stones to lucrative business jobs.''

PARENTHESES WITH FIGURES AND LETTERS. Parentheses are used to enclose figures or letters that comprise a list.

The authors present strong evidence to support their assertions that (1) education is used to raise rather than lower barriers between people, (2) the government has resisted all attempts to reverse this policy, (3) tax money raised from those with lower incomes subsidizes education for wealthier groups, and (4) poorer people are becoming increasingly restive about the educational system.

PUNCTUATION WITH PARENTHESES

1. If the parentheses come within a sentence, punctuate as if the parentheses were not there; that is, the punctuation should go *outside* the parentheses.

> Voting against the bill was Clinton Anderson.

> Voting against the bill was Clinton Anderson (Democrat, New Mexico).

2. If the parenthetical material is a complete sentence in itself, punctuation should go *inside* the parentheses.

> (Voting against the bill was Clinton Anderson.)

THE PERIOD

1. Use a period at the end of statements, indirect questions, and mildly imperative sentences, or those which are not exclamations.

Statement:	It has been necessary to reduce the amount of the fellowships.
Indirect Question:	He asked if it had been necessary to reduce the amount of the fellowships.
Mild Imperative:	Find out if it has been necessary to reduce the amount of the fellowships.

2. Use a period after most abbreviations. See p. 193, *Abbreviations.*
3. Use three spaced periods to indicate an omission (an ellipsis) in quoted material. See p. 233, under *Quotation Marks.*

THE QUESTION MARK

Use a question mark at the end of every direct (not indirect) question.

Direct:	What is the purpose of your visit?
Indirect:	He asked what the purpose of your visit was.

(NOTE: It is generally a poor practice to make statements by asking questions of your reader. He may be irritated by such rhetorical questions because they seem unnecessary, contrived, even condescending.)

Unnecessary Question: What is the theme of Frost's poem, ''The Pasture''?
The theme of the poem is the simple expression that the beauty of nature is better enjoyed by two people than by one person alone.

Concise Statement: ''The Pasture'' by Robert Frost states the simple proposition that the beauty of nature is better enjoyed by two people than by one person alone.

QUOTATION MARKS

WHEN TO USE QUOTATION MARKS

1. Use quotation marks only to enclose the *exact* words spoken or written by someone. You should not use quotation marks for an *indirect* quotation since the exact words are not reproduced.

   Direct: She said, ''It's cold today.''

   Indirect: She said that it's cold today.

2. Quotation marks are also used to enclose the titles of magazines and newspaper articles, songs, poems, and short stories.

   ''White Rabbit,'' by the Jefferson Airplane.

   ''Aspirin: Is It Addictive?'' reprinted in *Today's Medicine.*

3. Sometimes you may use quotation marks to exhibit a mocking tone.

   This ''man of honor'' became rich by peddling worthless stock to small investors.

   or to show that you are using an informal word in a formal context:

   In the room were found large quantities of barbiturates or ''reds.''

Notice that the quotation marks in the above sentence mean, in effect, "I am quoting the language of another group or another context. These are not, at this time, really my own words."

4. Fight the tendency to put quotation marks around words of your own. In a few years, sentences like the one below have a dated sound, making the writer appear somewhat foolish:

> Billy was really "cute." All the "chicks" wanted to date him.

If you are tempted to use quotation marks in this way, ask yourself why you need them. If you are apologizing for slang or a cliché, rewrite the sentence so that the need for quotation marks is eliminated.

5. If, on the other hand, you still want to use the expression in question, then use it but don't use the quotation marks. Don't apologize with quotation marks if it's your own word, your language, and it's what you want to say.

HOW TO USE QUOTATION MARKS

1. When quotation marks are required *within* a quotation, use single quotation marks.

> Joan said, "Yes, I heard 'Light My Fire,' but I can't seem to remember the words."

> Mr. Jones said, "I remember Roosevelt's words, 'The only thing to fear is fear itself.'"

2. If a quotation continues for more than one paragraph, that is, if the same speaker speaks for two or three paragraphs, use quotation marks at the beginning of every paragraph but at the end of only the last.

3. To quote dialogue, use a separate paragraph for every change of speaker.

> "Another brandy," he said, pointing to the glass. The waiter who was in a hurry came over.
> "Finished," he said, speaking with that omission of syntax stupid

people employ when talking to drunken people or foreigners. "No more tonight. Close now."

"Another," said the old man.

"No. Finished."—Ernest Hemingway, *A Clean Well Lighted Place*

PUNCTUATION BEFORE A QUOTATION

1. If the quotation is very short and emphatic, no punctuation is needed.

   The coach yelled "Shoot!" when the clock had run down to only three seconds.

2. A comma should precede a short quotation.

   Bill replied, "This omission stands out as the main deficiency in his theory."

3. A colon should precede a long quotation.

   One critic compares the two novels: "Just as *The Red Badge of Courage* is not a religious novel, neither is *Sister Carrie* concerned with the morality of man's actions. Like Crane, Dreiser interjects no heavy-handed preaching, either in direct commentary or through his characters. Both novels are decidedly amoral."

(Also see *Footnotes,* p. 127.)

PUNCTUATION AFTER A QUOTATION

1. Periods and commas are always placed inside the quotation marks.

   "I know," he said, "but I still can't wait."

   After the lecture he had but one comment: "Useless."

   The following words are misspelled in your paper: "tediously," "experiment," and "usury."

2. Colons and semicolons always go outside the quotation marks.

   All he says is, "Please pass the sugar"; perhaps those are the only words he knows.

There are two points worth remembering in the article "Skin Diving at Hanauma Bay": you should never attempt to cross the reef at low tide and you should avoid the rip tide just outside the cove.

3. Question marks, exclamation marks, and dashes are placed inside the quotation marks if they apply to the quotation only—that is, if they are a part of the quotation itself.

Ed threw down the book and yelled, "Don't bother me!" (Only the quotation is an exclamation.)

I picked up the book and asked him, "When may I talk with you without bothering you?" (Only the quotation is a question.)

They are placed outside the quotation marks if they apply to the sentence as a whole; that is, if they are *not* a part of the quotation itself.

Was it Mr. Pickwick who said, "If the law says that, sir, then the law's an ass"? (The entire statement is a question.)

When will you get it through your head that I don't want anyone ever to say "Please"! (The entire statement is an exclamation.)

LONG QUOTATIONS. If a quotation is less than four or five lines you may quote it without modification within the body of the paragraph. If it is longer than four or five lines, however, you should separate the quotation from the paragraph, indent five spaces for each line, and use single spacing. When a quotation is in this "block form," quotation marks should be omitted.

Both as a critic and as a writer, Virginia Woolf shared in the artistic concern for realizing the best artistic form into which a writer translates the matter of reality. She realized that art implies order, selection, and arrangement; her novels were cohesive and tightly controlled, and in statements of criticism she argued for adherence to literary standards.

If fiction is, as we suggest, in difficulties, it may be because nobody grasps her firmly and defines her severely. She has had no rules drawn up for her, very little thinking done on her behalf. And though rules may be wrong and must be broken, they have

this advantage—they confer dignity and order upon their subject; they admit her to a place in civilized society; they prove that she is worthy of distinction.

—"The Art of Fiction"

VERSE

Verse may be quoted within the body of the paragraph if it is no more than two lines. A line break is indicated by a diagonal line (/).

"This above all: to thine own self be true," Polonius advised his son Laertes. "And it must follow, as the night the day/ Thou canst not then be false to any man."

If the verse is more than two lines, you should quote it exactly as it appears in the original, indented and single spaced.

The chorus contrasts Dionysus, born of Zeus, to the "rabid beast" Pentheus:

With fury, with fury he rages,
Pentheus, son of Echion,
born of the breed of Earth,
spawned by the dragon, whelped by earth!
Inhuman, a rabid beast.

—Euripides, *The Bacchae* (tr. William Arrowsmith)

INSERTIONS AND OMISSIONS IN QUOTATIONS

BRACKETS. If you want to clarify or explain a part of a quotation, your insertions should be enclosed with brackets. For example, in the following quotation it might be unclear to your reader who "He" refers to:

"He was one of the first defenders of the theory of natural selection."

Clarified: "[Huxley] was one of the first defenders of the theory of natural selection."

ELLIPSES. An ellipsis is a punctuation mark of three spaced periods which indicates that a part of the quotation has been omitted.

If an ellipsis comes at the end of the sentence, you should use four spaced periods (the period at the end of the sentence in addition to the ellipsis).

> "It is important to analyse the methods by which Virginia Woolf worked out her critical theories. . . . *To the Lighthouse* . . . is an excellent model from which to work. . . ."

Many student writers needlessly preface quotations. For example,

> Sartre acknowledges the perpetual conflict which is the only possible outcome of human relations. He does so in the following quotation: "Everything which may be said of me in my relations with the Other applies to him as well. While I attempt to free myself from the hold of the Other, the Other is trying to free himself from mine; while I seek to enslave the Other, the Other seeks to enslave me."

The sentence, "He does so in the following quotation," is unnecessary and should be omitted. The reader knows that the quotation relates directly to the sentence preceding it. There is no need to point out the connection.

(NOTE. Do not use "quote" as a noun, as in "He used too many quotes in his paper." Use "quotation" instead.)

THE SEMICOLON

In most cases you should use a semicolon only where you could have used a period, or a conjunction like *and, but, or, nor, however,* or *therefore.* Ordinarily the semicolon, like the period, is used to separate main clauses. Because the semicolon is not as strong a break as the period, however, you can use the semicolon between main clauses that are closely related.

> Measham's book provides a thoughtful analysis of the problem of pain; the importance of his research can hardly be overstated.

1. A semicolon may separate any two main clauses, provided that they are not already separated by a coordinate conjunction (*and, or, but, nor*).

Incorrect: Jensen's work was welcomed by opponents of bussing; and they made no attempt to check the reliability of the evidence.

Correct: Jensen's work was welcomed by opponents of bussing; they made no attempt to check the reliability of the evidence.

Correct: It has been alleged that the Puritans felt a monstrous guilt for separating from their mother country; this guilt was probably little in comparison to the awesome responsibility they must have borne as they, the last best hope for mankind, sailed for an unknown wilderness to reconcile humanity with God.

Correct: Hawthorne is often criticized for his use of allegory; many of his literary devices take on no meaning other than a singular representation of one idea or thing.

2. The semicolon is placed before a coordinate conjunction if the first main clause already contains commas or is unusually long.

> Jensen's work, based on dubious statistical evidence, was welcomed by opponents of bussing; and they made no attempt to check the reliability of the evidence.

3. The semicolon is sometimes needed to prevent confusion in a sentence that contains many commas.

Confusing: The following persons perished in the shipwreck: Black Bart, a conniving pirate, Ensign Jones, Billy McTeague, the cabin boy and Commodore Faddle.
[How many died? Six? Five? Four?]

Clear: The following persons perished in the shipwreck: Black Bart, a conniving pirate; Ensign Jones; Billy McTeague, the cabin boy; and Commodore Faddle.

4. Note that semicolons should separate only elements that are of equal rank: two main clauses, two subordinate clauses, or two phrases.

Run-on Sentences

Here are the rules about run-ons. For extra practice in correcting them, see *Passages for Editing,* p. 246. A run-on sentence consists of two sentences improperly joined. For example, the following are joined with only a comma,

> The boy became ill, he went home.

an error sometimes labeled "comma splice."
These are joined with no punctuation at all:

> The boy became ill he went home.

The run-on is a liability to good writing because it may be confusing and difficult to read. These are a number of simple ways to correct the run-on.

1. Place a period at the end of the first sentence and capitalize the first word of the second.

> The boy became ill. He went home.

2. Place a semicolon between the two parts (If they are closely related in content).

> The boy became ill; he went home.

3. Place the proper conjunction between the two sentences, making one compound sentence.

> The boy became ill and (he) went home.

4. Subordinate one of the sentences, making one complex sentence.

> Because the boy became ill, he went home.

Admittedly, many run-on sentences are usually not as easy to diagnose as our simple illustration. Nevertheless, no matter how long or involved two consecutive sentences may be, they must be joined, or separated, correctly. Of the four possible ways to correct

a run-on, one is usually preferable to the other three. Take the following run-on sentence as an example:

> Many women are just as vehement as men in opposing the extension of legal rights to their own sex, they have the same cultural biases as the male chauvinists.

Possible corrections:

1. Place a conjunction between the two sentences. This remedy, to make a compound sentence out of the run-on, would be grammatically correct but illogical.

> Many women are just as vehement as men in opposing the extension of legal rights to their own sex, *and* they have the same cultural biases as the male chauvinists.

2. Place a period at the end of the first sentence and capitalize the first word of the second. This correction is both grammatical and logical. The connection between ideas in the two sentences is implied not stated.

> Many women are just as vehement as men in opposing the extension of legal rights to their own sex. They have the same cultural biases as the male chauvinists.

3. Place a semicolon between the two sentences. This correction has virtually the same advantages as the one immediately above. Moreover the use of the semicolon rather than a period suggests a close logical linking. This correction is probably the best here.

4. Subordinate one of the sentences. This remedy is grammatical, logical, and states clearly the connection between the related ideas in the two sentences.

> Many women are just as vehement as men in opposing the extension of legal rights to their own sex *because* they have the same cultural biases as the male chauvinists.

Sentence Fragments

Here are the rules about fragments. For extra practice in correcting them, turn to *Grammar,* p. 143, and *Passages for Editing,* p. 246. A fragment is an incomplete sentence. It may be incomplete because it lacks either a subject or a predicate.

> But to combat this feeling of hysteria.
>
> In the clutches of the sea monster.
>
> Hoping to change my major.

If a string of words has a subject and a predicate, but is introduced by a relative pronoun (*who, which, that*) or a subordinating conjunction (such as *although, when, if, because*), it still is a fragment:

> *Even though* I marked all the boxes with an X.
>
> *Which* sounds more interesting every time I hear it.

HOW TO CORRECT FRAGMENTS

If the fragment belongs with either the sentence before it or the one after it, make the appropriate connection.

Fragment: *Being afraid of the dark.* I frequently was unable to sleep.

Sentence: Being afraid of the dark, I frequently was unable to sleep.

Fragment: He respected DuBois. *Because he used language as if it were the last desperate weapon of the Black mind.*

Sentence: He respected DuBois because he used language as if it were the last desperate weapon of the Black mind.

You may choose to rewrite the fragment, inserting the necessary subject and predicate.

Fragment: *Hoping to attend the W. C. Fields festival.*

Sentence: I hoped to attend the W. C. Fields festival.

PASSAGES CONTAINING FRAGMENTS

Our arrival caused quite a stir in the sleepy Mexican fishing town. *The small children shouting in their foreign tongue while their bigger brothers and sisters silently stood by watching.*

Revised: Our arrival caused quite a stir in the sleepy Mexican fishing town. The small children shout*ed* in their foreign tongue while their bigger brothers and sisters silently stood by watching.

During the next two centuries conditions changed sufficiently to lead the Spanish monarchs to petition the Pope for a tribunal to aid in the investigation and punishment of heresy. *In hope of solidifying their control and guaranteeing the orthodoxy of the Spanish Church.*

During the next two centuries conditions changed sufficiently to lead the Spanish monarchs to petition the Pope for a tribunal to aid in the investigation and punishment of heresy. *They hoped to solidify* their control and *guarantee* the orthodoxy of the Spanish Church.

Spelling

Consult the dictionary for words you are in doubt about. Also learn, if you don't already know them, these general patterns of English words.

PREFIXES

Prefixes like *dis-, pre-,* and *re-* are simply attached.

dis . . . position	in . . . consistent
dis . . . appoint	in . . . coherent
pre . . . cede	in . . . numerable
pre . . . view	in . . . audible
re . . . instate	in . . . discriminate

The prefix *in-* changes before the sounds, *m, r* and *l.*

ir . . . reverent   im . . . measurable
ir . . . responsible   il . . . legal

SUFFIXES

Suffixes like *-able* and *-ment* and verb endings *-ed* and *-ing* are usually just added on:

bark . . . ing   walk . . . ed
base . . . ment   rent . . . able
cautious . . . ness   sure . . . ly

But a final *e* on a root word drops off if the suffix begins with a vowel:

crave   crav . . . ing
divo   div   ing
retrieve   retriev . . . ing

The *ing* form of *tape* is therefore *taping.* For words like *tap* and *rid,* where the vowel is short, an extra consonant has to be inserted to keep it short, hence, *tap-p-ing.* Compare *riding* and *ridding, spiting* and *spitting, doting* and *dotting.*

A corollary to this rule has to do with words like *occur.* Why does it double the *r* before adding *ed* or *ing?* (*occurred*) Other words, for example *cover* and *offer,* do not double their final consonant. (*offered* and *covered*)

The category of words like *occur* differ from other words in two ways. First, they end with a single vowel—single consonant. Second, the stress or accent is on the last syllable of the word. Thus,

admit'   admitted
refer'   referred
fib'   fibbed
demur'   demurred
compel'   compelled

Other words do not fit into the *occur* category:

merit	merited (accent on first syllable)
appeal	appealed (the vowel before the letter *l* is not single)
funnel	funneled (accent on first syllable)
resist	resisted (the final consonant, *t,* is not single)
sadden	saddened (accent on first syllable)

(Some consonants will not behave like the *r* in *occur.* For example, the *w* in *slow* will not double, nor would the consonants *c, x, y, h, j,* or *q.* These, however, do not pose problems for spellers.)

The sound of soft *c* and soft *g,* require an *e* or an *i* after them to keep them soft; *ci* and *ce* are soft *c* sounds, but *co, ca,* and *cu* are hard sounds. Thus:

Keep the *e* in *noticeable* to keep the *c* soft.
Keep the *e* in *courageous* to keep the *g* soft.

Notice that *picnic* and *frolic,* when they add *ed* or *ing,* need a *k* after the *c.* Compare the sound of *picniced* (incorrect) with *picnicked* (correct).

THE y AND THE i

Words ending in *y* often change the *y* to *i.*

1. Change *y* to *i* and add *es:*

candy . . . . . . cand*ies*
lad*y* . . . . lad*ies*

2. Change *y* to *i* and add *-al* or *-ness:*

deny . . . . . . den*ial*
lovely . . . . . lovel*iness*

3. Don't change *y* to *i* if, by doing so, you would produce a double *i* or a strange-looking string of three vowels:

valleys	(not valle*ies*)
toys	(not to*ies*)
rays	(not ra*ies*)
staying	(not sta*ii*ng)
relying	(not rel*ii*ng)
dying	(not d*ii*ng)

(NOTE: *Skiing* is an exception.)

THE i *AND THE* e

The old rule is still the best:

i before *e*:	*field, friend, grief*
except after *c*:	*receipt, perceive, deceive*

and when sounded like *ay* as in ''neighbor'' and ''weigh'':

freight, deign, heir, feign

(Also *height,* which doesn't sound like *ay*).
EXCEPTIONS: *leisure, weird, seize*
             neither, either, foreigner

Split Infinitives

It is usually awkward to split an infinitive—*to walk,* or *to communicate*—by slipping an adverb between the *to* and the verb:

to *effectively* communicate
to *gracefully* walk

Better to say:

to communicate effectively
to walk gracefully

Occasionally a writer's language sense, however, tells him that it is better to split an infinitive than not to split it. Earlier in this book we wrote about a writer's lack of control over his prose. We said that such a lack of control

> results from the author's apparent unwillingness to think,
> *to really think,* about McLuhan's ideas.

To decide whether it would have been better to write:

> *really* to think

we read it aloud both ways and decided to split the infinitive.

Word Division

You should only need to break a word if the lines at the right-hand margin of your paper would otherwise be unusually ragged. A wide right-hand margin can accommodate all but the most lengthy words. In the event that a word must be broken, follow these rules.

1. The hyphen should be placed at the end of a line, not the beginning of the following line.

2. Break words only in between syllables.

butter-cup	*not*	butte-rcup
im-plicate	*not*	impl-icate

   Obviously, one-syllable words cannot be broken

through	*not*	thr-ough
flipped	*not*	flip-ped

   nor can short words like *cheery* and *ferry.* You cannot break between every syllable in a longer word.

3. There should be at least two letters in a syllable to set it off from the rest of the word.

ador-able	*not*	a-dorable
elusive-ness	*not*	e-lusiveness

4. Words already hyphenated should be broken only at the hyphen.

self-assurance	*not*	self-assur-ance
ex-convict	*not*	ex-con-vict

5. In words containing double consonants, break in between the double consonants rather than just before or after them.

stop-ping	*not*	stopp-ing

6. When two different consonants occur together in a long word, they may be separated but only if the breaking does not interfere with natural pronunciation.

in-spire	*not*	ins-pire
de-flect	*not*	def-lect

7. You can usually place a hyphen before *ing*. But you should not separate *ble* from its root word:

drink-able	*not*	drinka-ble

Passages for Editing

Once a piece of writing is organized, coherent, and well developed with detail, it is ready for editing and final typing. The following passages can be used for preliminary practice in editing since, in most of them, there is only one kind of error to be corrected. The margin symbols, like *frag* or *agr,* will lead you to explanations of the rules involved. See the back inside cover for the appropriate page numbers.

There is always more than one way to edit out an error, so it may be helpful to discuss some of these passages in a class. Following this kind of class work, you should be able to keep on increasing your editing skill by going over copies of other students' unedited writing. Finally, you will become skilled enough to look at your own writing as an outsider does, editing carefully but without being unduly self-critical. You will also see editing as something that comes late in the production process and not something that need concern you at the first draft stage.

245

The passages will give help with the following problems:

fragments	agreement of subject and verb
run-on sentences	parallel structure
punctuation	active and passive
pronoun reference	wordiness and word choice

One passage near the end is harder to edit since it has several kinds of problems. The last passage may be the hardest to deal with since it needs more work before editing can even begin.

Editing for Fragments and Run-on Sentences

PASSAGE 1

Edit for fragments and run-ons (*frag* and *ros*).

Batman is much easier to believe than Superman. Although they are both crimefighters, Superman has superhuman powers while Batman relies on scientific means of fighting crime. Summoned to danger by his x-ray vision and super hearing, the big man in leotards with an "S" on his chest flies to the rescue. Using his superhuman strength, he beats up the bad guys and saves the day. While the masked man with pointed ears is called through his "Batphone" and jumps into his turbine-engined Batmobile. Using his highly developed scientific instruments, he tries to outwit and outfight his opponents. Superman, as Clark Kent, is not as rich as Batman but doesn't need money for his crime fighting expense, Batman, on the other hand, as a millionaire, uses his money to buy lots of computers, a car, and even his hideout. Whereas Superman is a mere newspaper man and has to become "Super" by magic, Batman doesn't need magic, he has money.

Editing for Tense Shifts, Fragments, and Run-ons

PASSAGE 2

Edit for fragments, run-ons and tense shifts (*frag, ros,* and *t*). (There is a legitimate tense shift from the past, in paragraph 1, to

the present in paragraph 2, and back to the past in paragraph 3. These shifts serve a purpose. Within paragraphs, however, tenses should be consistent.)

I stared stonily at the dirty beige wall of a single-story locker room. Just below some dirty broken windows divided into quadrants by plain steel frames. As I stood on the black-top basketball court I felt my shoes pinch my feet. At a rigid ''brace,'' the strictest position of attention, I gazed past the black brim of my service cap and watched my ex-pupil and friend, now the squadron commander, Cadet Lieutenant-Colonel David Valloy.

As he passes, I note that his uniform is in proper order. I pause, taking in his collection of ribbons and medals, to which he will add another by the end of the year. He paces back and forth addressing his junior officers. I find that I am not really listening to the content of his address so much as I am analyzing it, Dave has learned the art of command well. The use of his voice, pauses, and inflections are combined with clear, concise wording for maximum effect on the audience before him. Very often he uses his hands to stress his point. His short heavy frame seems to grow to larger proportions as he states that he will not tolerate inefficiency and/or disrespect by junior officers like that shown last year. His eyes are hidden under the service cap, but his face wears a mask of anger enhanced by his dark features. He has the manner of a drill instructor without the derisiveness of that type of character. I turn my attention to the rank of junior officers arranged four paces in front of me, a few of them just getting used to the idea of being called ''sir'' and to the annoyance of returning salutes. Each of the officers who held positions last year were in states of unease as Dave mentioned the types of goofing-off he had seen earlier, the new officers were apprehensive about this hard-line policy for officers. All of them almost visibly squirming at attention. Dave knows one of these people will replace him and all will hold senior staff positions next year. So he will have to shape them up before then.

From being an outside observer, outside of even myself, I was snapped back to reality, when Dave's voice cracked into a squeaky,

high-pitched tone. As I suppressed the urge to laugh, Dave cleared his throat. Imperceptibly at first, a change came over him. Fatigue was getting him. His work in planning the orientation session and the drinking contest the night before, combined with the emotional strain of his speech, took a heavy toll. As soon as he finished, he walked to his position, called the deputy commander to inspect the officers, and we walked back to the staff room.

PASSAGE 3

Edit for tense shifts (*t*). Note that this does not mean that every verb must be in the same tense.

After having spent ten weeks in Java, Indonesia, studying the dance forms of that area, I was asked by a professor who teaches Javanese music and dance here to be a teaching assistant in dance this semester. Having studied with native Javanese, I have been accustomed to their method of teaching the dance. The problem for me was to transfer my knowledge from one teaching method, that of the Javanese, to another, something that would be effective at the University.

In Java, the method of teaching is one of memorization by means of repetition. The teacher presented the basic dance movements first alone, and then has the student follow in imitation. After the student memorized the movement, the teacher then watches the student try the movement alone. When there was a mistake, the teacher "fixes" it: the raising of an arm or leg a little higher, or the tilt of the head a little more or less as needed. After the teacher fixes the student a number of times, he is expected to know the movement or position well enough so that he can feel the mistake if he makes it again.

PASSAGE 4

Edit for tense (*t*).

Students of the University should be persuaded to join car pools. If every two students who drive to school alone join together and take turns in bringing their cars to school, there would be a noticeable de-

crease of cars in the student parking areas. The Traffic Desk in the Auxiliary Services building issues the student parking permits. Parking permits are sold to any bona fide University student with a driver's license. If regulations were carried out to limit the number of these permits, fewer students may want to bring their cars to school. For example, permits should be issued to those who live quite far away—15 or more miles, those who bring at least one passenger, those who must work immediately after school, and those who live where there are no bus stops nearby.

Editing for Punctuation

PASSAGE 5

Edit for quotation marks and use of apostrophe to show possession (*p*).

The common denominator of all religions is mans search for an understanding of himself. The questions who am I? and where do I come from? are basic to all religions and are an attempt to give man knowledge of himself and his place in the natural order of the earth. The beginnings of religion came with early mans attempts to deal with what he viewed as a hostile environment. He needed to try to understand his environment to understand himself, so he invented stories or myths to explain the natural phenomena of the earth. The more powerful and awesome features of the earth were given names and usually had gender. This personalization made a relationship possible between men and their gods, and ritual made it possible for men to keep in touch with their gods.

PASSAGE 6

Edit for commas and quotation marks (*p*).

I was seventeen a girl in high school and Kathy was twenty-four a seasoned woman of the so-called ''hippie'' class. She was tall and thin and rather boyish looking except for her long blond hair. Her bright blue eyes always looked tear-washed and I could never speak to her

without looking straight into them. I felt if I didn't I was missing the best part of the conversation.

I would see Kathy walking through town usually looking typically "hippie" with her muslin shorts and light summer blouse. Whenever I stopped to talk to her she'd tell me about her latest hobby and invite me over to see her new projects. Her hobbies macrame tie-dying vegetarian cooking and sewing became my hobbies too for Kathy enjoyed giving me private lessons. I learned a lot from her not only from what she taught deliberately but from what she taught subtly. She was soft and gentle and her manner attracted me to emulate her. I went as far as attempting a soft and tinkling voice until someone told me I had begun to mumble.

Kathy lived with Carlton in a two-room house with an open garage that served as their living room. The door to their bedroom was painted purple and lavender and alongside a drawing of a sun was the word "shanti" which means peace. The room was always dark and smelled of incense and cannabis. Kathy had hung an Indian tapestry across the ceiling which made the room seem even more mystical. There were macrame wall hangings pictures of Lord Krishna shell mobiles and candles artfully placed throughout the room. Kathy made her own pillows out of velvet and knick-knack trays out of tuna cans. Though the blouses she sewed were made with the least amount of material she adorned them by attaching beads or shells. She frequented the beach and collected shells to make her own jewelry and driftwood to use in the macrame wall hangings. Her skill with her hands extended outside of her hobbies and home and into a beauty shop where she "made up" tourists five days a week. Kathy qualified as a hippie but was not free spirited by Thoreau's standards.

At home Kathy always worked in the living room and sat next to the 1950-style dining table. Though the floor in the garage was merely packed dirt and the flies made themselves at home in the heat of the day Kathy did her best to make her home comfortable. Every now and then she'd sweep out the loose pebbles and dirt and only once did I hear her talk of a new home. It's great she said in defense of the old one. Our friends can drive right up to our living room.

PASSAGE 7

Edit for commas and quotation marks (*p*).

The cannery was an enormous factory with long rows of tables
and millions of people. The sight of other new faces gave me a little
more confidence that what I had come with but I was still unsure of
myself as a forelady approached us with her red stripe of authority and
led us through the huge factory leaving one of the new people at each
table we passed. Finally it came to be my turn and I was left at table
12 the only new one there amidst a group of ''professionals.'' The
forelady told me to pick up one of the bunches of yellow circles going
past me. I slowly reached out to pick up the pineapple between my
two baggy-gloved hands but the table was moving too fast and the
middle of the stack slipped away and continued on its journey to the
end of the table. I felt everyone's eyes on me and was sure they were
all laughing at me. I managed to grab the next bunch that came
through and proceeded to separate the yellow circles and place them in
their right places. Noticing that the forelady was replacing all the pineapple that I so carefully tried to put in the correct can I began to lose
confidence. But then she left and I packed the pineapples according to
my own decision. Don't be so nervous, said the girl next to me and I
realized I was packing with shaking hands. Now came my turn to go
for a ten-minute break because the girl before me had returned and
had gone to the top of the table. I carefully stepped off the table and
pulled off my sticky gloves and proceeded to freedom.

PASSAGE 8

Edit for commas (*p*).

''When you use the paints don't forget to wash your brushes before changing colors'' I instructed the seven-year-olds. Normally other
children would dip their brushes in a color and after use wash them
and then dip them in another color but not Steven. He took his brush
and drowned it in green paint then immediately slapped it onto the

paper. Steven proceeded by painting a big green circle. Without remembering what I had said he dunked the paint brush into the red paint coming up with a purplish mixture. What made matters worse was that he didn't stop there. He took his brush which was covered with globs of red and green paint and soaked it in the yellow. The paint brush which was now dripping with different shades of colors was plastered onto the paper causing the assorted colors to run down and mingle with the bright green circle. Noticing that his hands were stained with paint he pressed them against the paper and smeared the colors together in a circular motion. Since the newspaper that was under the butcher paper had been torn it left the bare surface of the floor to be covered with the excess paint trickling down from the sides of the paper. Steven partially remembering what I had said took the brush and dunked it in the can of water. Instead of squeezing the excess water from the bristles of the brush he flicked it. The result was spatter marks on the paper and floor. Steven with smudges of paint and a great big smile on his face lifted his soggy paper and showed it to me. He had pride and self-accomplishment written in his eyes. Colors of red, yellow, and green seemed to blend in to produce a sort of shiny brownish blob. Long squiggly streaks ran from top to bottom. The water previously splattered onto the paper now created large round blotches where the paper was blistered and bumpy.

Editing for Vague "This"

PASSAGE 9

Edit for pronoun reference (*pro ref*). This passage contains a vague "this." Assume that you are the writer of this passage and know what you *intended* to convey. Rephrase the sentence containing the word "this" to make the meaning clear.

To a certain extent, I think we are all a product of our environment. Richard's striving for recognition through the entertainment field, his compulsiveness in buying cars, his choice of career, and insecurity are all effects of his upbringing. Richard is the middle child in the fam-

ily. The oldest one, Dennis, got much attention, being six years ahead of the next child. He was favored by my father, and, of course, I had much affection being the baby of the family. Wanting more attention, Richard probably fell into the habit of doing things out of the ordinary and was thought of as a "troublemaker." Meaning well but failing to realize what was happening, my parents had neglected this for many years. When he started school, he probably tried to prove himself better than other children by bragging and gained many enemies.

Editing for Subject-Verb Agreement

PASSAGE 10

Edit for agreement (*agr*).

Up to the present, says the speaker in this poem, their love has been spiritual. Their love, begun in purity, is based on the union of their souls. He likens their bodies to "sepulchrall statues," which retained the same posture for an entire day while the "negotiations of the souls" was in process. It is this comparison of their physical bodies to stone artifacts that show the lack of sensuality in their love. While their love possess spiritual immortality, it also possess the qualities of death and coldness. While their souls may ascend to communicate and unite, their bodies must stand by the grave.

PASSAGE 11

Edit for agreement (*agr*).

After the Second World War socialist forms of government of various kinds were adopted in various countries. Many of these countries now acknowledges complete equality for women. In Israel and Cuba, for example, women have to carry out military duties traditionally thought of as male tasks. Seldom is communist countries used as examples of women's position in society, but progress in socialist Scandinavia and Finland is gaining attention. As far as constitutional rights are concerned, total equality has been achieved there. In Finland, for

example, a woman can become the head of the Republic. Even there, however, the old attitudes towards the division of sex roles in society persists to a certain degree.

PASSAGE 12

Edit for agreement (*agr*).

By doing a proper automotive tune-up, these home mechanics increases engine performance, increases gas mileage, improves cold engine starting, reduces engine emissions, and helps prolong engine life. A full tune-up involves replacement of ignition parts, resetting of dwell, timing, choke, and carburetor, plus a full inspection of the engine and accessory parts. An examination of the distributor cap, ignition leads, and the ignition coil tells you if you have to replace any of these parts.

Editing for Parallel Structure

PASSAGE 13

Edit for parallel structure (| |).

Our junior high school was a Triple A school. Everything was superior: the students, and the equipment was superior, and they had superior teachers and cafeteria system. Our high school association had a certain curriculum for all its schools, but we were expected to perform above the requirements. Our textbooks were "advanced for our ages," a dress code more strict than usual, and there were punishments far more severe than at other schools. Comprehending the material seemed less important than to get a good grade, so it is no wonder that several students began to cheat. Good grades and if the teacher approved of you were the important things.

PASSAGE 14

Edit for parallel structure (| |).

Around the year 1940, scientists finally split the atom, and it gave us the power to do more than we ever dreamed we could do. What

peaceful uses have we put it to? As the most powerful country in the world, we have created a few token power plants for our own use and done minor experimentation in curing disease. We have, on the other hand, progressed from dropping the atom bomb, to build the Polaris submarine, to test the hydrogen bomb, and now into the cobalt bomb and its creation. Radiation has helped to cure perhaps 50,000 people through the world. The relatively small atom bomb dropped on Nagasaki alone killed 246,000 people.

Editing for Active/Passive

PASSAGE 15

Edit for active/passive. Which of the passives below would sound better in the context if they were active? (*act/pass*)

To stimulate our interest, Jefferson High had what they called "Alternative School Day." It was a day of school without classes. The entire day was filled with activities for the students. Movies were seen, field trips were taken, lectures with guest speakers were held, and a whole variety of other activities that could not be held on a regular school day were scheduled for this day. Half of the students were usually off campus either hiking, swimming, diving, surfing, bowling, or bike riding. There were also student recreation centers on campus, where the students could do whatever they wanted to. Rock groups and a band would be playing at one end of the campus, while the math department's simulated casino was in full swing at the other end of the campus.

PASSAGE 16

Edit for active/passive. Which of the passives below would sound better in the context if they were active? (*act/pass*)

My Saturday afternoons were spent babysitting a one-and-a-half-year-old boy called Josh, who moved into the house next door in the summer of 1972. He was considered adorable by everyone but mis-

chievous by me and the three hours I spent babysitting him proved my point. A typical afternoon would be spent playing hide-and-seek to keep him occupied and out of mischief. He liked to be found and the fun that he was having was reflected in the big smile on his face. Finding him was easy; I just followed his path of drools.

Editing for Wordiness

PASSAGE 17

Edit for wordiness (*w*).

The racist ideology holds that one ethnic group is condemned by nature to hereditary inferiority, and another group is destined by nature to hereditary superiority. Racism treats of the fundamental nature of human beings. As a doctrine concerning the fundamental nature of human beings, racism is a faith.

The racist trusts in his belief as the source of his personal value. His life has meaning and worth because he is part of the "good race," the "right race," the "*in*" race. His life fits into and merges with a valuable whole, the race. The white racist derives his worth and satisfaction from the belief that however deprived he may be, culturally and economically, he is still "better'n them." The racist at the same time is loyal to his faith for the value it possesses independent of itself. The race is the object of value, for even criminals, degenerates, and enemies can feel they have worth and goodness if they think they belong to the "in" race.

PASSAGE 18

Edit for wordiness (*w*).

In his book, *Tribesman,* Marshall Sahlins distinguishes between the primitive and civilized in terms of war and peace. He states that civilizations differ from tribes by virtue of their specialized political institutions. A civilization is a society especially constituted to maintain law and order, the guarantees of peace. Governments assume the power

and right to protect the citizenry and maintain peace within the state. In tribal societies control of force is not withheld from the people. Lacking these specialized political and law-enforcing institutions, the primitive tribesmen must mobilize their generalized institutions of agricultural economics, kinships, and rituals to make war, and war limits the complexity and all-around richness of their culture.

Although there is much truth in Sahlin's discussion of the meaning of the primitive, there is one matter in which I would like to discuss. This is his definition of the civilized in contrast with primitive societies. While it remains true that civilizations do have specialized political institutions to maintain law and order, thus attaining what Sahlins describes as higher levels of peaceful existence, how do we as citizens of the United States account for its problems associated with crime, overpopulation, political disruption, and wars, in naming just a few? The use of the terms ''peace'' in describing a civilized society and ''war'' in conjunction with primitive ones need to be carried into further discussion than what Sahlins offers in his explanation. Ironically, there are implications that range beyond the terms of war and peace, and beyond primitive peoples, to the ''civilized'' world in which we live, for we too live in a state of chronic warfare and are threatened by annihilation. Where then can we draw a line separating the primitive and the civilized, asking ourselves what is the difference between primitive and civilized peoples?

PASSAGE 19

Edit for word choice and wordiness (*ww* and *w*).

The men who resisted the draft and deserted cannot be conveniently categorized into one group. Their reasons for their course of action are as varied as the men themselves. Some resisted or deserted because it was conscientiously the right thing to do. There were others who were motivated by cowardice and others who could not fit into the military system. There are some like Terry Whitmore, a decorated soldier out of Vietnam, now living in Sweden. There is also Doug Griffin, who lives in Vancouver. They believe they ''were obeying a higher

law." [1] After a survey of exiles in Canada was taken, it showed a great proportion were college graduates, Ph.D's, and social workers.[2] So the people involved are of quality and not merely quantities. This source of valuable young leaders is being excluded from America.

(The footnotes are not included here.)

General Editing

PASSAGE 20

Here is a passage with several kinds of editing problems. The margin comments will help identify them. For more guidance, see the margin symbols on the inside back cover.

agr
lc

    p

active/passive

"what were probably"?

    s

    w

    w

pro ref

    p

The animal which I have selected for my primate behavior study is the Infant White-Cheeked Gibbons. These gibbons came to the zoo about the middle of last year, and are now about three years old. The data collected was done by means of observation of these gibbons on Tuesday, February 7, from 9 A.M to 10:30 A.M.

Observing the gibbons, I singled out one of the two, a black male. I found him eating probably the leftovers from his morning meal. There weren't many people around at the time, and he just sat there eating a banana. After finishing the banana, he grabbed a palm tree husk about four feet long, and by the use of his hands (having an opposable thumb, and feet also resembling the hands in that it seems as if it has an opposable big toe) he was able to manipulate the object. He first grabbed it with his hands then with his feet and secured it by grabbing it with his hands again. This shows that this animal had a manipulation of all his limbs.

After their meal they were quite active and playful. They played in the fashion of the male chasing the female around, both on the ground and above in the network of ropes and poles. This playful activity was carried on for a few minutes, until a crowd of people came. From their previous perch high up, they tumbled down the ropes to the ground and sat at the waters edge. The male sat there looking at the people

for a while then turned and returned to his frolics in the ropes. After
the crowd had passed a man eating french fries came by and the male,   p
seeing this, stoped all previous action and swung down to the waters   sp. p
edge possibly anticipating a hand-out of some sort. Now the primate   p
area became noisy with hoots and squeals from the neighboring adult
gibbons and chimpanzees. The noise seems to have stirred the male   t
gibbon, as he actively swung around and looked in all directions.

The noise having receded by now, the female gibbon went under
a cage enclosing a tree. The male tried to enter the cage the same way
the female had entered but was kept out by his companion. He then
stoped after a few tries and played with a stick about two to three   sp
inches long, tossing it from hand to hand without dropping or signs of   ᴎ ?
clumsiness.

Then along came a lady with a bag of grapes. She started throw-   sub
ing the grapes at the gibbons. While they, the gibbons, were standing
side by side, the lady threw a grape in the middle of the two. The male   ww "between"?
picked it up and ate it and while eating it another one fell between
them. But this time the female picked it up and ate it. The lady kept on
throwing grapes, and I noticed that either one could have it, depending
on which one got it first. This indicates that they knew that there was   s
probably more, and so there was no need to fight over it. So ended
the observation.

Passage Not Ready for Editing

PASSAGE 21

This passage is not ready for editing. What advice should be
given to the writer?

Finding that the old system was unsuccessful, the school introduced a change in instruction. Class size was cut down. This new system gave students the freedom to choose their subjects and teachers as
it is done in colleges and universities. Teachers were then given the
task of teaching subjects they themselves knew nothing about. When I
enrolled in a filmmaking class, I expected someone to teach me the

basic principles concerning the production of a film. I later found out that the teacher knew nothing about making a film, nor did she know how to run a projector. When asked questions, she gave out wrong information or sometimes admitted she didn't know. Most students chose a subject that involved little or no work. At registration, everyone made a mad rush to the ecology section. The ecology teacher gave A's to anyone who attended class at least a few times. Once in class, students were given the freedom of either listening to their stereos, roaming around campus, or loitering in the bathroom, which was conveniently located right next to the classroom. The teacher gave no lectures, class assignments, or homework. Though a majority of the classes were poorly run, there were a couple of classes where teachers gave lectures daily and quizzes regularly. From class assignments and exams, the teacher graded each student individually. One class like this was history. Another was political science. The political science teacher, at the time I was enrolled in his class, was running for mayor of the county. He continuously gave lectures. Most considered him quite boring and refused to have him for an instructor. Both political science and history classes had small enrollments. The grading system was poor. I received everything from A's to F's. I received an A from attending ecology class. I received an F for health class. In health, we were given a two-page worksheet containing simple multiple choice and fill-in blanks. At the end of the course, we were to hand in this paper in order to receive a grade. Unfortunately, my paper was stolen and there were no extra blank copies of this sheet made available by the teacher. I was forced to take an F for that part of the semester. Study hall was labeled "unstructured time." Students with study hall were to report to the office and check in. They were then able to go anywhere on campus as long as they made this free time useful. Many left the campus and persuaded others to cut class and leave campus with them. There were hundreds of cut slips turned into the vice-principal's office daily. Nothing was done.

INDEX

Abbreviations, 193–95
  degrees of, 194
  familiar, 194
  general, 194
  Latin expressions of, 195
  titles of, 193–94
  unfamiliar, 195
Accept/except, 180
Active/passive, 153–56
  editing for, 255
Adler, Irving, 62
Advice/advise, 180
Affect/effect, 180
Agreement, 196–204
  pronoun and antecedent, 200–204
    antecedents, collective nouns, 201
    compound nouns, 200

Agreement (*continued*)
  intervening phrases, 200
  pronoun form, 204
    in apposition, 204
    after prepositions, 204
    as subjects of clauses, 204
  shift in person/tense, 199–200
    pronouns, 199
    verbs, 199
  subject and verb, 196–99
    collective nouns, 197
    compound subject, 196–97
    intervening phrase, 196
    inverted sentence, 196
    nouns plural in form, 198
    pronouns as subjects, 198
    with *there* and *it*, 198

All ready/already, 180
All together, altogether, 181
Allusion/illusion/delusion/elusive, 181
Ambiguity
    dangling modifiers and, 145–47
    pronoun reference and, 147–48,
        202–203, 252
    see also This, vague use of; Vagueness;
        and Which, vague use of
Amount/number, 181
Antecedent, pronoun and, 200–204
Anybody, etc. as subject, 198
Apostrophe
    in contractions, 220–21
    in possessives, 219
Appositives and commas, 224
Approve of/approve, 181
Argument, *Generally the same as*
        Unifying idea *in this book. See*
        also Counterarguments
Articles, professional, samples of, 13–15
Assert/concede, 73–75
Assignments
    for course papers, samples, 22–35
    for essay exams, 16–22
    for writing courses, Preface, 8–12,
        Chap. 2 exercises
Attribute/contribute, 181–82
Audience, 2

Because of/due to, 183
Beginning of paper, how to write,
        50–53
Benjamin, Joe, 69
Bibliography
    arrangement of, 131
    sample, 125, 131–32
Bibliography card, sample, 113–14
Bracken, Peg, 84
Brackets, use of, in quotations,
        108, 227

Cahn, Edgar, 65
Capitalization
    in sentences and poetry, 205
    in words, types of, 205–207
Cause and effect, use of, in writing,
        64–67
Chomsky, Noam, 170
Choose/chose, 182
Chronological ordering, 59–61

Cite/sight/site, 182
Classification, 61–64
Clause reduction, 162–64
Clauses, 150–51. *See also* Relative
        clauses, Subordinate clauses, *and*
        Comma, main clauses with
Clichés, 187–88
Coherence, *see* Incoherence; *or* Mapping
Colloquialisms, 189
Colon, 221
Comma
    main clauses with, 222
    modifying clauses and phrases with,
        222
    nonrestrictive clauses and phrases
        with, 223–224
    parenthetical expressions with,
        224–225
    to prevent misreading, 226
    series with, 225
Comma fault, 236–37
Comma splice, 236–37
Comparison/contrast, use of, in writing,
        67–73
Complement/compliment, 182
Concession statement, in beginning
        paragraphs, 52–53
Conclusions, how to write, 53–55
Conscience/conscious, 182
Continual/continuous, 182
Contractions
    apostrophe in, 220–21
    appropriateness of, 221
Contrast, *see* Comparison/contrast
Contribute/attribute, 181–82
Co-ordinate adjectives and commas, 225
Correctness and grammaticality, 139–41
Correlatives, 215
Council/counsel/consul, 182
Counterarguments, dealing with, 73–76
Course papers
    how to organize, 43–50
    samples of
        anthropology, 22–28
        humanities, 28–32
        literature, 32–35
        science, 38–40
    see also Footnotes; Guide to
        punctuating quotations
Craft, Robert, 14
Credible/credulous/creditable, 183
Cross, Jack, 62

Dangling modifiers, 145–47
Dash, 226
Definition, use of, in writing, 61–64
Delusion/allusion/illusion/elusive, 181
Description
  sample assignment, technique, 8–9
  use of, in writing, 55–57
Descriptive words, fallacy, 167
Detail
  need for, 88–89
  ways of using for paragraph
    development, 55–77
Dialects
  spoken, 138–39
  written, 139
Diction, *see* Word choice
Disinterested/uninterested, 183
Due to/because of, 183

Effect/affect, 180
Either/each as subjects, 198
Elkins, Stanley, 67
Ellipses, 233–34
Elusive/allusion/illusion/delusion, 181
Embedders, 158
Embedding, 157–64
Emphasis
  sentence structure and, 137–38
  underlining for, 211
    see also Preposing; Subordination;
      Highlighting; Active/passive;
      Sentence structure, embedding;
      and Clause reduction
Ending of paper, how to write, 53–55
Essay exams
  samples/guidelines, 16–22
  and unifying idea, 46–48
Essays
  informal, samples of, 8–15
  narrative, 9–11
Euphemisms, 171
Everybody, etc. as subject, 198
Evidence;
  need for, 88–89, 97–100. *see also*
    Idea development
Except/accept, 180
Exclamation point, 226–27
Extraposition, 159–60

Finite verbs, 143
Focus
  sentence structure and, *see* Emphasis

Focus (*continued*)
  see also Unifying idea
Footnotes
  how to write, 128–29
  sample, 124, 130–31
  second references to source, 129
  when to use, 127–28
  where to place, 128
Formally/formerly, 183

Gardner, John, 71
Generalization, excessive, 97–100
General-purpose writing, 8–16
Gerundive embedder, 158
Grammar
  active/passive, 153–56, 255
  agreement, 196–204
  antecedents, agreement with,
    200–204. *See also* Pronoun
    reference
  "by" phrases, 156–57
  clauses, 150–51. *See* Relative clauses;
    Subordinate clauses; Comma,
    main clause with; and Clause
    reduction
  comma splice, *see* Run-on sentence
  complex sentences, 145
  correctness and, 139–41
  dangling modifiers, 145–47
  dialects and speech, 138–39
  embedding sentences, 157–64
  extraposition, 159–60
  finite verbs, 143–45
  gerundive, 158
  highlighting, 151–53
  infinitive, 158
  monster sentences, 164–65
  nominal, 157
  parallel structure, 214–216
  preposing, 148–49
  pronoun and antecedent, 200–203
  pronoun forms and, 203–204
  pronoun (person of), 199
  pronoun reference, 147–48, 201–203
  punctuation and, 220–37
  relative clauses, 160–64
  restrictive/nonrestrictive clauses, 161–62
  rules and, 139–41
  sentence fragments, 143–45,
    238–39, 246
  split infinitive, 242–43
  subjects and predicates, 141–42

Grammar (*continued*)
  subordination, 150–51
  syntax and, 137–38
  transformation, defined, 153–54
  verbs, shift in tense, 199, 246–49
  see also entries under individual
    headings
Guide to punctuating quotations,
  107–108

Harris, Alan, 62
Highlighting, 151–53
Human/humane, 183
Hyphens, 207–209

Idea development, 55–76
Idea linking, 65–66, 74, 76–77,
  79–85, 95–97
Idea relationships, *see* Mapping
Illusion/allusion/delusion/elusive, 181
Illustration, use of, in writing, 58–59
Implications of words, 168–70
imply/infer, 183
Incoherence, 95–97
Infinitive, split, 242–43
Infinitive embedder, 158
Introductions, how to write, 50–53
Irrelevance, 90–95. *See also*
  Incoherence
Irrelevant/irreverent, 183
Italic, use of, 210–11
Its/It's, 184

James, William, 62
Jargon, 170–71
Job assignments, samples of, 15–16
Judicial/judicious, 184

Körner, Stephen, 62
Kroeber, Theodora, 186
Kuhn, Thomas, 60

Lead/led, 184
Lie/lay, 184
Linking words, 76–77. *See also*
  65–66, 74
Literature course paper
  irrelevancies in, 92–95
  samples, 28–35
Logic, *see* Reasoning, confused;
  Incoherence; Irrelevance;
  Mapping; Overgeneralization;

Logic (*continued*)
  Oversimplification; and Undefined
    terms
Lorenz, Konrad, 72
Lose/loose, 184
Luxurious/luxuriant, 184

McCullers, Carson, 57
Main idea, *see* Unifying idea
Malcolm X, 85
Mapping, 79–85
Mayer, Martin, 14–15
Meaning, 137
  basic meaning, transformations, 153–54
  see also Idea relationships; Sentence
    structure; and Word choice
Mechanics of writing, 193–244. *See*
    also individual aspects of
Medium, 3–4
Metaphorical words, 185–87
MLA Style Sheet, 129
Monster sentences, 164–65
Moral/morale, 184

Narrative, samples of, 9–11
Narrowing a topic, *see* Unifying idea
Neill, A. S., 85
Nominal, 157–59
Nonrestrictive clauses, 161–62, 223–24
    249–52
Note cards, samples of, 109–113
Notes, as preliminary to writing, 4
Nouns
  collective, 197–98, 201
  compound, 200–201
  plural, 216–19
Number/amount, 181
Number, *see* Singular and plural
Numbers
  cardinal/ordinal, 213
  as figures, 212–13
  plurals of, 214
  spelled out, 212–13

One, none as subjects, 198
Organization
  beginning/ending paragraphs, 50–55
  cause and effect as, 64–67
  checking, 79–85
  comparison and contrast as, 67–73
  definition as, 61–64
  description as, 55–57
  developing ideas/paragraphs, 55–76

Organization (*continued*)
  in essay examinations, 16–22, 46–47
  illustration as, 58–59
  mapping as, 79–85
  plan/outline, 48–50
  preliminary suggestions, 1–5
  problems to anticipate, 87–104
  time sequence, 59–61
  transitions, 76–77
  unifying idea, 43–48
  see also General-purpose writing;
     Course papers; Science writing;
     Proposal writing; *and inside front*
     cover
Outline
  as plan, 48–50
  sentence, sample of, 116–17
Oversimplification, 100–101

Papers for courses
  anthropology paper, 22–28
  humanities paper, 28–32
  issue paper, 12
  paper about a poem, 32–35
  samples of, 22–40
  scientific paper, 38–40
Paragraph coherence, 95–97, 79–85
Paragraph development, 48–76
  by cause/effect, 64–67
  by comparison/contrast, 67–73
  by definition, 61–64
  by description, 55–57
  by illustration, 58–59
  by time sequence, 59–61
  taking note of counterargument,
    73–76
Paragraphing, relation of, to unifying
  idea, 48–50
Paragraphs, beginning and ending,
  50–55
Parallel structure, 214–16
  correlatives and, 215–16
  in sentences, 214–15
  in series, 215
Parentheses, 129, 227–28
  brackets and, 108, 227
  figures and letters with, 227
  punctuation with, 228
Passages for editing, 245–60
Passive/active, 153–56, 255–56
Period, 228
Person, shifts in, 199–200

Planning, 48–50. *See also* Stages of
  writing task
Plot summary in course papers, *See*
  Passage C, 92–93
Plural
  formation of, 216–19
  of numbers, 214. (*See also* Singular
    and plural)
Poetry
  how to capitalize, 205
  how to punctuate titles, 210
  how to quote, 233
  sample paper about poem, 32–35
Pompous words, 172–73
Possessive, 219–20
  apostrophe, position of, 219
  form to use, 220
Possessive embedder, 158
Practical, practicable, 184–85
Precede,/proceed, 185
Predicate, 141–45
Prefixes, 239–40
Preposing, 148–49
Prepositions, idiomatic usage of,
  177–80
Pre-writing, *see* Audience; Medium;
  Writing as speaking; Writing in
  stages
Principle/principal, 185
Pritchett, V. S., 84
Proceed/precede, 185
Pronoun reference:
  problems with, 147–48, 202–203
  pronoun and antecedent, 200–203
Pronouns
  antecedent and, 200–204
  appositives and, 204
  I, use of in course papers, 199–
    200
  Its and *it's*, 220
  person of, 199–200
  after prepositions, 204
  singular and plural, 198
  as subjects of clauses, 204
  who/whom, I/me, 203–204
  see also This; Which
Proper names
  capitalization of, 206–207
  hyphen with, 209
Prophecy/prophesy, 185
Proposal writing, 40–41
Proofreading, 5

Punctuation, 220–35
  apostrophe, 220–221
    in contractions, 220–221
    in possessives, 219–220
  colon, 221
  comma, 222–26
    main clauses with, 222
    modifying clauses and phrases
      with, 222
    nonrestrictive clauses and phrases
      with, 223–24
    parenthetical expressions with,
      224–25
    to prevent misreading, 226
    series with, 225
  dash, 226
  exclamation point, 226–27
  parentheses, 129, 227–28
    brackets and, 108, 227
    figures and letters with, 227
    punctuation with, 228
  period, 228
  question mark, 228–29
  quotation marks, 229–34
    how to use, 230–33
    long quotations, and, 232–33
    punctuation after, 231–32
    punctuation before, 231
    when to use, 229–30
  quotations, 233–34
    brackets in, 108, 227, 233
    ellipses in, 233–34
    indenting of, 232–33
    verse, 233
  semicolon, 234–35

Question mark, 228–29
Quotations
  in block form, 232–33
  brackets, for insertions in quoted
    material, 108, 227, 233
  and dialogue, 230–31
  direct and indirect, 229
  ellipses, for omissions in quoted
    material, 233–34
  how to use quotation marks, 229–34
  indenting of, 232–33
  of poetry, 233
  punctuation after, 231–32
  punctuation before, 231
  punctuation/footnoting/course papers,
    107–108, 119

Quotations (*continued*)
  quotation within quotation, 230
  when to use quotation marks, 229–30

Reasoning, confused, 101–103
Reduction of clauses, 162–64
Redundancy, *see* Wordiness
Reference, *see* Pronoun reference
References, standard library, 132–33
Relative clauses, 160–64
  clause reduction and, 162–64
  commas and nonrestrictive relatives,
    223–24
  converting sentences into, 160–61
  extraposed, 159
  restrictive and nonrestrictive, 161–62
Relevance, *see* Irrelevance
Repetitiousness, 89–90
Research papers
  basic rules about, 105–107
  bibliography, 113–14, 125, 131–32
  footnotes
    when to use, 127–28
    how to write, 128–29
    sample, 130–31, 124
  punctuating quotations in, 107–108
  sample of
    bibliography, 125, 131–32
    bibliography card, 113–14
    footnotes, 124, 130–31
    note cards, 109–113
    paper, body of, 118–23
    sentence outline, 116–17
  suggested topics, 133–35
  standard library references, 132–33
Respectfully/respectively, 185
Restrictive clause, 161–62, 223–24
Revision
  for change of emphasis in sentence,
    148–64
  for mechanical, grammatical errors,
    *see margin symbols inside back
    cover*
  for organization, 43–76
  for practice in editing, *see* Passages
    for editing
Rhetoric, *see* Idea development;
    Description; Illustration;
    Definition; Classification; Cause
    and effect; Comparison/contrast
Rhetorical question, 54
Run-on sentences, 236–37

Sample papers, assignments
anthropology paper, 22–28
description, 8–9
essay exam
botany, 16–20
history, 21–22, 46–47
humanities paper, 28–32
issue paper, 12
job writing assignments, 15–16
narrative, 9–11
passages for editing, 245–60
passages for mapping, 84–85
poetry paper, 32–35
proposal, 40–41
science
lab report, 35–37
paper, 38–40
Samuelson, Paul A., 84
Science writing
lab report, 35–37
proposal, sample, 40–41
references on technical writing, 37
scientific article, 36–37
theoretical science paper, sample of,
38–40
Semicolon, 234–35
Sentence structure
active/passive, 153–56, 255–56
complex sentences, 145
embedding, 157–61
extraposition, 159–60
highlighting with *It, What,* 151–53
inverted sentence, 196
monster sentences. 164–65
nominals, and, 157–59
parallel structure, 214–16, 254–55
preposing, 148–49
relative clauses, 160–64
run-on sentences, 236–37, 246
sentence fragments, 143–45, 238–39,
246–48
subordinate clauses, 73–76, 150–51
Singular and plural
collective nouns, and, 197–98,
201
compound nouns, 196–97, 200–201
it is and, 199
nouns ending in *s,* 218
plural of nouns, 216–19
of pronoun and antecedent, 200–201
pronouns and, 198
subject and verb, 196–99

Sight/cite/site, 182
Slang, written, 189
Somebody, etc. as subject, 198
Speaking and writing, 1
Spelling
double consonants, 240–41
i and *e,* 242
prefixes, 239–40
suffixes, 240–41
y and *i,* 241–42
Split infinitive, 242–43
Stages of writing task, 4–5
Subject
compound, 196–97
predicate and, 141–43
see also Topic
Subordination
for dealing with counterarguments,
73–76
Subordinate clauses
and main clauses, 150–51
position of, 150–51
Suffixes, 240–41
Syntax, defined, 137–38

Technical writing
bibliography for, 37
job assignments and, 15–16
Tense, shifts in, 199, 246–49
Terms, undefined, 103–104
Theme, *see* Unifying idea
There is/are, 198–99
There/their, 185
Thesis statement, *see* Unifying idea
Thesaurus, 2
This, vague use of, 147–48, 202, 252
Titles
abbreviation of, for names, 193–94
punctuation of, 210, 229
Topic sentence, 50
Topics
narrowing, 4
relation to unifying idea, 43–50
suggested, for papers, 133–35
Transformations
active/passive, 153–56
adjective, 163
defined, 153–54
extraposition, 159–60
highlighting, 151–53
relative clause reduction, 162–64
sentence embedding, 157–60

Transformations (*continued*)
  sentences into relative clauses,
    160–61
  sentences into nominals, 157–60
Transitions, 76–77

Underlining and emphasis, 211
Unifying idea, 43–48
Uninterested/disinterested, 183

Vagueness, 88–89
Verbs, agreement with subject, 196–99
Verbs
  complex sentences and, 145
  finite verbs and fragments, 143–45
  tense, shifts in, 199, 246–49
Verse, *see* Poetry

Which
  clauses, use of comma with, 222–24

Which (*continued*)
  vague use of, 147–48, 202–203
Whose/who's, 185
Williams, Gertrude, 62
Wylie, Lawrence, 58–59
Word choice, 167–92
  clichés, 187–88
  colloquial English, 189
  euphemisms, 171
  grammatical context and, 173–77
  implications of, 168–70
  jargon, 170–71
  metaphorical words, 185–87
  pompous of, 172–73
  prepositions, usage of, 177–80
  slang, written, 189
  word pairs often confused, 180–86
  wordiness, 190–92
Word division, at end of line, 243–44
Wordiness, 190–92

Margin Symbols

ab	Unnecessary abbreviation	Abbreviation 193
agr	Agreement	Agreement: Subject and Verb 196 Agreement: Pronoun and Antecedent 200
awk, k	Awkward sentence. Read it aloud and revise.	See also Parallel Structure 214, Writer's Grammar 137–164
cap	Capital	Capitals 204
cliché	Overused, empty expression	Clichés 187
coh	Not coherent; reader loses sense of focus or direction	Incoherence 95
colloq	Language too informal	Colloquial English 189
d m	Dangling modifier	Dangling modifiers 145
def	Undefined terms	Undefined Terms 103
dev	Idea needs detailed development	Idea development 55–76
emph	Sentence could be rephrased for better emphasis on main idea	For more help, see Writer's Grammar 148–164
focus	Lack of focus or sense of direction; reader is lost	Unifying idea 43–50
frag	Sentence fragment	Sentence fragments 238, 143 For practice, see 246
ftnt	Footnote needed	Footnotes 127
inf	Split infinitive	Split Infinitive 242
intro, con	Introduction, conclusion	Beginning / Ending Paragraphs 50
jarg	Excessively complex language	Jargon 170
lc	Lower case	Capitals 196
mm	Mixed metaphor	Metaphorical Words 185
org	Lack of apparent structure, organization	Chapter 2. Also see Sample Papers in Chapter 1
overgen	Overgeneralizing: broad - claims not justified	Overgeneralization 97
oversimp	Oversimplification of complex idea	Oversimplification 100
⅄	Parallel structure	Parallel Structure 214 For practice, see 254
¶ (no ¶)	Should (should not) be a new paragraph	
pass / act	Passive / active: try rephrasing	Passives 153 For practice, see 255
pl	Plural / singular error	Plurals 216
plot sum	Plot summary only	Relevance, Passage C, 92 Also see sample paper 28